Chicago Hustle and Flow

Chicago Hustle and Flow

Gangs, Gangsta Rap, and Social Class

Geoff Harkness

University of Minnesota Press
Minneapolis
London

Portions of this book were previously published as "Gangs and Gangsta Rap in Chicago: A Microscenes Perspective," *Poetics* 41 (2013): 151–76; copyright 2013; reprinted with permission from Elsevier. Portions of chapter 3 were previously published as "Get on the Mic: Recording Studios as Symbolic Spaces in Rap Music," *Journal of Popular Music Studies* 26 (2014): 82–100; copyright 2014; reprinted with permission from Wiley Blackwell.

Published by the University of Minnesota Press
111 Third Avenue South, Suite 290
Minneapolis, MN 55401–2520
http://www.upress.umn.edu

Harkness, Geoffrey Victor.
   Chicago hustle and flow : gangs, gangsta rap, and social class / Geoff Harkness.
   Includes bibliographical references and index.
   ISBN 978-0-8166-9229-3 (pb : alk. paper)—ISBN 978-0-8166-9228-6 (hc : alk. paper)
1. Gangsta rap (Music)—Social aspects—United States. 2. Gangsta rap (Music)—
Illinois—Chicago—History and criticism. 3. Gangs—Illinois—Chicago. I. Title.
   ML3918.R37H27 2014
   306.4'842490977311—dc23

2013049673

Printed in the United States of America on acid-free paper

The University of Minnesota is an equal-opportunity educator and employer.

20 19 18 17 16 15 14   10 9 8 7 6 5 4 3 2 1

Contents

Preface

There is a growing awareness that class-based stratification is among the most pressing social issues of the day. This can be seen everywhere from the Occupy Wall Street movement to debates over tax cuts for the wealthy, the flow of transnational labor, and the growing disparities in income between wealthy and poor. Social class may be more salient than ever because upward class mobility—the cornerstone of the American dream—has become increasingly difficult to achieve.

The promise that through hard work, motivation, and sacrifice one can achieve upward mobility is central to understanding Chicago's rap underground. Chicago's underground rap microscenes—encompassing socially conscious and gangsta rap—are bounded by social-class divisions. This book considers how social class shapes meaning, interpretation, and opportunity for young men involved in rap, particularly those who are also members of street gangs. While I focus on social class throughout the book, readers are cautioned that social class and race are inherently linked. To a large degree, any discussion of social class is also a discussion of race, and the young people in Chicago who were involved in both gangs and gangsta rap were nearly all people of color. Gang members and gangsta rappers are two widely maligned and misunderstood groups, and assuming the identity of gang member or gangsta rapper is not without consequence. My hope is that readers will come away with new understandings of these cultures, as well as the role of social class in shaping the young people involved in them.

I did not arrive at these topics in a linear or straightforward manner. Ethnography, like life, is complicated. I was raised by a single mother, lived in government-subsidized housing as a child, and remember waiting in line for food stamps. Mom tells stories about how she used to position our groceries at the front of the refrigerator shelves so it would look like we had more food. The family car only had one working gear—reverse. Yet I don't remember especially feeling poor, at least not in the melodramatic way that poverty is often portrayed in the media. Yes, my clothes and my sister's came from the Salvation Army, and we knew the taste of government cheese, but we were no better or worse off than anyone else on our block. No one had much, but I never saw anyone wring their hands in poverty-stricken despair, either.

When I was six, the family moved to the heart of Kansas City, Missouri. It wasn't a great neighborhood—our house was robbed three times in the first year—but it wasn't the worst, either. We still didn't have much money. We slept on the floor and cooked meals on a hot plate. We survived.

Eventually, Mom got an entry-level job in marketing, and our financial position began to improve. It wasn't an instant leap forward, but slow, steady upward mobility over several years. In the middle of fourth grade, I transferred from the local public school to a private institution. A year later, my sister followed suit. We stopped buying clothes at the Salvation Army; we slept on mattresses. Things were improving.

Growing up, I was heavily into music, obsessed with KISS and the Beatles. Every penny of my Kool-Aid stand money went toward the purchase of records. My sister was into disco and made sure kids in the neighborhood memorized every line of "Rapper's Delight." Fast forward a few years, and mom landed a job at a concert promotion company. Suddenly we had front-row tickets and backstage passes for every concert in town. I was an eighth grader, running around backstage at the Clash, Van Halen, and Duran Duran. Heaven.

When I was thirteen, I got my first job, stocking shelves at a record store. Most of my salary went towards the purchase of more records, and I became immersed in all things music. I bought a guitar, started taking lessons, and joined a punk band. My sister had graduated from disco to Run-D.M.C. and Whodini. I loved the sound of Eddie Martinez's guitar on "Rock Box," which was, with apologies to Aerosmith, the *real* first rap-rock tune.

At seventeen, I'd had enough of the Midwest and moved to Los Angeles with my band's drummer, Skunkhead. Being under eighteen meant limited employment opportunities, so I took the only thing I could find, telemarketing. Skunkhead, his drums, and I shared a one-room studio apartment with two other guys. I still have nightmares about the smell.

The day I turned eighteen, I applied for a job at a record store. It paid minimum wage, so I continued to put in night shifts at the telemarketing company. But at least I was working around music again. This was a great time to be living in Los Angeles, playing in a band, and working in a record store. West Coast gangsta rap was just beginning what would come to be known as its golden era, and the record store gave me a front-row seat. N.W.A, Cypress Hill, DJ Quik, Kid Frost, and A Lighter Shade of Brown were in heavy rotation. Oakland party crew Digital Underground dropped an EP that had everyone debating the merits of Shock G versus the group's new recruit, a young upstart named Tupac. The East Coast was holding its own with everything from classic Public Enemy and LL Cool J joints to the native tongue twists of De La Soul, A Tribe Called Quest, and Black Sheep. Even the pop rap of the day was new jack swinging— MC Hammer, Heavy D, Bobby Brown, PM Dawn, Guy, Young MC, Kid 'n Play. And everyone loved "Ice Ice Baby" without so much as a trace of irony. I devoured it all.

On April 29, 1992, everything changed. The media blamed the Rodney King beating, but in Los Angeles we knew that it was only part of the story. We knew that the Latasha Harlins shooting was just as significant. And we knew why Korean businesses were specifically targeted for destruction. Public Enemy got credited for its ability to address important social issues, but in Los Angeles we knew that Ice Cube was the real voice of the people. Not the black man's CNN, as Chuck D famously described rap music, but everyone's.

Cube's 1991 opus *Death Certificate* perfectly captured the range of discussions that were taking place in Los Angeles in the year that preceded the uprisings. "Black Korea" got all the attention, but "Us," "A Bird in the Hand," "Man's Best Friend," and "My Summer Vacation" were equally important points of dialogue, all set to the most head-bobbing rapstrumentals ever committed to tape. While "conscious" groups like De La Soul and A Tribe Called Quest rhymed about roller-skating and Bonita's apple bum, gangstas like Cube were rapping about subjects that really mattered.

I returned to the Midwest in October 1992, ready to change the world. I knew working in record stores wasn't going to accomplish that, so I enrolled in community college and waited tables on weekends to pay the bills. In my second semester, I enrolled in intro to sociology, where I was assigned to read articles that analyzed rap music and the LA uprisings. I'd found my calling.

In 1999, I began graduate training in sociology at the University of Kansas. I also landed an entry-level job as a music journalist for the local newspaper. It paid next to nothing, but I would have done it for free—CDs, concert tickets, and the chance to interview musicians were payment enough. Another breakthrough was the purchase of a $300 video camera. This was the advent of the digital revolution, the first time amateurs like me could make movies for almost no money. Armed with a camera and more enthusiasm than talent, I made a documentary film about pawnshops, work that eventually formed the basis of my master's thesis.

Pawnshops were interesting to me for a number of reasons. As someone who had to pawn my TV from time to time to cover the rent, I was personally familiar with how they provided loans to people who couldn't get them anywhere else. I also knew how these "fringe banks" charged interest rates that were far higher than those paid by people who had access to traditional credit. It was obvious that there was a two-tiered system of credit, one for the working and lower classes and one for everyone else. The poor paid more, which didn't seem fair.

Around that time, I was assigned to review a U-God concert for the local paper. I showed up that night and caught the last few songs of the opening act, a gangsta-rap quintet called DVS Mindz. I was blown away. They were one of the most amazing bands I'd ever seen, in any genre. I assumed they were from New York and touring with U-God. It turned out they were from Topeka, Kansas, about twenty miles down the road. I passed my number to their manager, and wrote how impressed I was in my U-God review. Okay, I raved about them. They were that good.

A couple of weeks later, I interviewed the band and penned a feature article about them for the newspaper. I also made sure to attend their next concert, and because I had just purchased a video camera, I decided to videotape it for posterity. The footage looked okay to me, so I edited together a quick music video for fun. The group loved it, and we decided to make a real music video, something none of us had attempted before. Over the course of the next three years, we made dozens of music videos and a short film, and I shot and edited a two-hour documentary that told the group's history from start to finish. It was an interesting story. A couple of band members had been to prison, one of them had gang ties, another sold drugs for a living. But they seemed normal to me, nothing like the caricatures of black, gangsta rappers found in the media.

My work with DVS Mindz had nothing to do with my academic studies; I just loved the band's music. I started out as a fan, then became a collaborator, and eventually a friend. I still keep in touch with some of the guys, and to this day, DVS Mindz remains my favorite rap group of all time. You can find some of the videos we made on YouTube. You should check them out.

When I arrived in Chicago in the fall of 2003 to attend grad school at Northwestern, I had spent the previous three years hanging out with DVS Mindz, filming their concerts, interviewing them, and watching them record. Relocating to Chicago meant that my time spent hanging out with gangsta rappers was finished. Unless . . .

Within months of my arrival, I was out videotaping Chicago rap concerts, interviewing rappers, and had decided that this was going to be the topic of my dissertation. Moving from Lawrence's rap music scene to Chicago's wasn't much of a stretch. The city was bigger and there were more venues and musicians, but I basically picked up right where I'd left off. I didn't encounter the classic "outsider" dilemma described by some ethnographers. Because I was new to Chicago and unknown to the musicians, I was not an insider, but being part of this setting was not unusual or uncomfortable either.

The fieldwork conducted for this book began in January 2004 and concluded six years later. I was not new to gangsta rappers or music scenes, but I was new to Chicago, and it took time to locate and penetrate the heart of the city's rap underground. From the outset, I utilized the traditional qualitative methods of observation and in-depth interviews. I attended concerts, introduced myself to rappers, arranged interviews, and used snowball sampling to find others.

I also utilized social networking, beginning on MySpace and later moving to Facebook. MySpace, which launched in August 2003, had only been online for a few months when my fieldwork began, but was already growing in popularity with local rappers in Chicago. Social networking made it easier to find the "center" of Chicago's rap underground, including events not held in mainstream venues. Eventually, I tapped into an ever-expanding network of local rappers with whom I could make contact. This network would have been difficult, if not impossible, to connect with via traditional strategies.

Although I occasionally relied upon traditional qualitative methods such as observation, audio recordings, and field notes, most of my fieldwork was videotaped. This enabled me to analyze this material in greater detail, often noticing new phenomena after repeated viewings over time. Over the course of six years, I interviewed 135 participants, mostly rappers but also a few music producers who did not rap. Some interviews were conducted one-on-one, but many were group interviews. With some sub-jects, particularly those who had been part of group interviews, I conduct-ed one or sometimes two follow-up interviews using questions personally created for that interview and specific to the participant.

Of the 135 participants, 23 claimed to be active gang members. Throughout the book, I focus on them, but also include insights from the vast majority of participants who were not gang members. Many were part of the gang-rap network, and offered additional insights about the relationship between these groups; others were members of the backpack microscene, and provided both contrast and context. Due to the substan-tial risks involved for gang members, I have altered the names and some identifying features of some of those described in this book, primarily gang members but also some members of Chicago's rap undergound who were not part of gangs.

In addition to formal interviews, I also spent hundreds of hours chat-ting informally with the participants in this study. These conversations took place at nightclubs, in cars, at birthday parties, barbeques, softball games, and any number of formal and informal events. I did not record these conversations, but wrote down their salient points in field notes after the fact. These informal conversations lent invaluable insight into the activities of gang members because they were not being videotaped and were often far more candid than those that were.

In writing the book, I set aside what is often the focal point of many studies of rap music: song lyrics. Doing so forced me to focus entirely on the cultural aspects of the music rather than scrutinizing its lyrical con-tent. The musical output of Chicago's rapping gang members did not waver significantly from a good deal of that created by mainstream rap musi-cians, or even their peers in the microscene. Typical of the subgenre, the songs were filled with the usual gangsta-rap tropes: guns, gangs, drugs, money, women, hard-knocks, street life, criminal activity, and so on. (I counted at least a dozen Chicago rap groups that had a song entitled "Get Money.") I am not implying that this music was not enjoyable, merely that it was not unique. This analytical compartmentalization enabled me to consider not what these musicians did in their songs, but what their songs did for them. Ultimately, my interest is not in how their rhymes reflect—or perhaps exaggerate—their lived experiences, attitudes, or aspirations, but how assuming the liminal identity of gang member and musician impacts their lived experiences, attitudes, and aspirations.

Directing my attention away from the lyrics also enabled me to sidestep much of what has so often been maligned about gangsta rap: its hypermasculinity, misogyny, and glorification of the so-called thug life. Women are underrepresented in this book. Only six participants were women, reflecting a general dearth of female involvement in local music scenes, and in rap music, despite women's important role in the establishment of the genre. The lack of female participation in rap music, in Chicago and elsewhere, can be attributed to the genre's hypermasculinity and misogyny (Dyson 2007; Adams and Fuller 2006), the limited, stereotypical roles available to female rappers (Keyes 2000), and larger societal systems of sexism and patriarchy that inhibit female participation in many arenas of social and economic life (Rose 2008). Therefore, while this book offers a platform for a limited number of female voices, its findings should be understood as stemming primarily from a (heterosexual) male perspective.

Acknowledgments

Howard Becker once wrote that creative endeavors are not the result of individual effort, but collective products authored by dozens of people. There are numerous individuals who deserve thanks and credit for their contributions to my intellectual and personal development, and I want to acknowledge them here.

Thanks to Jason Weidemann, Ana Bichanich, Alicia Gomez, Danielle Kasprzak, Anne Wrenn, and everyone at the University of Minnesota Press. I appreciate your support of this book from the beginning. James Cappio was a fastidious copy editor, and my production editor, Edward Wade, helped shape the book in important ways.

I would like to thank the Department of Sociology at Northwestern University for supporting my graduate education. In particular, I would like to thank the members of the Culture and Society Workshop, the Ethnography Workshop, and others who took my work seriously, and pushed it in directions I could not have otherwise imagined. This includes Elisabeth Anderson, Jean Beaman, Kieran Bezila, Ellen Berrey, Japonica Brown-Sarcino, Michaela DeSoucey, Kerry Dobransky, Gabrielle Ferrales, Gary Fine, Lynn Gazley, Amin Ghaziani, Ashlee Humphreys, Marcus Hunter, Stacy Lom, Erin Metz McDonnell, Terence McDonnell, Michelle Naffziger-Hirsch, Lori Delale-O'Connor, Liz Onasch, Wenona Rymond-Richmond, Heather Schoenfeld, Nicole Martorano Van Cleve, and Berit Vannebo.

I was fortunate to have Wendy Griswold, Mary Pattillo, and E. Patrick Johnson on my dissertation committee. This outstanding group of scholars believed in me and allowed me to pursue my research with passion and autonomy. I appreciate their support, encouragement, kind words, and brilliant ideas.

Living in the Middle East for three years, the time during which I wrote this book, was life-changing. The experience was made all the better thanks to the smart, funny, worldly colleagues and friends I met in

Qatar: Anahita Alivand, Sean Burns, Sandy Choi, Mary Dedinsky, Kira Dreher, Bijan Esfahani, John Gasper, David Gray, Jennifer Gray, Erik Helin, Blake Hounshell, Abe Kamarck, Kristy Kamarck, Joe Khalil, John Margolis, Silvia Pessoa, David Phongsaven, Mohana Rajakumar, Kulsoom Rizvi, Richard Roth, Trish Roth, Trish Seapy, Jeffrey Squires, and Zachary Wright. I would also like to extend my thanks to the incredible students at Education City, who enriched my time in Qatar. Hassan Asif, Samira Islam, Rana Khaled, Omer Mohammad, and Zaina Salemeh taught me at least as much as I taught them.

To the many professors who encouraged me, pushed me, and generally pointed me in the right direction, I thank you for your knowledge, wisdom, and inspiration. Being your student instilled in me a desire to teach, to follow in your path, and to make a difference in the lives of others. Robert Xidis, Bill Staples, David Smith, Carol Warren, Joel Morton, and so many others, I thank you.

Thanks are also due to Anthony Kwame Harrison and Peggy Levitt, intelligent, creative scholars who I am fortunate to count as friends. I appreciate your comments on my work, your wisdom, and your friendship.

To my friends and partners in crime, Greg Douros, Kathryn Kollett, Doug Lerner, Paul Marinescu, Jon Niccum, Ken Perreault, Eliott Reeder, Jeff Roos, and Spencer Wright, I am grateful for your cheer, inspiration, assistance, encouragement, and good times over our many years of friendship. I am lucky to have such a talented, eclectic group of friends, and I am so glad that you are part of my life.

I am lucky to have a family filled with wonderful, unique, interesting people. Orlo, Maxine, Dad, Harriet, Julie, Mark, Nathan, Adelyn, Nick, Sam, Pari, Steve, and Anne, I thank you for enriching my life, inspiring and encouraging me from the moment we met.

To my son, Benjamin, you changed my life the instant you entered it. You are a small person with big eyes, and even bigger things ahead. I cannot begin to express how much I love you.

To my wife and partner, Laura, your love and support have changed and transformed me in more ways than I can name. You are an incredible human being and have the kindest and most generous heart of anyone I've had the fortune to know. I am absolutely devoted to you, and look forward to our next great adventure.

Finally, to all of the talented, hardworking Chicago artists and musicians who contributed their energies to this research, I thank you so much. Your desire to succeed at all costs, despite the odds, served as inspiration to me. You live and breathe your art with passion, and you motivated me to pursue my own work in a similar manner.

None of this would have been possible without each and every one of you, and I thank you all.

Welcome to the Terrordome

Chicago's Gangsta-Rap Microscene

Lupe Fiasco, Common, and Kanye, that's all fine and dandy, but that's a Hollywood type of Chicago picture right there. You need to get to the underground, to the actual 'hood, the heart of it. Then you'll come to understand it.

—Adeem

On September 4, 2012, Joseph Coleman, an eighteen-year-old aspiring gangsta rapper who went by the moniker Lil JoJo, was gunned down in the Englewood neighborhood of Chicago, the victim of a drive-by shooting. Chicago police immediately began to investigate the connection between Coleman's murder and an online war of words and music he was having with another Chicago rapper, seventeen-year-old Keith Cozart, better known by his stage name, Chief Keef. The feud between Coleman and Cozart had all the trappings of a media sensation, as evidenced by breathless headlines in the local press: "Chicago Hip-Hop War of Words Turns Violent" (Kot 2012), "Chief Keef and Lil JoJo: A Rap Feud Straight Outta Englewood" (2012), "Cops Investigating Whether Hip-Hop Feud Linked to Slaying" (Kot and Gorner 2012).[1] *New York Times* writer Jon Caramanica (2012) noted the "long history of overlap between Chicago's gangs and Chicago's rap" in a lengthy article about Coleman's slaying.

By any measurement, Cozart's music career was on the rise. While under house arrest for a gun charge earlier that year, he had inked a deal with Interscope Records, a powerhouse label and home to rap superstars such as 50 Cent, Dr. Dre, and Eminem. In August 2012 Cozart performed in front of tens of thousands of revelers at Lollapalooza. His homemade YouTube videos had received millions of hits, and a movie deal was purportedly in the works. "Street buzz, his criminal record and the Internet hit 'I Don't Like' have conspired to make Keef the most notable new face of Chicago hip-hop," opined *Chicago Tribune* music writer Greg Kot (2012).

Cozart also wrought attention from songs and Twitter posts that made frequent reference to the number 300, a known reference to the Black Disciples street gang. According to investigators, Cozart was a member of the Lamron faction of the Black Disciples, whose long-standing rivalry with another Chicago gang, the Gangster Disciples, dates at least to the 1970s. Coinciding with Cozart's rise in fortune, the hostilities between the Gangster Disciples and the Black Disciples heated up online, with members from the two gangs using rap songs, social networking sites, and YouTube to insult and goad one another. In May 2012 Coleman posted a music video entitled "3 hunnak" (translation: "300 killer") that appropriated the backing track for Keef's song "Everyday" and added new lyrics over the top. In the original song, Cozart regurgitated gangsta-rap clichés (making money, having sex with "bitches," smoking marijuana) over a crawling beat. Coleman's remake replaced the words "every day" with "BDK," meaning Black Disciples killer. "These niggas claim 300 but we BDK," Coleman taunted repeatedly. The accompanying video featured Coleman and a number of associates rapping to the camera, dancing, and waving an armory's worth of automatic weapons. According to Coleman's aunt, Coleman was attempting a "Tupac and Biggie thing [to] get under the skin" of Cozart and his associates (Konkol, Janssen, and Horton 2012). "They were feuding in the rap game," Coleman's mother added (Kot and Gorner 2012).

Criminologist John Hagedorn is among the few scholars to denote the "crucial role of gangs in the history of hip-hop culture" (2008, 86). Rap's past is strewn with musicians who were gang members or ex–gang members, including Afrika Bambaataa (Black Spades), Ice-T (Crips), Mac Dre (Romper Room Gang), Boo-Yaa T.R.I.B.E. (Bloods), Cypress Hill founders Sen Dog and B-Real (Bloods), Snoop Dogg (Rollin' 20 Crips), MC Eiht (Tragniew Park Compton Crips), Tone Lōc (Westside Tribe Crips), and The Game (Bloods). "How can anyone understand the outlook of gang members today without exploring the meaning of gangsta rap?" Hagedorn asked (85). Skeptics assert that rappers emphasize their gang connections to engender publicity and record sales, but the Coleman–Cozart incident illustrates how mixing gangs with rap music can be deadly.[2]

Scholars of rap music have done little to illuminate the genre's relationship with street gangs. Yet this association is well known to members of Chicago's local rap-music scene, who for years have witnessed feuds similar to the Coleman–Cozart dispute. In part, this is due to the sheer number of local Chicago rappers who are also affiliated with gangs. "This is the home of the gang, so out of ten rappers, seven of them bang," estimated Black Soldier, who has been part of Chicago's local gangsta-rap music scene for more than a decade.

> If seven out of ten rappers are motherfucking gang niggas, that's gonna come out in the music. Gang niggas are *angry*. Most of the time, motherfuckers feel like there's no way out. So you're gonna get gangsta music from a bunch of angry gangstas: young niggas that ain't got shit, they fathers are locked up. Of course it's gonna come out in the music.

There is a degree of demographic commonality between gang members and practitioners of gangsta rap. The former tend to be young, lower-class Latino and African American males who reside in urban areas (Tapia 2011; National Gang Center). The latter appeals to a broad audience, but gangsta rappers are popularly perceived to be young, lower-class African American males from inner-city environs (Collins 2006; Perry 2004). In Chicago, there are about seventy active street gangs featuring between 68,000 and 150,000 members, more gang members per capita than any other city in the United States (Chicago Crime Commission 2012; Attorney General's Report 2008).[3] A number of active gang members are also part of the city's gangsta-rap music scene. "Chicago is the gangbang capital," insists Habit, a rapper and gang member from Chicago. "There's no fakin'. All us gangbang for real; we really in the street." This book explores the connection between gangsta rappers and active gang members. While these collectives have been considered separately, this book examines cultural practices at their intersection, as occurring within a local music scene.

Haterville

Chicago was once home to a thriving music industry, including scores of recording studios, performance venues, and major labels such as Chess Records and Vee-Jay Records. In the wake of economic decline and music-industry consolidation in the 1960s and 1970s, these companies shuttered their doors, were bought out by larger companies, or relocated to the coasts. Today's up-and-coming Chicago rap musicians enjoy far fewer opportunities to engage with the corporate music infrastructure that once supported famed denizens such as Muddy Waters, Howlin' Wolf, Bo Diddley, and Curtis Mayfield. Chicago-bred rap superstars such as Common and Kanye West only achieved fame after moving out of town to be closer to key industry figures and major-label record companies.

Today, there are three tiers to Chicago's rap music scene. The corporate tier consists of internationally established artists, such as Kanye West, Common, Twista, and Lupe Fiasco, who are tied to the major music corporations. The independent tier includes locally and regionally successful rappers who operate without aid from the major labels. These artists, whose number is very few, earn a modest living from music sales, live performances, and merchandise. The underground tier consists of rappers who are trying to launch careers in the music industry, hoping to be the next big name out of Chicago. This book is set in Chicago's underground rap-music scene.[4]

Chicago boasts the fourth largest underground or "grass roots" music scene in the nation (Rothfield et al. 2007, 39). The musicians constituting this scene have no affiliation to the large music corporations, but occasionally have contracts with small, independent record labels. They hold concerts in local nightclubs and makeshift, unlicensed settings such as warehouses and house parties. Chicago's underground gangsta rappers perform at the handful of clubs willing to hire gangsta-rap acts, venues often situated on Chicago's West and South Sides, as well as some inner-ring suburbs.

In part due to this scarcity of resources, most rappers describe Chicago's rap underground as highly competitive, with artists vying with one another and doing whatever it takes to gain any possible advantage over their peers. "Crabs in a bucket" is the phrase many used to depict interactions among members of Chicago's rap underground, and the city is often referred to as "Haterville." As with any competition for meager resources, infighting, envy, and backstabbing are widespread and common. Artists are reluctant to collaborate or even praise one another, because doing so may hinder their own chances at success. Those who do join forces often stick together in small groups that have little interaction with other cliques.[5]

Some believe that this dynamic is the natural outgrowth of the city's geographical, racial, and class-based stratification. Despite its diverse population and large size, Chicago is America's most racially segregated city (Glaeser and Vigdor 2012, 6). "Chicago is segregated on so many levels," says Grant Parks, a rap producer. "It's segregated on race, segregated by gangs, all kinds of stuff. Why would you expect the music to be any different?" Others attribute the crabs-in-a-bucket milieu to a unique "Chicago mentality," born of the city's industrial history and gritty, hard-nosed way of life. Many underground rappers view personal effort and gaining advantage over one's peers to be the only realistic routes to success.

Local Rap Music Scenes in Three Settings

Scholarship on music that takes place in local settings has moved away from earlier theoretical frameworks such as communities and subcultures and instead viewed them as "scenes" (Straw 1991). Music scenes are "space[s] of a specific (often urban) location formed by social networks of interacting individuals and groups with multilayered, but overlapping identity" (Císař and Koubek 2012, 6).[6] Music scenes "designate the contexts in which clusters of producers, musicians, and fans collectively share their common musical tastes and collectively distinguish themselves from others" (Peterson and Bennett 2004, 1). The scenes perspective, which draws upon Howard Becker's research on art worlds and Pierre Bourdieu's concept of fields of cultural production, has been applied to local (Grazian 2003; Mitchell 1996; Shank 1994), translocal (Dowd, Liddle, and Nelson 2004; Schilt 2004; Thornton 1995), and virtual settings (Kibby 2000; Lee and Peterson 2004; Vroomen 2004). The scenes perspective is useful because it explains the development of music scenes under conditions unique to a particular setting.

The scenes perspective figures heavily in three recent ethnographies of rap music, set in the Mississippi Delta (Neff 2009), San Francisco (Harrison 2009), and Los Angeles (Morgan 2009). These works are important because they illustrate contextual variation: how rap-music culture plays out in specific locations, producing not only stylistic variations, but also unique sets of behaviors and attitudes on the part of scene members. For example, cultural studies scholar Ali Colleen Neff (2009) explored the small rap-music scene in Clarksdale, Mississippi, whose aspiring MCs drew upon an extended history of regionally specific music traditions: slave hollers, spirituals, folk psalms, and the Delta blues. "Techniques of oral/ musical improvisation remain deeply embedded as the stylized cultural life of the Delta is passed from one generation to the next. From preaching to toasting, the traditional verbal practices of the Mississippi Delta have set the stage for the contemporary development of the region's distinctive hip-hop style" (113). Neff described a Southern rap music scene in which local styles and sensibilities imbued every aspect of her participant's identities. Neff's primary research subject and collaborator, a rapper named Top-Notch the Villain, even linked local fashion, regional cuisine, and ideology, asserting that all reflected a unique Delta "flavor" (69).

Neff noted, however, that Delta rap music was created within a context that also incorporated the translocal and virtual aspects of scenes: "Hip-hop in the Mississippi Delta is defined by the interaction of Black Atlantic aesthetic practice, local cultural tradition, and global networks. . . . These rural artists are engaged in a global call and response with the greater Black Atlantic diaspora, a network of cultural practitioners who draw from and, in turn, replenish the shared well of global creativity" (10). This included the styles and sensibilities of LA gangsta rap circa the late 1980s and early 1990s, which informed the rap-music scene in Clarksdale: "crunk" rappers appropriated the "script of gangsta identity to stake their claim as southern hip-hop artists" (102). The Clarksdale MCs used "aspects of thug life in their raps, echoing the strains of Tupac Shakur or Snoop Dogg" and sported "shiny gold teeth and expensive pimped-out clothing" (104). Neff noted that this "gangsta posture" was designed to appeal to fans of the popular gangsta/crunk subgenres, and served as markers of resistance (102). Today's local rap-music scenes—whose tech-savvy members make full use of ongoing digital developments in the realms of communication and music creation and distribution—are informed and shaped by translocal and virtual forces, which in turn inform and reshape the local. In result, the boundaries between these once-disparate geographies, as well as the traditional distinction between audience and performer, have been all but eliminated.[7]

The Bay Area underground rap-music scene explored by sociologist Anthony Kwame Harrison (2009) was informed by San Francisco's legacy of 1960s and 1970s countercultural politics and activism (anti–Vietnam War protests, the Black Panther Party, Haight-Ashbury hippies) and antiestablishment ethos (35). Legendary Oakland rapper Too $hort, who began his career by creating bedroom recordings that he manufactured and sold to local audiences, was another key influence (36). The Bay Area's combined legacy of countercultural practices, antiestablishment ideology, and street-level entrepreneurialism produced what Harrison termed the "Bay Area hustle," described as a "savvy, independent-minded business approach to life that willfully embraces nonconventional means of pursing artistic and career ambitions" (35). The Bay Area scene was also informed by the region's ethnically diverse population, leading to Harrison's creation of a rights-based racial hierarchy for underground rap music, which ranked fourteen distinct ethnic categories into three major clusters (107). During his participative ethnography, Harrison spent time freestyling at Rockin' Java, a café that hosted a weekly open mic for local rappers. The relatively relaxed norms of this event (free of charge, no sign-up sheet or set order) combined with an ethos of equality ("everyone should get a turn before someone went twice") further illustrated the impact of local ideologies on cultural practices (75).

African American studies scholar Marcyliena Morgan (2009) explored Los Angeles's rap-music scene in the mid-1990s by conducting ethnography at a single performance venue, a weekly workshop known as Project Blowed where local rappers, breakdancers, DJs, and graffiti artists could hone their skills. As with Neff and Harrison, Morgan demonstrated how local cultural forces shaped (and were shaped by) the content and character of LA's rap-music scene. Project Blowed was, to some degree, a response to N.W.A's nihilistic vision of Los Angeles. "It did not fan the flames of urban decay and societal attacks. Project Blowed was putting out the fire" (5). As with Harrison's study of the Bay Area, the cultural practices at Project Blowed reflected LA's ethnic diversity: rappers blended Jamaican Creole and Mexican and Chicano Spanish into their rhymes (96). Contrasting with Harrison's account of Rockin' Java were Morgan's descriptions (88–91) of the cultural practices created by and for the Project Blowed participants: the somber "work rituals" enacted to prepare the room, the strict norms related to performance (rappers were required to enroll and pay a small fee to perform, and were to make a formal introduction before beginning their rap; signs directed, "Do not bite styles"), and the locally specific calls for nonviolence ("Take that stuff to Westwood"). Morgan's study illustrated how local music scenes can produce specific sites, populated by certain scene members, where collective ideologies, attitudes, preferences, practices, customs, and memories took place. All of this rendered Project Blowed distinct from the LA rap-music scene, while still occurring within the context of it.

These three studies of local rap scenes, while exploring different locations from disparate perspectives, shared some common features. (1) All authors paid careful attention to local and regional influences. They detailed how a confluence of locally specific cultural factors manifested in the production of sounds, styles, aesthetics, ideologies, and cultural practices unique to that setting. (2) None of the authors treated their chosen sites of study as removed from larger discourses and practices of rap music, but rather considered the larger dialogue between local rap-music scenes and what Motley and Henderson (2007) termed the "global hip-hop Diaspora." This was exemplified by Harrison's and Morgan's analysis of open mic and freestyle performances, whose norms combined site-specific dictates and local customs in dialogue with a more general set of rap-performance norms followed by MCs the world over. As Morgan wrote, participation at Project Blowed required "hip hop knowledge" as well as "local knowledge shared by those active in hiphop and in Project Blowed in particular" (101). (3) Methodologically, the three authors utilized ethnography and situated themselves into their research settings. Harrison did so most explicitly by working at a popular Haight-Ashbury record store and freestyling at open mic nights. By continually expressing the emotions, doubts, and desires of the ethnographer in the field, Neff never let readers forget that she was right there, experiencing Delta rap firsthand. Morgan did not just observe the happenings at Project Blowed, she worked directly on various community and art projects with their founders and coordinators. (4) All authors placed a premium on observation, as well as interviews and the words and expressions used by their participants. They also placed considerable emphasis on the analysis of cultural objects, particularly performance, with Neff and Morgan scrutinizing song lyrics.[8] (5) Finally, and perhaps most significantly, none of these authors examined music scenes as holistic, but scrutinized some portion of the larger entity. Harrison examined the socially conscious element of the Bay Area's underground rap scene; Morgan focused on a single venue in Los Angeles; Neff used a lone rap artist as a springboard for exploring portions of the Clarksdale scene. This implicit "scenes within scenes" approach—what I term a "microscenes" perspective—allowed for more nuanced understandings of their chosen settings.

Microscenes

A microscenes perspective should be made explicit because it offers a more comprehensive understanding and conceptualization of music scenes than the broader scenes perspective. The microscenes perspective does not replace scenes as a theoretical construct, but allows music scenes to be interpreted as members experience them. The scenes perspective implies the existence of a cohesive, collective entity, yet this is not how members of a music scene encounter it, nor is it the level of analysis by which the aforementioned scholars approached their research. As units of analysis, microscenes are more precise because they better describe the composition of music scenes, which consist of a number of microscenes, in large music scenes perhaps dozens or even hundreds.

Microscenes do not exist in a bubble. Because they are components of larger music scenes, they occur in dialogue with one another and often share overlapping characteristics. Members of a music scene (musicians, producers, fans) may move from one microscene to another, as evidenced by Neff's journey through the Mississippi Delta with TopNotch. At the same time, core microscene members often desire to remain distinct from the parent music scene, and do not necessarily seek assimilation, as evidenced by the rappers at Project Blowed. In these instances, microscene insiders rely on tropes such as authenticity and artistic purity to protect their threatened cores (see McLeod 1999).

Microscenes are not fixed in time or location. They represent shifting allegiances, trends, tastes, and values. They explain how key music venues can shutter their doors, signature bands can break up, and fans can come and go, while the parent music scene remains intact. They also elucidate how advances in technology can lead to the formation of new microscenes, and the attendant expansion of parent music scenes, exemplified by the proliferation of virtual microscenes that arose in the wake of the Internet (Peterson and Bennett 2004, 10–12).

A microscene can be defined as a distinct component of a music scene located in a delimited space of mutual social activity, where certain clusters of scene members assemble and generate sociocultural cohesion through collective ideologies, attitudes, preferences, practices, customs, and memories that distinguish them from the larger scene. The characteristics of a microscene are as follows:

1. It is a recognized component, branch, or faction of an existing, larger music scene. It is a scene within a scene. For example, the goth scene consists of microscenes populated by traditional, cyber, romantic, industrial, vampire, and candy goths (Haenfler 2012, 93). Because the various goth microscenes can be found in specific cities or locations, as well as online and in the translocal form, the microscenes perspective holds up under the same conditions that define the scenes perspective, but with added nuances that help explicate their distinctions.

2. It differs from the parent scene in ideology, attitude, preference, cultural practice, custom, collective memory, and/or style. For example, the straightedge faction of punk rock is a microscene that materialized out of the Washington, D.C., hardcore punk scene circa 1980 in response to "some segments of the punk scene; straight edgers appreciated punks' questioning of the status quo, aggressive music, and unconventional ideals but didn't like the heavy drinking, drug use, and cynical 'no future' attitude" (Haenfler 2012, 33).

3. It has a link to a certain space, be it local, translocal, or virtual. Morgan's study of a single performance space, Project Blowed, is a microscene par excellence, demonstrating how the microscene as a unit of analysis can be applied at many levels. At the other end of the spectrum, sociologist David Grazian's (2003) study of the Chicago blues scene is also enhanced by the microscenes perspective. Grazian conducted fieldwork in thirty-six different blues-oriented performance venues throughout the Chicagoland area. The downtown microscene consisted of venues that catered to tourists eager to hear well-known blues standards. This was distinct from the South Side microscene, which attracted a mix of locals, business travelers, and college students seeking what they perceived to be a more authentic blues experience, one that took place away from the downtown tourist traps and featured a different type of blues.

4. It has ties to a specific musical or artistic subgenre. Most forms of music can be divided into a range of distinct subgenres that appeal to different audiences in varying locations (see Lena 2012). For example, Harrison (2009) noted a division in the Bay Area's local rap scene, based upon subgenre: "underground hip hop" and "thug" rap. "Both formats form a branch of Bay Area independent hip-hop music, yet together they embody competing definitions of hip-hop authenticity that cannot always be reconciled. Regardless, the two are not mutually exclusive since underground artists and thug rap artists do collaborate. They are rather

mutually implicated in defining one another through notions of sameness and difference" (37). The microscenes perspective accounts for these types of differences. 5. It has an idioculture that distinguishes it in some way from the larger scene. An idioculture is "a system of knowledge, beliefs, behaviors, and customs shared by members of an interacting group to which members can refer and that serves as the basis of further interaction" (Fine 1979, 734). For example, at Project Blowed, MCs generally did not resort to homophobic slurs or excessive name calling during rap battles, as such behavior denoted lack of skill (Morgan 2009). Music festivals are better viewed as microscenes, too. Because music festivals are "components of broader music scenes" (Dowd, Liddle, and Nelson 2004, 149; emphasis added), they sometimes develop festival-specific idiocultures. For example, males over the age of ten were not allowed to attend the Michigan Womyn's Festival, a prohibition that distinguished the festival from its larger scene (157).

Chicago's rap underground is bounded by two large microscenes, divided by social class. One microscene consists of gangsta rappers and the other of socially conscious or "backpack" rappers.[9] This division is not unique to Chicago, but has a history that extends to rap music's inception.

Backpackers and Gangstas as Class-Based Analytical Frameworks

"Showdown!" proclaimed the cover of a 2007 edition of *Rolling Stone* magazine. The words were pasted across the faces of rappers Kanye West and 50 Cent, who squared off and glared at each other as if poised for war. West, a Chicago hit maker whose thoughtful lyrics hinted at his art-college background, and 50 Cent, a former crack dealer turned gangsta-rap superstar, could not be more distinct. It was their contrast that provided the article's hook: two rappers from opposing ends of the spectrum release new CDs on the same day in a battle to sell the most copies. The *Rolling Stone* feature dutifully reported the cultivated images of the two celebrity rappers: West was described as a "pink-Polo-wearing preppy with a positive message," while 50 Cent was likened to a menacing hustler. These differences cannot be explained through racial analysis—Kanye West and 50 Cent are both dark-skinned African Americans. The dichotomous presentation of these two superstars, backpacker versus gangsta, reveals key social-class distinctions that continue to define and divide rap music.

Understanding the backpacker-gangsta divide is important because it is *the* site of contention in rap music. As ideal types, backpackers are progressives whose lyrics espouse social responsibility, racial unity, and gender equality; gangstas are nihilists whose lyrics are brimming with violent and misogynistic themes. The division between these opposing categories is rap's most enduring symbolic boundary, and continues to separate rappers and their audiences into distinct, if overlapping, sub-groups.[10] From the genre's inception and throughout its history there has been a split between socially conscious MCs and so-called street rappers, who represent two distinct, polarized elements of rap.[11] During rap's formative years a culture war was waged between groups such as Run-D.M.C. (a trio from the borough of Queens in New York City that dressed in black leather street gear and rapped in an aggressive style that was new at the time) and Public Enemy (a political outfit from suburban Long Island that rapped almost exclusively about social problems within the black community). In the late 1980s and early 1990s, backpacker acts such as De La Soul and A Tribe Called Quest stood in stark contrast to the gun-toting gangsta rap created by N.W.A, the Geto Boys, and Cypress Hill.

Backpack rap arose from the "nation conscious" acts of the late 1980s. "Using the rhetoric of the Nation of Islam, Rastafarianism, the styles and expressions of Black Panthers and Black Nationalist poets of the 1960s, and the wearing of African garb, nation-conscious rappers address the political and economic disenfranchisement of black people in mainstream America. Their songs [were] designed to promote empowerment, aware-ness, and ethnic pride among black youths" (Keyes 2002, 158). Updated for today's more racially heterogeneous rap-music landscape, backpacker rap eschews black nationalist ideology and focuses on social and person-al issues related to race, class, gender, and politics. The split between back-packers and gangstas was further concretized in the early 1990s, as some rap artists strayed from the nation-conscious sound and "began using rap as a vehicle to glorify a gangsta image, utilize gendered expletives (e.g. 'bitches and hoes'), and exploit drug lore, violence, and sexual promiscuity on and off the stage" (158). The mid- to late 1990s ushered in a fresh set of backpackers (The Roots, Jurassic Five) and gangstas (Tupac Shakur, The Notorious B.I.G.), and the new millennium continued apace with socially conscious MCs such as Talib Kweli, Mos Def, and Common opposite commercialized street rappers such as Ludacris, Lil Jon, and The Game. Today's backpackers and gangstas are represented by superstars such as

Lupe Fiasco and Rick Ross, but these archetypes are found in every facet
of rap music, including underground microscenes where unsigned artists
perform for small, local audiences.

Corporate media outlets tend to focus on gangstas and ignore conscious rap altogether. Critiques of rap music are typically aimed at the
culture's baser (gangsta) elements: violence, misogyny, sexual promiscuity, drug and alcohol abuse, cursing (including use of the "N word"), nihilism, and other forms of antisocial behavior. Politician and anti-rap
crusader C. Delores Tucker spent a good part of the 1990s disparaging the
genre and its purveyors. In 2002, conservative talk-show host Bill O'Reilly
criticized Pepsi for featuring gangsta rapper Ludacris in television commercials. O'Reilly asserted that Ludacris's music glorified a "life of guns,
violence, drugs and disrespect of women. The man can rhyme many words
and some of them are 'Glock,' 'crack,' 'hos' and, most frequently, the 'f-
word' in an amazing array of forms." Scholars sometimes echo these sen-
timents. For example, a 2006 study reported that listening to gangsta rap
led to a variety of social problems, including "alcohol use, malt-liquor use,
potential alcohol-use disorder, marijuana use, club-drug use, and aggression" (Chen et al. 2006, 378).[12]

Criticisms of gangsta rap overlook its positive elements, but also
echo class-based critiques of broader black American culture, illustrating the increased cultural and socioeconomic disparities described by
scholars of the black middle class. The notion that there are two "types"
of blacks was the source of an infamous 1996 routine by Chris Rock, a
black comedian of the hip-hop generation, who distinguished between
what he called "black people" and "niggas." In Rock's routine, black people
represented the upstanding black middle class (backpackers), while
niggas represented the criminal-minded black lower class (gangstas).[13]
"There's like a civil war going on with black people," Rock declared in
the routine. "There's two sides: There's black people, and there's niggas."
Similarly, sociologist Elijah Anderson (1999) separated "decent" and
"street" black families in his study of poor Philadelphia neighborhoods.
Thus, reflected in rap's split between backpackers and gangstas are the
same class-based divisions described as polarizing the larger black community. These class-based differences can be extended to other ethnic
groups as well, including the emerging Latino middle class, and those
who distinguish "white trash" from whites of higher economic and sociocultural status.

Divergent Characteristics of Backpackers and Gangstas

As iconic figures of pop culture, backpackers and gangstas are class-based identity types through which various forms of culture are shaped. They represent two extremes on a continuum that allows for plenty of ideological, cultural, behavioral, and symbolic variation. These are not hard, fixed categories; there is often considerable overlap between back-packers and gangstas, and no rapper belongs strictly to either category.[14] Most rappers draw upon and select aspects from elements of both the backpacker and gangsta models. For example, it is somewhat rare to find a backpacker who never curses in her music, and many backpackers project larger-than-life auras that rival those of their gangsta counterparts. Tupac Shakur may be considered the quintessential gangsta rapper, but some of his lyrics were stridently political, demanding social justice for women and people of color. When Kanye West claimed on wax to be the "first nigga with a Benz and a backpack," he positioned himself at the center of the backpack–gangsta continuum and illustrated the polarization of these two schemas.

Virtually all rappers—regardless of ethnicity, artistic style, or individuality—can be consigned to one of these two broad categories. To which category one belongs is signified by a number of cultural cues, including clothing, hair, jewelry and other accessories, aura, body language, musical influences and aesthetics, lyrics, on-stage banter, political outlook, activism, and degree of social consciousness. There is not always agreement on what constitutes morality in these arenas; many backpackers view gangstas with derision and vice versa. Even the terms "backpacker" and "gangsta" are sometimes perceived to be or used as insults. Backpackers in Chicago rarely self-identified as such, nor did every gangsta appreciate the label. Most members of the city's rap underground, however, referred to others using these categorical terms. By defining each other in this manner, backpackers and gangstas created class-based symbolic boundaries that impacted the content and character of Chicago's rap underground.

Sociologist Pierre Bourdieu (1984) pointed out that any division of a population into two groups has consequences: an "us versus them" mentality arises whereby each group favors itself and acts in ways that are hostile and discriminatory towards the other group. In her study of for-profit workers and cultural specialists, sociologist Michèle Lamont (2002) discovered both groups were quick to invoke moral boundaries in relation to each other: "The opposition between the two groups is often expressed under the cover of political attitudes, symbolic and political boundaries being drawn at one and the same time" (101). In part, this type of class-based boundary work is functional. As communications scholar Kembrew McLeod (1999) noted, divisions such as these maintain in-groups and out-groups, and help preserve the allegedly "pure" core of hip-hop culture. By drawing class-based distinctions between and among themselves, backpackers and gangstas were equally able to make claims to cultural purity.

The backpacker–gangsta dichotomy is useful for understanding how social class functions differently within collectives. Chicago's rap underground was bifurcated at every level by this class-based symbolic boundary: there were bands composed of various ethnoracial groups and there were mixed-gender acts, but there were no groups that blended backpackers and gangstas. It was rare for backpackers and gangstas to perform together onstage, to appear on each other's recordings, to attend each other's shows, or to lend meaningful support to one another.[15] This resulted in two rap microscenes, divided by social class, with differing sets of norms, ideologies, and cultural practices that both shaped and constrained the interactive processes and social exchanges that occur within them. Chicago's backpacker and gangsta microscenes diverged along eight characteristic dimensions: social class, race, style, musical aesthetics, lyrics, performance, audience, and aspirations.

Social Class

In Chicago, backpackers and gangstas tended to come from different social class backgrounds.[16] Of the 135 rappers I interviewed, 57 were backpackers and 78 were gangstas. Table 1 demonstrates basic class indicators for both groups. The rappers came from a variety of backgrounds, but overwhelmingly the gangstas were lower in measures of social class relative to backpackers. Backpackers had higher rates of education than gangstas.[17] The average backpacker had some college training, but gangstas were likely to have gone no further than high school. Twenty-five percent of backpackers had a college degree, as opposed to five percent of gangstas. (Of the gangstas with college degrees, most were earned through prison education programs.) Backpackers were slightly more likely to be

---

TABLE 1

Social-class indicators for backpackers and gangstas

SOCIAL-CLASS INDICATOR	BACKPACKERS	GANGSTAS
Level of education (average)	2.97	2.25
Level of education (median)	3	2
Has college degree	25%	5%
Currently a student	22%	23%
Ever married	15%	12.5%
Ever divorced	3%	5%
Has at least one child	41.9%	40%
Has more than one child	16%	22%
Median number of children	1	2
Parents married	53%	52%
Parents divorced	47%	48%
Father's level of education (average)	2.64	1.97
Father's level of education (median)	2.0	2.0
Father has college degree	45%	13.5%
Mother's level of education (average)	2.91	2.75
Mother's level of education (median)	3.0	2.0
Mother has college degree	43%	32.5%
Two parents with college degrees	25%	11.6%
Average number of siblings	2.9	4
Median number of siblings	2	3

---

married, but gangstas were almost twice as likely to have been divorced. About 40 percent of both groups had children, but gangstas had twice as many children as backpackers.

Both groups were about equally likely to come from a single-parent home as they were a home with two parents. Parental level of education (a more reliable class indicator, given that this was a relatively youthful cohort and more than 20 percent of participants in both categories were college students) for backpackers was also higher than that of gangstas. Nearly half the fathers of backpackers had a college degree, but the fathers of gangstas were likely to have only a high school education. Furthermore, backpackers were more than twice as likely to come from homes where both parents held a college degree. Backpackers also had on average about one less sibling than gangstas, implying greater access to parental resources, be they financial, emotional, or otherwise. The social class differences found here imply a structural element to the division between backpackers and gangstas. The available choices one made when assimilating into either the backpacker or gangsta-rap microscene were influenced by one's social class background.

Perhaps unsurprisingly, backpackers and gangstas employed the rhetoric of social class to describe their differences. Gangstas described backpackers as coffeehouse intellectuals who rarely put in an honest day's work. Gangstas believed that they were more authentic than backpackers because they were from the "streets" and told real-life stories from the perspective of society's have-nots. Backpackers were depicted as suburbanites without the day-to-day problems found in the 'hood. Conversely, the backpackers described their counterparts as inauthentic studio gangstas who inflated their 'hood tales to the level of fiction and glorified violence and misogyny. According to the backpackers, the gangstas pretended to be members of the lower classes to boost their credibility to their potential audience, when in reality most were middle class.

Race

Chicago provided a unique setting for researching underground rap music. Previous studies of rap music have taken place in more racially heterogeneous settings (Harrison 2009; Morgan 2009), less racially heterogeneous settings (Jeffries 2011; Schloss 2004), or have focused on a single ethnoracial group (Neff 2009; Rodriquez 2006; Sharma 2010), but Chicago's demographics offered a relatively even split between the three largest ethnoracial groups in the city, the metropolitan area, and the United States.[18] Table 2 shows race as a percentage of the total population for Chicago, Cook County, and this study. According to the 2010 census, 32.9 percent of Chicago's population was black or African American, 28.9 percent was Hispanic or Latino, 16.1 percent was white, and 5.5 percent was Asian (1.6 percent Chinese, 1.1 percent Asian Indian, 1.1 percent Filipino, and less than 0.5 percent of citizens fit either the the Japanese, Korean, Vietnamese, or Other Asian categories). 13.4 percent of residents identified as "some other race" and 2.7 percent as two or more races. Providing

TABLE 2

Race as a percentage of total population

RACE	CHICAGO	COOK COUNTY	CURRENT STUDY
Black or African American	32.9	24.8	34
Hispanic or Latino	28.9	24.0	36
White	16.1	31.4	22
Asian	5.5	6.2	-
Some other race	13.4	10.6	-
Two or more races	2.7	2.5	8
Total percent	99.5	99.5	100

additional context were the ethnoracial demographics of Cook County, which contained most of Chicago's larger metropolitan area, and was the setting in which all of my fieldwork took place. In Cook County, home to about 5.2 million people, 31.4 percent of the population identified as white, 24.8 percent as black or African American, 24 percent as Hispanic or Latino, 6.2 percent as Asian, 10.6 percent as some other race, and 2.5 percent as two or more races.

The racial demographics of my participants aligned closely with that of the city and the larger metropolitan area. Of the 135 subjects, 49 (36 percent) self-identified as Latino, 46 (34 percent) as African American or black, 29 (22 percent) as white, and 11 (8 percent) as biracial or multiracial. Compared with the city of Chicago, blacks, Latinos, whites, and those of two or more races were overrepresented, and Asians and those fitting the "some other race" category were underrepresented. Compared with Cook County, blacks, Latinos, and those of two or more races were overrepresented, and whites, Asians, and those of some other race were underrepresented.[19]

While my research does not purport to contain a representative ethnoracial sample of Chicago's underground rap scene, in six years of observation I noticed a fairly even split between blacks and Latinos. There was also a smaller yet noticeable white population, although whites tended to assume auxiliary roles (DJs, producers, promoters, fans) more often than they took the stage as rappers. Because Latinos had a visible presence

TABLE 3

Racial differences between backpackers and gangstas (percent)

RACE	BACKPACKERS	GANGSTAS
Black	26	40
Latino	28	42
White	35	11.5
Bi/Multiracial	11	6.5
Nonwhite	65	88.5

in Chicago's rap underground yet are underrepresented in rap-music scholarship, I actively sought Latino participation.[20]

Given the inseparable relationship between social class and race, it comes as little surprise that the backpacker and gangsta musicians in Chicago also differed on this dimension. Backpack rap was created by a variety of ethnoracial groups, whereas the gangsta subgenre was predominated by blacks and Latinos. Table 3 illustrates the racial differences between backpackers and gangstas as a percentage of the total number of participants for each microscene. Table 3 demonstrates that gangstas were primarily black or Latino; backpackers were a mixture of black, Latino, white, and those who identified as biracial or multiracial. Blacks and Latinos were more likely to be gangsta rappers than backpackers. More than one-third of backpackers were white, but less than 12 percent of gangstas were white. Those who identified as biracial or multiracial were found in both categories, but the larger portion was backpackers.

Rap music, in Chicago and elsewhere, is still very much rooted in black American culture and tradition. Chicago's backpackers and gangstas, regardless of race, drew upon a long history of black cultural practices, and incorporated them into their lyrics, live performances, speech, and dress. But backpackers and gangstas used blackness differently. Backpackers drew upon one set of ideas about blackness and gangstas another. These ideas were rooted in social class differences found within the black community.

In his study of conscious rap microscenes in Massachusetts, sociologist Jason Rodriquez (2006) found that white fans justified their participation in a culture popularly defined as black by employing color-blind discourse: subjective concepts such as "skills" were said to matter and race was deemed unimportant. In Chicago, nearly all rappers employed a similar rhetoric. Rap was no longer an exclusively "black" thing, they said, it belonged to everyone. Yet race served as a symbolic boundary that impacted the array of cultural choices available to members of various racial and ethnic categories. Blacks and Latinos could freely participate in either the backpacker or the gangsta microscenes, but there were constraints for whites (and perhaps some multiracial groups) who aspired to be gangsta rappers. Of course, whites could assume a gangsta persona, and some did, but this symbolic boundary was much more difficult to transgress. For white rappers, being a backpacker was the path of least resistance, one that afforded them the best chance at fitting in with scene members and finding an audience.

This strategy also came with its own claim to authenticity: whites were "keeping it real" by not "acting black." On some level, of course, all white rappers are "acting black" in that they are participating in a culture rooted in blackness. In Chicago, the white rapper performance of blackness was not problematic in and of itself, and white MCs deployed a host of rhetoric- and practice-based strategies to deemphasize race (see Harkness 2011, 2012a). It was difficult, however, for whites to assume a certain *type* of blackness, the gangsta persona, a category distinguished by social class.

A latent function of this dynamic was that blacks and Latinos were more likely to get caught up in the gangsta image and lifestyle. The risks associated with adopting a gangsta persona can lead to any number of problems, especially for artists whose gangsta image is incongruent with their lived experiences. "Artists who assume a gangsta posture on stage, or the so-called studio gangstas, are often confronted by rivals who fail to distinguish artists' real selves from their fictional ones" (Keyes 2002, 173).

Style

A primary identifier of subcultural membership is style: clothing, jewelry, shoes, hair, and body language, all of which are important demarcations of subcultural membership and identity. Subcultural scholar Dick Hebdige (1979) believed that members of subcultures used style to communicate group identity and difference. For example, by sporting a Mohawk haircut and a leather jacket held together by safety pins, punk rockers used fashion to project a distinct identity to the world. This style did not merely connote fashion preferences, but also an ideology: the punk rocker's rejection of "normal" hair, for example, denoted an anticonformist worldview and rejection of the mainstream.

Likewise, Chicago's underground rappers projected collective identity and ideology through style, but backpacker and gangsta styles were quite different. Rap style is derived from assorted archetypes including the hustler, the gangsta or thug, the working-class man, the militant, and so on (Keyes 2002, 125). The varied uses of style by Chicago's backpackers and gangstas communicated class-based differences, including divergent group identities and ideologies.

The archetypical Chicago gangsta dressed in baggy jeans and professional sportswear; shirts, hoodies, and hats emblazoned with corporate logos; and "celebrity" clothing lines such as Sean Jean (Sean Combs), G-Unit Clothing (50 Cent), and Roc-A-Wear (Jay-Z). They sported massive "bling" rings, thick watches, chunky bracelets, and long platinum or gold chains weighted down by flashy medallions. Some wore sunglasses onstage, or sported grills—elaborate metallic dental veneers constructed from faux gold or platinum. Color-coded bandanas were tied strategically around necks and wrists. Timberland boots or name-brand tennis shoes, such as Nike or Adidas, were the preferred footwear.[21] Embedded within gangsta style was an ideology: the prison and gang look connoted a close association with criminality, violence, and danger. The diamond jewelry accentuated the ability to acquire and display material wealth. The corporate logos emphasized consumerism; the sportswear, masculinity and competition. The boots and denim shirts implied a blue-collar work ethic, and sunglasses projected an aura of distance and cool.

The archetypal backpacker dressed less flashily than his gangsta counterpart, an antifashion statement that illustrated a bohemian ethos. Blue jeans, army or cargo pants were worn with a T-shirt, buttoned-up polo shirt, sweatshirt, or sweater. Backpackers avoided ostentatious jewelry, although some wore small earrings or watches. Beanies, Kangols, and applejack hats perched atop domes; eyeglasses and neckties added an intellectual, businesslike look. Some toted backpacks or messenger bags, even on stage. Like gangsta rappers, backpackers favored boots and name-brand tennis shoes. Embedded within backpacker style was an ideology: the backpack and its contents denoted a connection to the nonmusical elements of hip-hop culture, such as graffiti and breakdancing. The lack of jewelry and overall flash underscored an ethos of nonmaterialism. The hats accentuated a playful, optimistic outlook, and eyeglasses signaled intellect. The buttoned-up, collared shirts, neckties, and sweaters were adapted from the white-collar day jobs held by many of the Chicago back-packers. The boots underscored the working-class, everyman aspects of backpacker ideology, while the army fatigues were a throwback to the Black Panther dress code as well as hippie protestwear, aligning the back-packer ethos with the civil rights and peace movements of the late 1960s and early 1970s.

For both groups, style was aligned with markers of social class. Gang-stas, lower on the class strata relative to backpackers, used fashion to dis-play high-status indicators of wealth and consumption, augmented by signifiers of criminality and violence.[22] Backpackers, higher on the class strata compared to their gangsta counterparts, used fashion to downplay their class position, but augmented this with signifiers of white-collar, intellectual, and political culture. Hebdige (1979) referred to such amal-gamations as *bricolage*, referring to the processes by which subcultural members appropriated bits and pieces of mainstream culture and blend-ed them together to create new meanings. Contained within the styles of Chicago's rap microscene were distinct class-based ideologies: the gang-sta's based on the rap-hustler version of capitalism, and the backpacker's rooted in intellect, cultural pride, and social justice.

Musical Aesthetics

From an aesthetic perspective, the sounds of backpacker and gangsta music rap were divergent and unique. Gangsta rap is hard hitting, with thundering beats, sinuous bass lines, and moaning keyboards. Producers such as DJ Magic Mike, Dr. Dre, and Mannie Fresh built the foundation for gangsta-rap sonics, each adding signature flourishes and regional twists to the basic format. Consider historian Robin Kelley's (1994) vivid description of an instrumental by legendary gangsta rap outfit Compton's Most Wanted: "Mixed in are the sounds of automatic weapons, a looped sample of blood-curdling screams . . . would-be assassins hollering, 'You Die, motherfucker.' This disturbing cacophony of sound captures the fra-gility of human life, the chaos of violent death, and the intense emotions young murderers and their victims must feel" (128). Gangsta rap was de-signed to be played at top volume, preferably blasting from an elaborate, bass-heavy car stereo system. According to Kelley, black rap fans deploy loud music strategically as a means by which to control or take ownership of public space. The backpackers in Chicago were generally appreciative of gangsta rap's musical aesthetics, but the reverse was not true. The sound of backpack rap dates to rap music's origins, but was popularized in the late 1980s and early 1990s by "Native Tongue" acts such as De La Soul and A Tribe Called Quest. Other forerunners of the backpackers' less street-styled productions include Dana Dane, Doug E. Fresh, Biz Markie, DJ Jazzy Jeff, and the Jungle Brothers. The musical aesthetics of backpack rap were refined, sparse and "low fi" or wildly experimental, with samples appropriated from an array of sources. Live and acoustic instruments were not altogether uncommon, and producers of backpack rap drew influence from the history of black American popular music, including jazz, blues, soul, and funk. Backpack rap was designed to sound great through headphones, where close scrutiny of the music was possible. The gangstas decried the backpacker production as paper-thin and lightweight, with tinny beats that had little sonic or emotional resonance. Not all backpackers disagreed with these critiques.

Like style, embedded within these divergent musical aesthetics were polarized ideologies rooted in social class. Gangsta rap's thumping bass lines, booming beats, and "street" noise emphasized power, physicality, hypermasculinity, and the dangers and thrills of criminality. Conversely, backpack rap's easygoing, subdued beats downplayed machismo, while its incorporation of various black American musical genres endorsed shared history and collaboration.

Lyrics

Lyrics are the principal signifier of a rapper's identity. In Chicago, backpack and gangsta rap varied widely in terms of lyrical content, reflecting divergent ideologies in stated terms. Lyrics were also used to create and maintain class-based symbolic boundaries. Embedded within these descriptions was a class-based ethos used for identity building and boundary work.

Gangsta lyrics espoused misogyny and conveyed the violent and sometimes criminal elements of "street" life: drug dealing, gangbanging, pimping, and gunslinging. Yet gangsta lyrics also contained first-person narratives that offered poignant critiques of social problems such as police brutality, racism, and poverty. Drawing on the work of Elijah Anderson, criminologist Charis Kubrin (2005) discovered that gangsta-rap lyrics contained a street code that touted respect, violence, material wealth, retribution, and to a lesser degree, nihilism and misogyny. Images of toughness, violence, and guns were prevalent. The functions of this code, Kubrin concluded, were to demarcate social identity and reputation and wield social control. The lyrics provided "both a formula and a justification for violent street identities" (372). In Chicago, the gangstas insisted that their rhymes reflected the harsh realities of the urban poor, and described their lyrics as more realistic, meaningful, powerful, and authentic than backpacker rap.[23] Backpackers were critical of gangsta-rap lyrics, and argued that the subgenre's themes were tired and unoriginal. Inadvertently echoing the criticisms of Bill O'Reilly and his ilk, backpackers believed that the gangstas glorified violence, criminal activity, sexism, and hypermaterialism. They believed gangsta rap lacked any real message, and was dumbed-down music for the masses.

If gangsta lyrics adhered to a code of the street, backpackers might be said to have a code of the suburbs, one that espoused unity, equality, and social consciousness, and warned against the dangers of violence, racism, drug abuse, and political apathy. Backpack lyrics were described as positive, Afrocentric, motivational, abstract, analytical, scientific, educated, and political. The backpackers believed their rhymes to be more creative, artistic, original, intricate, realistic, passionate, intelligent, and beneficial to audiences than gangsta rap. Both backpackers and gangstas generally described backpackers as lyrical "artists," purists who eschewed commercial considerations in favor of creating art for art's sake. While many gangstas expressed admiration for backpackers, some criticized conscious rap lyrics as lacking street-level authenticity, and believed that eccentric backpack rhymes were difficult to comprehend or take seriously. Other gangstas chided the backpackers for overthinking their raps, trying too hard, or being effete.

Performance

In concert, gangstas projected a larger-than life aura, and had dangerous, crazy, hypermasculine, and/or swaggering "pimp" vibes. Stalking the stage, gangstas took cues from gang and prison culture, employing a complex series of coded hand gestures and signs. During performances, gangstas did not use DJs or live musicians, but rapped over prerecorded tracks. Onstage they were sloppy and boisterous; they drank alcohol, smoked cigarettes, cigars, and/or marijuana. A somewhat common practice during performances was to pull out a wad of cash, peel off bills and throw them into the audience. Their performances reflected an ethos of violence, masculinity, materialism, and competition.

Conversely, backpackers were practiced and professional, emphasizing nimble displays of verbal prowess and encouraging the audience to have a good (and safe) time. Backpackers projected a low-key aura and had a relaxed vibe that put the audience at ease. Some backpackers were high energy, but in an upbeat, nonthreatening way. If backpackers drank onstage, it was bottled water or soda. Live instrumentation was not uncommon, and some backpackers were supported by full bands, augmented by a DJ. The DJ generally played a key role at backpacker shows, scratching and mixing the sonic backdrops on the spot, using vinyl records rather than digital derivations, and creating an old-school atmosphere.

Some backpackers were critical of gangsta-rap performances, stating that gangstas tended to angrily stalk the stage and say very little. Backpackers were especially critical of gangstas for the somewhat common practice of rapping accompanied not by instrumental tracks, but over preexisting recordings of their songs that included vocals. Conversely, gangstas chided backpackers for putting too much emphasis on wordplay during performances and not devoting enough attention to pleasing the audience.

Audience

Backpackers and gangstas catered to different audiences; fans of gangsta rap attended gangsta-rap shows and fans of backpack rap attended backpack rap shows. Race seemed to play a role in the audience composition. In Chicago's rap underground, gangsta-rap shows were typically attended by blacks and Latinos, and there was also segregation within those categories. For example, Latino gangsta-rap shows often took place before almost exclusively Latino audiences. An ethnically heterogeneous crowd typically attended backpacker shows, a phenomenon also found in Harrison's (2009) study of the Bay Area backpack microscene. While there was a relatively large white audience for backpacker concerts, gangsta-rap shows were sparsely attended by this demographic. Beyond racial makeup, however, in Chicago a percentage of the audience had some connection to the rap-music microscene. Becker (1982) witnessed this same phenomenon in his study of art worlds: the audiences for local artistic events were composed largely of members of the local artistic community. In Chicago this was also true, but there was little commingling between the backpacker and gangsta art worlds. On the rare occasions that the two audiences did mix, there was often indifference or even outright hostility between them.

Aspirations

Backpackers and gangstas in Chicago diverged in terms of career aspirations. At the modest end of the spectrum were "hobbyists" (who made music for enjoyment and had little or no expectation of receiving money from it) and "realists" (who hoped that rap music would provide a living wage, that they could earn enough income from music to avoid outside employment).[24] The hobbyists and realists were uniformly backpackers. Realists had slightly higher aspirations than hobbyists, but were still modest in their goals. A realist backpacker named Doctor Who told me that he "would like to just make a living off of this, just a middle-class living, pay my bills that I got now." The backpackers were largely pragmatic about their chances of making it in the music business. Even those backpackers (and there were many) who hoped to become wealthy enough to earn a living from music were practical about their prospects and modest in their goals. Backpackers defined success using a rhetoric of artistic purity, stating that conscious rap was untainted by monetary considerations and therefore morally superior to gangsta rap. Backpackers described themselves as being in it for the love of the music rather than the money.

Comparatively, the gangstas had grandiose ambitions that included chart-topping albums and sold-out stadiums. The high aspirations of the gangsta rappers, combined with their position at the bottom rungs of the hegemonic class structure, resulted in a different relationship to commercialization than backpackers. The gangstas typically had no problem commercializing their lyrics, sound, or image in order to appeal to the masses. Selling out or going commercial was a nonissue; it was the goal. Getting signed to a major label—perhaps the ultimate sign of selling out, to a backpacker—served as an indicator of success to gangsta rappers.

The more CDs you sold, the more endorsement deals you signed, the more T-shirts you hawked, the greater your success. Many of the gangstas in Chicago were adamant that they were in this as much for the dollars as for the art. This did not mean that artistic merit was unimportant to the gangstas; commercial success *represented* artistic merit to them. If anything the gangstas viewed themselves as more authentic than backpackers because mass acceptance signaled making it. To achieve this, the gangstas subscribed wholeheartedly to the American-dream ideology: through hard work, motivation, sacrifice, and personal effort, success was virtually guaranteed.

There were two factors that helped account for these class-based differences in ambition. One explanation was that the backpackers, who were more educated, had a better sense of the actual odds of making it in the music business. Knowing that their chances of success were small, they hedged their bets and created modest goals that were better aligned with their realistic potential for achieving their goals. A second explanation was that the gangstas had more to lose by not making it. If music didn't pan out, backpackers could rely on their college degrees, day jobs, or even their parents. Many of the gangstas believed that making it in the music industry was their only legal opportunity to achieve upward mobility. With little to lose and everything to gain, the gangstas were fully invested in the belief that hard work would pay off. This may have spurred them to take greater risks in pursuing success. For a portion of the gangstas, these risks were compounded by their status as members in local street gangs.

Gangbang Capital

There is a degree of overlap between Chicago's street gangs and its gangsta-rap microscene. Some believe that it stems from Chicago's extended history of crime and corruption. A rapper named Cipher told me, "That's always been a big part of Chicago: gangs, gangstas, pimps. So it's always gonna be a big part of the music." Participants who were gang members sometimes had difficulty keeping the two worlds separate. "I try not to engage gangbanging with rapping," said Dustup, a member of the Spanish Cobras. "But it's fucked up because when I rap I'm around nothing but gangbangers."

While national rates of crime have steadily decreased for more than a decade, gang membership has grown every year since 2003 (National

Gang Center). In 2010, there were 30,550 violent crimes reported in Chicago, including 437 murders. Of the murder victims, 88.3 percent were male and 95.4 percent were either black or Latino (Chicago Police Department 2010). Street gangs are responsible for approximately 70 percent of all crimes in Chicago (National Drug Intelligence Center 2008). Unsurprisingly, members of Chicago's gangsta-rap microscene claim to feel unsafe; they often carry weapons or travel collectively for protection. The number of gang members and the patchwork distribution of gangs, they said, made Chicago uniquely dangerous. "Every three blocks is a different gang," a gangsta rapper named Ikon insists. "You go three blocks, it's MCs, the next block is BDs, the next three blocks is GDs, the next block is Vice Lords. Stones over there, Latin Kings over here."

Chicago gangs are divided into two adversarial umbrella confederations, the People Nation and the Folk Nation. In part, this organization was a response to the number of gangs in Chicago. "Instead of scores of street gangs all fighting one another for turf and honor, two major coalitions were consolidated to absorb all the internecine hostilities and rearticulate them along one fundamental Us/Them divide: the symbolically constructed border between People and Folks" (Conquergood 1994, 30). The People and Folk Nations are not gangs; rather "they are alliances under which gangs are aligned. A simple comparison might be the National and American baseball leagues. The National League is not a team—it is the alliance under which teams like the LA Dodgers and Atlanta Braves are aligned. The American League is the alliance under which the Baltimore Orioles and New York Yankees are aligned" (Security Threat Intelligence Unit). The symbolic boundary between these groups is not based on race, ethnicity, or geography. "People Nation and Folks Nation gang branches are distributed throughout the city, thus making Chicago a patchwork quilt of continuously alternating Nation turf" (Conquergood 1994, 31). The piecemeal distribution of People- and Folk-affiliated gangs in Chicago adds an element of danger for gang members who travel the city—allied and rival territories can change on a block-by-block basis.

Gang members "represent" or display their gang affiliation and People/Folk alliance using a series of coded symbolic exchanges that involve some combination of hand signs, gestures, clothing, jewelry, hairstyles, language, colors, and tattoos, and left/right alignment. To declare their affiliation to the public and fellow gangs, members of People-associated gangs display to the left, "turning their hat bill to the left, wearing earrings in the left ear, tying their left shoe in a certain way, cuffing their left pant leg, etc. Folks gang members do the same, but to the right" (Chicago Crime Commission 2012, 16). The People/Folks alliances continue to carry considerable weight in the Illinois penitentiary system, where publically displaying gang affiliation is forbidden. Chicago gangs still declare People/ Folks affiliation, but these alliances have less meaning than they did even a decade ago (ibid.). Furthermore, rivalries sometimes occur between gangs supposedly united under one of the two Nation coalitions.

The People/Folk Nation alliances continue to crop up in gang-related graffiti throughout the city. For example, People draw a five-pointed star or crown, and Folks paint a star with six points. According to a rapper named Platinum, the divisions between these two factions remain a source of tension for gang members who are part of Chicago's gangsta-rap microscene. "You got a lot of these inner city kids that come from the People and the Folks. And each section's got a representative right now out there, every mob has got someone out there that's spittin'," he said. "You have these two crowds, and on the streets, they're enemies, they shoot, they kill. When we do shows, we have a lot of opposition that come out. I bring my guys, they bring their guys."

In Chicago, gang members who rap enjoy a vaunted position in the city's gangsta-rap microscene. Countering hegemonic class structures, gang membership is a desirable status, a demarcation of authenticity in rap music, where "keeping it real" is imperative. Chicago's rapping gang members derive tangible benefits from their gang affiliations, yet these associations also contribute to a host of difficulties, including violence and the threat of arrest and incarceration. To navigate this rocky terrain, Chicago's rapping gang members utilize gang membership selectively, sometimes emphasizing this status to accrue resources, in other instances downplaying it to diminish risk.

It is my position that the gang members described in this book were largely risk avoidant vis-à-vis violence. While gang members are often portrayed in the mainstream media as willfully savage, it is my observation that they—like most people—do their best to avoid violence in most circumstances. Many joined gangs as teenagers to manage the risks of growing up in dangerous neighborhoods, and emphasizing their gang ties was a means of gaining advantage in the risk-laden music business. Rappers with felonious pasts are often glorified by the media—and marketed by record companies—as authentic street poets. Thus, it made perfect sense for the rappers studied here to play up their criminal backgrounds. They did so, but in order to manage the attendant risks, they did so strategically.

Rap Hustlers

Street gangs and gangsta rap are youth cultures predominated by working- and lower-class black and Latino males. Recent national survey data found that in larger cities, 45.5 percent of all gang members were Latino/ Hispanic, 39 percent were black/African American, 9.7 percent were white, and all other racial categories accounted for 5.8 percent (National Gang Center). About 93 percent of all gang members were male. In large cities like Chicago where there are long-standing gang problems, gang members are more likely to be over the age of 18.

I interviewed 135 people interviewed for this book, 23 of whom claimed to be active gang members.[25] Of the 23 gang-member participants, 8 were African American (34.8 percent), 13 (56.5 percent) were Latino, and 2 (.09 percent) described themselves as multiracial. All were male. Their ages ranged from 18 to 35, with an average age of 24 at the time of our first interview. Most of them did not have legitimate jobs. Many still lived with their parents or other relatives, and wives or girlfriends typically supported those who did not. Many earned a few dollars from low-level drug dealing. Compared to the larger sample of 135 participants, the gang members had lower rates of education, were less likely to have a job or be a college student, were more likely to have fathered a child, had more siblings, and were the offspring of parents with lower rates of education and jobs with lower occupational prestige. The few who had taken college courses or obtained postsecondary degrees had done so while serving time in prison.

There was a trajectory that marked most of the gang members' entry into rap music. Most were gang members well before they started rapping. For example, Swag was part of a drug-dealing street gang before he became interested in music. "I never, ever thought about being a MC," he told me. "I was just on the street all the time doing my dirt. We started as a street crew: selling drugs, selling weed, selling all that shit. That's where it all started. Motherfuckers makin' bread. It's like a bunch of drug dealers off the street came back with that hip-hop essence."

In the postindustrial era, jobs have increasingly moved out of the inner city and into inner- and outer-ring suburbs. The minority youth population of inner cities has grown, resulting in greater competition for fewer jobs (Wilson 2009). The available jobs tend to pay low wages and have little or no opportunity for advancement. Poor, inner-city ethnic minority youth are among the hardest hit by the trends (Watkins 2012). Many of these young people are forced to seek alternate means of employment. Sociologist Sudhir Venkatesh (2006) studied the underground economy in Chicago's inner city, looking at those who did "off the books" jobs, including cleaners, cooks, mechanics, hairstylists, and small-time entrepreneurs of all stripes. In addition to the potential risks related to unreported income, many of these jobs involved a relatively high degree of risk, including drug dealing, prostitution, pimping, and gang-related economic activities such as money laundering.

Many of the rapping gang members had run afoul of the law, generally beginning in their early teens. Most had been incarcerated, some for short periods of time, others for as long as a decade. Convictions ranged from petty narcotics crimes to attempted murder. Their lack of legitimate employment and encounters with the criminal justice system encouraged the young gang members to seek alternate routes to economic freedom. Their options, they insisted, were limited to sports and music, two winner-take-all industries with slim odds for success. Bleek, a Gangster Disciple, quoted rapper The Notorious B.I.G., telling me, "Big said it: If you ain't got no wicked jump shot or you ain't flowin', I don't know where you goin'. So yeah, rap is my way out."

Poor and working-class inner-city residents have increasingly turned to sports and rap music as means of escaping poverty. These ambitions carry a high risk of failure, but there are social and economic rewards for those able to reach the elite level. Individual talent and motivation are highly subjective, but athletes can be ranked quantitatively. An aspiring basketball player who is seven feet tall has a measurably better chance of playing professionally than a player who is 5′5″. Becoming a good rap musician, however, is far more subjective. There are no quantitative measures that render one's chances of success better or worse. Rather, there are only idiosyncratic measurements, such as talent, personal ambition, motivation, and work ethic.

The rapping gang members described in this book believed their firsthand experiences with gangs and crime gave them a leg up on the competition. Gangsta rap's obsession with authenticity meant that those at the bottom of society—those who were poor, were raised in crime-plagued neighborhoods, those who had been shot, been arrested, served time, or were gang members—had résumés perfectly suited for gangsta rap. Following a rap-hustler blueprint popularized more than twenty years ago, the rapping gang members fully intended to go from streets to stages. Subscribing to the American dream ideology that through hard work one could achieve unlimited success, these young men saw rap as their ticket out of poverty. This rap version of the Horatio Alger myth was doubly appealing because it enabled them to flip the script on hegemonic structures of social class, and get rich in the process.

1

Who Shot Ya?

A Tale of Two Gangsta-Rap Rivals

When a man who served nine years in prison for armed robbery, assault on a police officer, and unlawful use of a weapon tells you to be there at 8:30 p.m., you get there at 8:25. I'm standing at the address Habit gave me on the phone earlier, a nondescript two-flat with faded side paneling and a small yard surrounded by a rusty chain-link fence. Habit is Puerto Rican and lives in the Logan Square area of Chicago. Logan Square—which boasts a Latino population of more than 65 percent and where the median household income is below the city average—is an uneasy juxtaposition of petty street crime, gang warfare, and encroaching gentrification.

For the last few years, young, urban hipsters have moved into the neighborhood, followed soon after by a gaggle of condo developers and yuppie first-time buyers. The building next to Habit's went condo last year. The tenants were evicted and the apartments were gut-rehabbed with hardwood floors, granite countertops, and stainless steel appliances.

I met Habit after attending a concert whose lineup featured his group, Xcons. It marked a turning point of sorts, a chance to journey deeper into the gangsta-rap underground. When Habit texted me, asking for a ride to an Xcons concert on the South Side, I saw it as an opportunity to get to know him better and jumped at the chance. At this point, I knew very little about Habit, only that he was a rapper with a lengthy criminal pedigree and a reputation for trouble in the gangsta-rap microscene.

I stand on Habit's front porch, shivering in the February cold. The wind is tsunami-like tonight, blocking out the sounds of late-model cars, tires spinning their way through what looks to be about a foot and a half of snow. Despite the white noise, from the bowels of Habit's apartment I hear the steady thump-thump-thump of rap music pounding at top volume. I push the buzzer but no one answers, so I dial Habit's cell phone. A dozen rings later, he picks up.

"I'll be out in two minutes," he shouts over the din. "Just hang tight."

Twenty minutes later, Habit appears on the porch, seemingly unaware of the elapsed time. Maybe he just doesn't care. Guys like Habit don't have to hurry.

Habit seems immune to the cold. He's dressed in a lightweight yellow-and-white madras jacket over a white tank top and baggy jeans tucked into a pair of unlaced tan military boots. A set of dog tags, a few rings, and two earrings are his only jewelry. It's pitch black tonight, but Habit's sporting a pair of oversized sunglasses, and two long braids wind around from his nape to the middle of his chest.

I'm a big guy, but Habit looks like he could take me out with a casual backhand. Six-feet-something, with the granite physique of a man who's spent more of his adult life behind bars than performing in them, Habit cuts an imposing figure. Some of this comes from his build, but most of it stems from the mischievous, slightly maniacal energy that he emits at all times. He puts you on edge and keeps you there; you don't know what's coming but it's probably going to be some form of trouble.

"Where are you parked?" he asks. Even his questions sound like orders. We hop in my car and slush our way to Fullerton, heading east towards Lake Shore Drive. We're going out south tonight to Chicago Heights, at the extreme southern end of the city. I settle in for a long drive. Habit talks. And talks.

This is a prison rap group. We was all in penitentiaries together for years. I'm talking about six, seven, eight *years*. We started rapping in jail so we already jailhouse legends. There's nothing you can say that could ever blemish our character or our image whatsoever. In jail, there's no question about are you real or are you fake. Nigga, if you in jail, you as real as it gets. So can't nobody never take that away. That's why I strongly feel that there's no way we can't make it. Because rap is urban; rap is the tale of the have-nots. And there's nobody that can represent the have-nots better than us. Everybody can say they can represent 'em, everybody can rap about representin' 'em. But when it comes down to the black and white, you can pull my record off the computer, and it's gonna tell you what I was locked up for and how much time I did. And if that's not representing the streets, then ain't no such thing.

Habit is a gangsta rapper. A real one. A longtime member of the Spanish Cobras. Habit's hardcore rhymes are as gritty as they come. He and every member of the Xcons have served time in prison, doing lengthy bids for such crimes as attempted murder, armed robbery, assault, and a string of gun and drug-related offenses.

Habit began rapping when he was a kid, but it was in prison that he started to take it seriously. Bored with a monotonous routine of weightlifting, cutting heads in the prison barber shop, and watching TV, Habit started freestyling to pass the hours.

When you in jail, literally, the walls are gray. They paint the motherfuckers gray for a reason: to make you feel dull as shit. At the end of the day, there was nothing to shoot for. I already know I got cases on my back. I can't even get a job at McDonald's; I can't get a job nowhere 'cause I'm convicted for a violent crime. The only thing I loved more than doing the dumb shit I was doing, was rapping. And I just started doing it and taking it serious in there, started dreaming and hoping and shit.

Rap not only gave Habit a way to pass the time, it gave him a goal: the promise of a better life beyond the prison walls. Habit's felony convictions would deny him access to even menial work in the Chicago labor market, but he had the perfect pedigree for gangsta rap, where pen time serves as the ultimate stamp of authenticity. He began to hone his craft, performing reps of raps like a weightlifter, and building his vocabulary through classes in the prison school. Slowly, and without much fanfare, he got better.

While rapping in the exercise yard one day, Habit's freestyles caught the attention of a young man with cappuccino skin and crimped hair that flowed halfway down his back. Tattoos of every variety adorned a physique sculpted from a daily routine of heavy weights, and his cocked eyebrow split the difference between threatening and playful. Even in drab prison blues, he had a hustler's swagger. His name was Bleek and he rapped, too.

Bleek

Bleek was born in the Uptown neighborhood of Chicago's North Side. At age five, he was taken from his family by the Department of Children and

Family Services and placed into a group home on the city's South Side. Bleek immediately began getting into trouble. By age nine he had joined the Gangster Disciples, Chicago's largest and most notorious gang. Bleek embraced the Disciples' lifestyle head-on, brawling, robbing, and selling drugs by the pound. He was arrested in eighth grade for stealing a car, and his teenage years were spent in and out of Cook County jail on various drug and weapons charges. He also started rapping around this time, drawing inspiration from the hardcore rhymes of N.W.A, Scarface, and Spice 1. He enjoyed rapping, but not nearly as much as he liked hustling drugs and making money, a career strategy that soon caught up with him.

"It just all hit me in '99," he recalls. "Blue City, by Belmont and Clifton. Back in the late '90s nigga, we was gettin' it like twenty stacks [i.e. $20,000] a day. We out there killin' 'em. Catch a dope case. Two months later, catch another dope case. I'm out on two different bonds. I cop out for seven-seven [i.e., a plea bargain], intensive probation. Two weeks later, it's war time. Nigga gotta get the iron, shoot a coupla niggas, let 'em know that we not just rappers. We do this for real, we gangstas."

Bleek's victim testified against him in court, and on his nineteenth birthday Bleek was found guilty of first-degree attempted murder and sentenced to six years in the Illinois state penitentiary system. Looking to avoid trouble and cut some time from his sentence, Bleek enrolled in college courses through a program sponsored by Southeastern Illinois University, where he eventually earned degrees in business management and applied science. This is a notable achievement given that in 1999, only about 3 percent of prisoners in Illinois earned such degrees (Street 2002, 5). Bleek also started taking rap more seriously, filling dozens of notebooks with gritty street prose. He wrote more than three hundred songs during his imprisonment, arranging the best ones into eleven separate albums that he hoped to release someday.

Before I went to prison, I was just like a freestyling kid, around the way, getting into the cipher with the guys at high school. But when I went to the penitentiary, when I really sat down and started writing, it was like write every day. You ain't gonna get no wicked jump shot if you don't shoot 300 shots a day; you not gonna get good if you don't write raps every day. And us being in prison, that's all we had to do. When we'd come back in from school and working out, it's writing. For hours. That's all it was:

write, write, write, write, write. If I hadn't started writing every day and doing what I was doing, trying to better myself as an artist while I was in there, I'd be back in the penitentiary. That ain't no secret. That or a nigga slump me over or something. Music is what saved me. It keeps me focused. Something to live for, something to chase; my dream.

Bleek's jailhouse dream included the formation of a rap group, Xcons. As he was transferred to different institutes within the Illinois system, Bleek recruited new members along the way. The burgeoning band was based out of Vandalia when Bleek met Habit. "When a new rapper comes on the scene and you a rapper in the joint, everybody wants to see a battle," Bleek recalls. "They wanna put money up, put cigarettes up on his buddy against this guy. So they was like, 'Yeah, there's this new Latino. He over there.' So we meet and we just clicked."

Reflections

As we drive south of Chicago's downtown Loop, Habit starts to open up, dropping some of his rough exterior and revealing a side of himself that I had not seen before and did not expect. It is disarming and makes both of us feel uncomfortable at first, but we settle in to a pattern: I drive, Habit talks. He talks about his childhood and how he was wreaking havoc from day one. "I was always a troublemaker," Habit remembers. "I got suspended from kindergarten, man. How you gonna get suspended in *kindergarten*?" Habit's tumultuous upbringing included living in a poor neighborhood with a single mother who struggled to raise three children on a bus-driver's salary. Habit's father wasn't in the picture at all.

"He's a wise guy," Habit muses. "Before I was born, he was already gone. Got a new family and shit. I'm twenty-eight now and I seen him probably about ten times in my life. Never on a birthday or nothing like that, only when it didn't count. I know where he at, but ain't nothing to say."

In grade school, Habit was diagnosed with attention deficit hyperactivity disorder, and was subjected to a series of counselors, therapists, and psychologists. They unanimously recommended medication but Habit's mother refused. Her brother, Habit's uncle Wiki, was medicated for similar reasons as a child, and grew to be a serious drug addict, eventually dying of AIDS. Not wanting to put young Habit on the same path, she endured her son's hyperactivity and mood swings.

Habit started rapping when he was ten, and even then, he says, the dark side of his personality was evident. Today, he tells me, he wants to explore the furthest realm of his creative powers, to make music from the soul, but when he tries to write uplifting, positive lyrics, nihilistic themes arise out of nowhere. "That dark shit always take over, that street shit," he intones. "Motherfucker really don't be wanting to, but it somehow gets its way in there. I want to express something else, I wanna get a little bit deeper, but I always end up doing the street shit."

Habit talks at length about a track he wrote years ago in prison entitled "Reflections." The number, he says, is an autobiographical account that contains some of his most personal lyrics. I ask Habit if he'll recite a few lines and he resists, changing the topic to something about how Xcons is going to take over the industry within five years. Ten minutes later, out of nowhere, he launches into the song, delivering an a cappella version so powerful I almost drive off the road. Habit's gift is his ability to convey pain in every line he raps. Like the legendary blues, gospel, and soul singers of yesteryear, Habit moans every word as if it were being dragged from him against his will. The song details the self-hatred and hopelessness Habit felt behind bars, how the shattering of his dreams led to suicidal thoughts, and how he blamed himself for his failings.

There are no plans to release "Reflections"; it's not a commercial song, according to Habit. Radio won't embrace the track and clubs are only interested in playing danceable party music. Habit tells me that he feels constrained by the commercial demands of the rap-music industry, which is focused on candy-coated hit making. With Xcons, Habit says, the goal is to meet these demands squarely and make the most commercial music possible. I ask if his definition of success is financial, rather than artistic.

"In my current situation, in my current mind frame, yes," he states flatly.

> Don't get it fucked up. Of course I'm trying to be mainstream, I'm trying to get some money. That's what this is about, some money, man. I love the art. That's embedded in me, I feel like I was born with that shit. But what the fuck good is it if you ain't got no money? What good is it if you ain't reaching a million people?

Then your art doesn't get heard. That's like a painter that paints for himself only. What the fuck you gonna paint for? So you can look at it? You put that shit in galleries, you put that shit around the world. You got Mona Lisas and Michaelangelos. They paint, man. I'm doing the same exact thing.

The Prison-Industrial Complex

Between 1980 and 2001, the number of prisons in Illinois grew by more than 266 percent (Street 2001). As the War on Drugs locked up increasing numbers of young, black males, the state built twenty new correction facilities to create room for a massive influx of inmates, 65 percent of whom were black and nearly half of whom came from Cook County. This included Bleek and most of the other members of Xcons. As these young men entered the prison system, they brought the sounds of the street with them, and prison walls across the state reverberated with Chicago rap. While locked up at Vandalia, Xcons began "touring," traveling en masse from exercise yards to lunchrooms, challenging all comers to impromptu rap battles. With no music to back them, the group members would pound on chairs and stomp their feet in unison to create beats. This is where Xcons built and cemented its reputation, according to Bleek.

We been in prison since '99, '98, '97 doing this. Behind the wall, where you gotta wake up every morning to the sound of "break-fast." Here come the SWAT team, everybody asshole naked. Back to the yard, we hitting 275 [makes weightlifting motions], we banging it out. We would go from building to building with our rap crew and just dare anybody to come across our path. Anybody who did, they was murdered lyrically. If the penitentiary was the streets, we woulda been like the Roc-A-Fella or the Bad Boy or the Death Row of the music business. We was all the way down state in the furthest penitentiary you can go, Vienna, but you got people all the way across state in Danville, and Victorville, and Jacksonville, and our name is ringing in them penitentiaries. Because people that came down to see us in one prison, done transferred to another, and then the word about our rap group done spreaded like germs.

Boss Bee

The first time Boss Bee was arrested, he was in sixth grade. Growing up on Chicago's West Side, it seemed as if Boss Bee was in trouble with the law at birth. Boss Bee grew up in K-Town, a section of North Lawndale notorious for gangs and crime. Raised by a strict single mother who was generally too busy working to keep a close eye on her wayward son, Boss Bee was running in the streets at an early age as a sometime member of his neighborhood gang, the Four Corner Hustlers, a division of the larger Vice Lords gang. But even then there was another side to Boss Bee. His sad, brown eyes and reserved demeanor made him appear a bit more thoughtful than his rowdy peers. "I had a short temper," he admits. "But I was always the quiet type, the thinking, observing type."

When Boss Bee was thirteen, his mother remarried and the family relocated to Rogers Park, a neighborhood on the far end of Chicago's North Side. The hope was that the move would keep young Boss Bee off the streets and rein in his proclivity for trouble. A few weeks after settling in, Boss Bee was playing basketball at a local park when members of the Four Corner Hustlers approached him with an offer he didn't refuse.

> I was already fuckin' with the Fours when I was a shorty out west.
> So it happen my mom move, and there's Fours right up the street.
> A guy got in my ear. He was like, "Man, you can get out here and
> get some money." He used to tell me, "I could see you with jackets
> and hats with diamonds on it. We come through in cars. You see
> that over there, you can have that." He was strokin' me. He was
> really influencing me to fuck with them up north. And I started
> fuckin' with the Fours. We started pushin' and shit.

In the ensuing years, Boss Bee was arrested countless times on drug and weapons charges. No one besides his mother seemed overly concerned about it, because as a juvenile, Boss Bee's record was expunged the day he turned seventeen. Unfortunately, hitting that milestone didn't slow him down any. Boss Bee was arrested in 1998 after being caught trying to sell three ounces of marijuana. He was sentenced to four years in prison, which—per Illinois law at the time—was immediately reduced by half. He served eighteen months in a boot camp before being transferred to the Cook County Juvenile Temporary Detention Center, where he spent another six months in lockup. The state's efforts to reform Boss Bee failed. Upon release, he picked up right where he had left off. In October 2001, less than three months after gaining his freedom, Boss Bee was arrested for attempted armed robbery. The judge was not amused and sentenced Boss Bee to fifteen years in the state penitentiary. Due to his previous conviction, the sentence was "enhanced" by the state. Rather than being charged with a class 1 felony—typical for armed robbery at that time in Illinois—Boss Bee was charged with a class X felony, reserved for the most serious offenses. Class X felons still had their sentences automatically cut in half, but could not earn additional "good time" for upstanding behavior or attending vocational classes. Boss Bee was facing more than seven years of incarceration. "I pretty much got railroaded," he recalls.

Being in prison didn't diminish Boss Bee's membership in the Four Corner Hustlers. "When you go to jail, either you affiliated or you get [killed]. Everybody's affiliated except the neutrons." Before entering the state penal system, Boss Bee assumed he would have to join forces with the larger Vice Lords gang for safety reasons, but the Hustlers had a large presence, and the two gangs remained separate entities. "Fours is they own thing out on the streets," Boss Bee explained. "Once I went to the joint, I was under the impression that it was just Vice Lords once you got in there. But even that was a lie. It was like all Fours and they wasn't even fuckin' with the Vice Lords. That's how much of a bunch the Fours created outside of Vice Lords. It was enough Fours for me not to even go in there looking for Vice Lords. But don't get me wrong. We all ride together when we in jail, unless we got into it with some other motherfuckers who was Vice Lords and we was Fours and you want to get down."

Upon entering prison, Boss Bee became, in his words, a "jailhouse lawyer," spending every spare hour outside his cell in the library, poring over law books with the help of a fellow inmate, who worked as the prison's de facto legal clerk. The pair discovered that in order for Boss Bee's sentence to be enhanced, he had to be at least twenty-one years old at the time of arrest; Boss Bee was only nineteen when he was arrested. He immediately filed an appeal and the state was forced to reduce the class X charge to a class 1 felony. As a result, Boss Bee's fifteen-year sentence was reduced to ten, meaning that he would serve five years in prison and be allowed to shave off an additional few months by earning good time.

With nearly five years of prison ahead of him, Boss Bee did what many young prisoners did to pass the time: he started rapping. Like Bleek and Habit, Boss Bee had always done a bit of freestyling in his spare time for fun, but started to take it more seriously in prison. Boss Bee honed his rap skills around the clock and began to earn a reputation as one of the better MCs on his cellblock. He started to see rap as an opportunity to turn his life around.

When I was growing up, I used to rap, but I was always insecure about it because everybody around me was so much better. I got serious when I got sentenced in 2001. I started writing. And it became a *passion* in jail. I really didn't want to do the streets no more. I wanted to find a vessel that could get me out the streets, other than trying to sell drugs and get rich like that. So I'm telling myself, "It's time to find something that's gonna get you out of here, man. I don't think you can do the streets and make it rich. I think you can get rich right here." I'm telling myself I got this talent, and I know I got it, but I'm holding myself back. (This is my good conscious talking to me, not my bad conscious.) So I had to make a choice. And I'm still struggling with that choice, falling off here and there. But that's how my passion for rap started: me going to jail and conditioning my mind and knowing what I want. Jail was a blessing in disguise. I mastered my craft in jail. Thank god for jail. That's why I am where I am. Jail sharpened me. Jail forced me to get in my cell and condition my mind.

One way that Illinois prisoners could earn good time was by taking educational courses. A high-school dropout, Boss Bee earned a GED in his spare time. Doing so enabled him to apply for a transfer to Vienna Correctional Center, a minimum-security facility where prisoners could earn college credits—and therefore good time—through a program at Southwestern Illinois College. In 2003, Boss Bee's transfer was approved.

On the bus to Vienna, a couple of inmates were talking enthusiastically about a rap group that was making serious waves, a reputation that reverberated through the various branches of the Illinois Department of Corrections. "They was like, there some motherfuckers down here that be smashing," Boss Bee recalls. "We been hearing about these niggas all the way in the county, in Chicago. They go from patio to patio, deck to deck, and *smash* motherfuckers."

At the Crossroads

After more than an hour of driving, Habit and I arrive at The Crossroads, a cavernous barn of a nightclub located at the far end of Chicago Heights. We pull into the parking lot and are greeted by Boss Bee and an Xcons affiliate named Stretch, both of whom traveled here with Bleek in his tricked-out powder blue Chevy. Fist pounds, hugs, and handshakes are exchanged, and we all go inside. The Crossroads is mostly empty and it will only fill to about a third of its capacity by the end of the night. Tonight the club hosts its weekly open-mic rap competition. Groups or solo acts sign up and receive three and a half minutes of stage time. Those wishing for an additional three and a half minutes can acquire them by purchasing a $65 bottle of Moët champagne. The winner of tonight's competition receives a $50 cash prize and advances to the next round. At a later point, the finalists will compete for a grand prize of $300 and a track recorded by a local producer. The Xcons crew orders two bottles of Moët and settles in at a table near the bar.

I ask Bleek if he gets nervous before a performance and he shakes his head. "I never get stage fright, man. The more people, the better my performance. I spent six years in the pen doing this in front of a hundred of the hardest motherfuckers you'll ever meet. Throwing apples, and oranges, and tomatoes at you."

"You gotta know this," Stretch adds. "Everybody in the squad, goddammit, is real niggas! Everybody in this motherfucker right here on parole or just got off parole. That's what's so different, man. When we spit, we speak real shit."

Less than 10 percent of newly incarcerated gang members leave their gang once they are behind bars, and many of those go on to join different gangs. Approximately 25 percent of male inmates in America's penal system have some form of gang affiliation (Knox 2005). In prison, rap groups and their audiences tend to be divided by gang affiliation, and there is little opportunity for crossover. It was to their advantage that the seven members of Xcons represented seven different street gangs: Gangster Disciples, Spanish Cobras, Four Corner Hustlers, Black Stones, Unknown Vice Lords, Vulcan Hustlers, and Two-Two Boys. This created a no-fly zone of sorts at its prison-yard performances, a strategy that reduced the risk of gang-related violence and increased the band's potential fan base.

Audiences at these performances were notoriously fickle, according to Stretch, who insisted that "If you can rock a penitentiary crowd, a cappella with no beat, nigga, you a motherfuckin' *beast*. You a MC. That's real talk. There wasn't no beats, there wasn't no crowd, no microphones, no clubs, no alcohol, no bitches to cater to. We rapping in front of the grimiest niggas, convicts, the biggest haters in the world. Packin' penitentiary patios, spittin' a cappellas."

Prison rap is as gangsta as it gets. It's unusual, according to Xcons, to hear socially conscious backpack rap in prison. To rap about subjects that are anything less than hardcore is to be labeled effeminate, a recipe for disaster in prison. Bleek described the competitive environment:

It's hardcore. You got to be good in there. You're surrounded by all these dudes. That's the most hateful place; everybody in there hating on each other. It's hard to impress somebody in prison. When we used to get patio or get yard, we'd go out there and rap, and have a whole bunch of inmates wanting to come out there and see us. I'm talking about fifty, sixty, seventy, a hundred inmates at a time. If you could do that in prison, then it should be easy out here. Because if somebody's mediocre out here, they're garbage in the penitentiary. The best artists have been locked up.

Each year more than 600,000 prisoners are released from state and federal prisons. The majority of these inmates "return to a relatively small number of heavily disadvantaged minority neighborhoods, where they remain largely beyond the sphere of the mainstream society's awareness and concern" (Street 2002, 7). A 2003 study (Visher, La Vigne, and Farrell 2003) of prisoners returning to Chicago from the Illinois penitentiary system found that 60 percent of participants reported that prior to incarceration, a portion of their income was derived from criminal activities. Nearly 30 percent claimed that crime was their sole means of income.

In 2003, Habit was finally released from prison after nine years in and out of the pen. He found the initial adjustment period unsettling.

Everything changes. When you live most of your life in the prison, and you return to the street, the streets are not familiar to you. Nothing in my personal life was going how it was supposed to go. Financially, things weren't going how they was supposed to go, and I was just really shaky out here, on the verge of going back. I was so comfortable with being in jail. Going to jail, in a sense, you're running away from something, something in your life. So it's real easy for me to go back to jail, it's real easy for me to get locked up. I could get locked up again in a minute. I know a million things you can do to go to jail, and I'll do every single one of 'em.

One by one, the other members of Xcons were paroled, and by mid-2006, the group was fully reunited on the outside. The band began recording tracks in Habit's claptrap bedroom studio. They had no money and few prospects, but they had spent years sharpening their rhyme skills and writing material. Now they just needed an audience. "When we got out, it was like, you know what, there was no reason in dreaming and making all these plans if we wasn't gonna do it," Habit says. "We got out here and we started with nothing. We started with beats and a piece of paper."

They also had Habit's computer, with which they created a MySpace profile for Xcons and individual pages for each group member. The profiles included each member's prison mug shot alongside the usual selfies and snapshots taken with friends and peers. They began posting tracks online and networking. People listened. Some liked the group's music, others didn't. Xcons began performing at local nightclubs, trying to establish a following.

However, success eludes even the hardest-working musicians, and Xcons was frustrated by its inability to get from the streets to the limelight. There was concern that the street life would catch up with them before they could make it in the music business. Bleek explained:

> The longer it takes for us to get on, the greater the chance it is that we see ourselves back in prison. It's harder to stay out than it is to go back. If it takes me five years to get on in the music business, I might not last. I might catch a weed case or a thumper [i.e., gun] case and I'm back in. It's gotta happen *immediately*. We point-three seconds away from going back to the penitentiary. There's point-three left on the clock. Can you get this shot off?

Xcons had an additional problem on its hands: a growing feud with a rival rap act that hailed from Logan Square, an outfit as streetwise as Xcons was prison hardened. The up-and-coming group's recently released debut—CDs that the band burned themselves and sold for $5 apiece—was the talk of the Chicago gangsta-rap microscene. The group's name was Bully Boyz.

Bully Boyz

The first time I saw Bully Boyz in concert was at the Capitol Club, a venue located on Chicago's Northwest Side that I attended regularly. Performing as part of a showcase featuring up-and-coming Latino gangsta rappers, the lineup included Bully Boyz, Xcons, and Sissero, all rappers whom I would come to know during the course of my research. As nightclubs went, the Capitol raised an eyebrow or ten. Still in transition from its previous incarnation as a strip club, the Capitol was awash in mirrors and tacky neon, and a tarnished brass dancer's pole ran floor-to-ceiling through center stage.

Bully Boyz had just released its debut CD and it seemed to be everywhere. In a few short months, the group sold or gave away nearly 5,000 copies. Local clubs played its signature songs nonstop, and the disc's bass-heavy gangsta rap bumped from car trunks around the city. "The response was just crazy," remembers Grafta, who produced and created the music for Bully Boyz's debut. "It started off with a thousand CDs to like I need to re-up. Almost like the street business with drugs. Motherfuckers keep coming for this shit. We had to get more and more and more. Then it just turned out like I'm walking down the street or riding around and I hear our song. And I'm just like what the fuck? Motherfuckers is riding around the city listening to this shit. With that many people, I knew it was gonna happen."

The crowd at the Capitol Club was wall to wall that night, 300-plus mostly Latino gangsta-rap fans crammed into the venue's large main room. When Bully Boyz took the stage, ten members strong, the audience erupted in frenzy. Most of the band members were draped in brown and gold clothing, colors I would later learn were associated with the Insane Orchestra Albany street gang. "I know all my gangbanging ass niggas ride to this shit," declared Phantastic, one of the group's spotlight MCs, introducing one of Bully Boyz's many odes to gunplay. "This that grimy grimy gutta shit right here." Those in the front row roared and raised their hands to the ceiling; I noticed dozens of forearm-length Bully Boyz tattoos of varying design. Superfans.

"That shit was crazy," recalls Shank, one of the members of Bully Boyz. "That shit started happening once the CD started flooding all the area, locally. We got a crazy buzz, a lot of local people were just popping up with these tattoos. A lot of females, a lot of dudes. Even outlandish people that you wouldn't think of with tattoos. We got a female out there just got a tattoo that's bigger than half of us. We're like what the fuck? That's crazy. That's when you know people are dedicated to the movement. Those are fanatical fans."

One of rap music's shortcomings is its inability to translate in a live setting. The sonic subtleties of its production disappear when blasted through club PA systems. Over the cacophony, MCs bark lyrics at top volume, offering little of the nuance found in even low-budget studio recordings. Bully Boyz's performance at the Capitol that night defied these drawbacks. There was a tangible exchange of energy, a rare synching of audience and performer that I had not witnessed during the numerous rap-music shows I had attended in Chicago. The group pounded out a twenty-minute set of hardcore gangsta rap, with the songs taking on a life of their own as the audience shouted along to each line. I was sold; an instant fan.

"That show was crunk, crazy," Shank remembers. "That shit was off the roof. We got onstage and everybody in that motherfucker went crazy. Like the exorcism happened to the whole club. When we hit the stage it was like bombing Baghdad. It was like something blew the fuck up, and everybody in the world had to be scared. It was like the world ended or something like that. See Bully Boyz tattoos popping up that I'd never seen. See screaming, shirts, everything."

One of the great things about Bully Boyz—also true for iconic rap outfits such as Wu-Tang Clan, and even rock bands such as the Beatles—was that the members' personas were distinct. Bully Boyz's key players—Grafta, Phantastic, Shank, and Hymnal—were like a modern-day Super Friends, a cartel of unique talents and personalities that melded together into a whole that surpassed the sum of its parts.

Grafta was the musical boy genius behind Bully Boyz's sound. A production whiz from an early age, he melded the group's thunderous backing tracks, memorable hooks, and sing-along choruses into sonic gold. Diminutive and laid back to near comatose, Grafta tended to sport sunglasses at all times and say very little. But his powerful music spoke volumes, and everyone in Bully Boyz readily acknowledged him as the leader and

"CEO" of the group. Grafta spoke, everyone listened. Grafta gave an order, it was carried out without question. It was a power he carried quietly. Grafta didn't need to raise his voice to get things done.

Phantastic was the smooth cat, the fly guy. With skin the color of caramel and always dressed to a T, Phantastic was as cool as they come. In concert, he positioned himself directly at center stage and led the show, interacting loosely with the audience and urging the group's performance to higher levels of energy. Behind the scenes, he was described as the "foot in the ass" of the band, the one who kept everyone pushing towards what he saw as inevitable success. Contrasting with Phantastic's larger-than-life persona were his strict Muslim upbringing and his belief in the redemptive power of music.

Shank was three hundred pounds of boisterous fun and good times. While many gangsta rappers spent their time scowling, Shank was never less than a joy to be around. With an animated, gregarious flow and a perennial wink in his eye, Shank's raps were reminiscent of Big Pun and The Notorious B.I.G. in the best possible way. But Shank had his own thing going and it was a sight to behold. He was one of those MCs who could rap a word like "stupendous" and make it sound like the Bard. His rhymes hit with the force of a freight train, but offstage Shank could be found mingling with the fans and making sure the vibe was positive and upbeat.

Hymnal was the hotheaded little brother of Bully Boyz. A cocky eighteen-year-old with movie-star looks, a punctuated unruly streak, and a persistent case of acne, Hymnal was a wild card you didn't want to draw. While his bandmates occasionally inserted humor into their rhymes, Hymnal delivered every line at face value. His rhymes were gleefully violent and willfully aggressive, with nary a sense of irony or humor to temper the homicidal images.

Bully Boyz was founded by Grafta's cousin Max, a shadowy figure who remains somewhat elusive in the Bully Boyz story. Bully Boyz was Max's vision, according to the group. Grafta was always musically inclined, and got into rap music when he was six years old after seeing a Geto Boys video. He acquired a small Casio keyboard and starting recording beats into an old cassette deck. Grafta was equally attracted to gangbanging and was deep into the lifestyle by the time he was twelve years old. Max initially discouraged his cousin's interest in criminal pursuits, but soon took the youngster under his wing. "I thought that was the coolest shit in the world, gangbanging," Grafta recalls. "That's what I looked up to. Max kind of pulled me in, showing me what this shit really is about."

Grafta continued to make beats, too, and Max began to appreciate the potential in his young cousin. "He was like, 'If you're gonna do this shit, do your shit for real,'" Grafta recalls. "So I got on my little hustle. I started lookin' into shit. I started buying little pieces. My first little trip to Guitar Center, let me get that, let me get this. And I started going at it."

Grafta teamed up with another cousin, Focus, who was already developing into a fierce MC with a street reputation to match. By the time Grafta arrived on campus at high school, he had a full-fledged studio in his bedroom and was flourishing as a producer. At school, he met Shank, CapPeela, Nfamous, and Ikon, fledgling rappers who would become early members of Bully Boyz. Initially, the group had few serious ambitions; it was an excuse to get together, hang out, and have a good time.

"We all went to school together, so everybody was cool," Shank remembers. "We became friends. Catching sessions, smoking. We ended up going to the studio with Grafta. He introduced us to the studio: the microphone, the lyrics, the bars, the music. Before that, we was just rappers, that's all we did. We battled, we didn't know shit about music."

"It was a hobby," Grafta recalls. "That's what we would do after school: go to the crib, make some music. These motherfuckers would go home, do they homework, smoke some weed, don't do their homework. And then wake up and just keep doing this shit. It became a little more serious when motherfuckers started hearing about what we was doing. 'Cause we was just bullshitting, and motherfuckers were like, 'Ya'll should step it up. Ya'll got the potential to be somebody.' So that kind of gave everybody a little motivation. And we just started going at it, doing this shit."

Bully Boyz began writing in earnest, developing real songs instead of merely freestyling and joking around. The group recalls this period as among its most creative, an intense burst of songwriting that fueled everyone's desire to continue. "Songs were coming out like crazy," Shank recalls. "I was tweaking. I'm listening to songs at thirteen years old on the radio that weren't even comparing. I was like what the fuck? We're thirteen! Young as hell. How're you doing this? So we just all started writing to the shit Grafta was making, and then the shit we were writing was crazy as well. And it just started building. When it started it consisted of three MCs, and then four MCs, and then five MCs. It was like the Gremlins. You put water on them, they start popping out everywhere."

As Bully Boyz began to take its music more seriously, members came and went. Two notable recruits were Phantastic and Hymnal. Unlike the other members of Bully Boyz, Phantastic hailed from a middle-class background and was raised in a strict Muslim household. In his teens, he attended a private Roman Catholic high school with a twelve-to-one student-teacher ratio. "He was really quiet, kept to himself," remembered a friend. "He was really lovable." The backpack rhymes Phantastic was writing reflected this, and when he initially auditioned for Bully Boyz, the group was skeptical. Phantastic was persistent, though, and the Boyz eventually brought him into the fold. This experience proved transformative for Phantastic, according to Shank.

He had a whole different demeanor and a whole different type of music. But we embraced him and he came to the family. He molded with us and became Phantastic. He got the knowledge of us, our lifestyle, and became a Bully Boy. We basically built a monster. All we did was show him certain shit, and he had it. It was like he had it in him, it just wasn't open, like a locked door. We opened that door and he just came out like crazy. Boom! He found himself.

Hymnal's entrance was decidedly more organic.

I was in the 'hood, actually, in a trap [i.e., crack] house. And we were making money and shit like that. I was chilling with a dude they went to high school with. And I was rapping and he was like, "Man, you got a talent. I'm gonna take you to the studio." So he bring me that weekend, and everybody was there. Shank was there, Phantastic was there, Grafta was there. I spit a quick sixteen [lines of rhymes] and they was like, "Oh, hold on. Where did he come from?" I was already part of our secret society; I was involved with a lot. So they was like, "Fuck it, he's part of the circle anyway. This little nigga got talent, he a loyal-ass little nigga." So I ran with it. Started fuckin' with these niggas. Once you're in this shit, if you really that nigga and you really loyal for the shit, you'll breathe this shit every day.

Mixtapes

In underground rap music, there are two types of CDs. The first is the "album," a disc consisting entirely of original music or music created with authorized samples drawn from the works of others. An album is like any other "regular" CD. It comes shrink-wrapped in a case, has a bar code, and can legally be sold anywhere, typically for prices ranging from $10 to $15. In the Chicago rap music microscene, CDs are sold at record stores, performances, and through online retailers such as Amazon .com. The second and far more common type of CD is the "mixtape," a format unique to independent rap music. Mixtapes typically rely on unauthorized samples taken from major and minor rap hits. Sometimes producers remix the samples into "original" material, much like major-label rap artists do, but they don't purchase the rights to them. At other times, previous material is used wholesale, and the rapper merely offers his interpretation of another's song, adding new lyrics, but changing little else. At still other times, DJs create a mix of popular songs that highlight their particular tastes. Major-label rap artists fork over huge sums for the right to use or sample material from others. With mixtapes, these samples are not paid for and are unauthorized. These crude discs are generally burned onto CD-ROM, do not come shrink-wrapped and do not have bar codes. In Chicago, they are often handed out for free, although many artists and stores sell them for prices ranging from $3 to $10. Mixtapes are illegal, but typically sell so few copies that they are difficult to prevent. Mixtapes are distributed through various online means (generally for free download), sold at flea markets and swap meets, at concerts, out of car trunks, and under the counter at mom-and-pop record stores.

The popularity of mixtapes in rap-music microscenes around the country spurred an increasing sonic regionalism within the genre. Mixtapes allowed independent rap artists to bypass the music industry's corporate infrastructure and create music that was "informed more deeply by [a] region's particular terrains and tastes" (Dimitriadis 2009, 40). In the late 1990s and early 2000s, the widespread circulation of mixtapes in Southern rap microscenes—those found in cities such New Orleans, Houston, and Memphis—gave rise to Southern rap subgenres such as "bounce," "crunk," and "chopped and screwed." In the face of rap music's growth and international appeal, this "reclaiming" of rap music at the community level "solidified the notion of mixtapes as an alternative model for regions off the major-label radar" (41).

While it is widely reported in the media and most academic studies that a vast majority of rap music is purchased by whites, this statistic overlooks mixtapes, which are not counted by SoundScan, the company that tracks the sale of music through the major record-store chains, retail outlets such as Walmart, and online music retailers. Some mixtapes sell thousands of copies, and artists such as Danger Mouse from the multiplatinum group Gnarls Barkley began their careers with mixtapes. As mixtapes gained increasing street credibility, even major-label artists started releasing them. Lil Wayne, among the biggest stars in rap today, often takes years in between albums, but has released more than a dozen mixtapes since 2005, an astonishing collection totaling hundreds of tracks. There are even mixtapes of Lil Wayne's mixtapes. Lil Wayne was already famous, but it was mixtapes that made him a superstar.

Grafta had a similar strategy for Bully Boyz: to release a mixtape that would create a huge splash and launch the group's career. "When we dropped that, we weren't looking for no money," he said. "We had the plan already: let's get the streets, let's market this shit, let's do this."

The Bully Boyz debut mixtape consisted almost entirely of original music created by Grafta. He did, however, swipe a couple of samples, which prevented the distribution of the disc through mainstream channels. "A mixtape can only take you so far," Grafta told me. "That's one thing we learned. When you do a mixtape, the way you do it, it's like fuck all the paperwork, fuck all that shit, let's just do it. Throw it out there, let's go."

Bully Boyz's mixtape offered a wide variety of sonic sounds and styles. There were jazzy, laid-back tunes that wouldn't sound out of place on a De La Soul album, and salsa-inflected numbers that paid tribute to the group's Latin roots. There was even a sultry thug-love song as good as the ones Tupac recorded, as well as a mystical closing track that had religious undertones and pondered the afterlife. "The most responses I got were young teens: thirteen, fourteen, fifteen, sixteen," Grafta said. "They were just crazy about this shit; it was floating around high schools like crazy. That's what created that buzz was the young motherfuckers that were listening to our shit, who then turned it over to their older sister. We put so many styles of music and so many different artists on that mixtape that everybody could relate to it, from any color, race to any age group. From the forty, fifty-year-old lady to the young."

It was, however, the mixtape's violent, unabashed gangsta-rap tracks that caught the ear of Chicago's rap underground, and these were the songs that became most associated with Bully Boyz. The popularity of this material wasn't surprising. The tracks featured huge beats, sing-along choruses that stuck to the brain like cranial fluid, and vivid, prose-packed images of gang life seemingly drawn from the group's day-to-day experiences.

La Orquestra Albany

Bully Boyz attracted hordes of devoted fans and heaps of trouble every-where it played. The band had direct ties to the Insane Orchestra Albany (also known as IOAs, OAs, Aces, or just A's), a Folks-affiliated Latino gang whose roots date to the early 1970s. Interestingly, there has always been a relationship between the IOAs and music. As legend has it, the IOAs began as a group of salsa musicians who resided on or near Albany Street in the Logan Square neighborhood. La Orquestra Albany, as the band was known, was performing at a local block party when members of the Latin Kings street gang showed up and started a fight that resulted in the gun-related murder of one of the Orquestra Albany members. Seek-ing revenge, the band formed into a Folk Nation–affiliated street gang whose primary intent was to wage war on the People Nation–affiliated Latin Kings. (The enmity between these two gangs continues unabated today.)

In the 1980s, the Spanish Cobras, one of Chicago's largest and longest-running street gangs, formed an alliance with a number of fellow Latino gangs known as the Insane Familia. Every gang under the alliance added the word Insane to the front of its name to denote membership. Thus, La Orquestra Albany became the Insane Orchestra Albany, the name it con-tinues to use today. "We *are* them," Shank said when I asked him about the relationship between the IOAs and Bully Boyz. "This is my life. I am what I am for whatever I am forever. As far as that OA shit goes, that's me. That's what I am. I am a OA. I've never *not* been a OA. I'll die one of those. That's with me for my life."

Bully Boyz's ranks, however, were not limited to the IOA street gang. The group also featured members of the Gangster Disciples. "Bully Boyz got GD Folk, you dig what I'm saying?" Shank told me. "It ain't all just OAs. We got GDs, too, baby, from the [Robert Taylor Homes housing project]. This is the city of mobs. This is the gangbang capital. It ain't just go to one block and you see one thing. Every other block you step on is somebody else's territory. You dig what I'm sayin'? So if you survive here like we survive a nigga, you a fuckin' animal. A million gangs out here. You can't put your shit to the right [adjusts hat], to the left, none of that."

Hymnal explained why the gang situation in Chicago was unique in comparison to other large cities: "In New York, either you're a Blood or a Crip, right? In Chicago, it ain't like that. There's a whole different branch of gangs. This is gangbang central. . . . We the Middle East of Chicago in Logan Square. That is our university, LSU: Logan Square University. You go there, you learn shit, move forward from that shit, graduate, you do what the fuck you gotta do."

Hymnal had already earned a PhD in street life. A few months before the Capitol Club show, he was ambushed coming out of his front door. Shot twice, Hymnal spent a month in bed, "smoking my fuckin' brain out" and writing raps. Hymnal's survival only boosted his credibility in the overlapping gang and gangsta-rap circles. The incident didn't seem to rattle him much; he described it almost philosophically: "You're in the 'hood, you get what you get," he said. "What goes around comes around. You get money in the 'hood, niggas hate on you if you're out there like that. So I was out there, doing me. I didn't give a fuck about nobody. I thought I was untouchable. I got mine, but got blessed and shit. I'm good, I'm here."

I asked Hymnal if he was concerned that he wouldn't be so lucky next time. "I don't know," he replied. "The life I live, that shit, you choose you life, your lifestyle. You know when you gonna get into something, you know the consequences and shit that's involved with that shit. And my theory is, God's got a plan. If your ass is supposed to die that day, you're already dead. Your shit's been wrote in a book. If you gonna die that day, you gonna die. If you gonna survive that shit, you gonna survive. If it's gonna come again, it's gonna come again. There ain't no stopping it. You can't stop death."

Due to the band's association with the IOAs, Bully Boyz performances attracted dozens, sometimes hundreds, of gang members, many of whom were from rival sets. This uneasy commingling of adversaries, fueled by alcohol, women, and hardcore rap music, often led to fights at Bully Boyz shows. "We unite gangs," group member Escobar explained.

"We have about five, six different gangs at our performances. They choose to fight. When they first get there they shakin' each other's hands, and learning who's who. They get drunk, something happens."

Bully Boyz at the VIP Room

For a live-music venue so small it doesn't even have a stage, the VIP Room is surprisingly packed. The nondescript nightclub, located a few miles west of Logan Square, is crowded wall to wall. Patrons cluster near the bar and shout orders at two overworked staff members, who barely look up as they rush to mix drinks, collect cash, and make change. The youthful crowd consists primarily of Latinos, with a smattering of blacks interspersed throughout.

Bully Boyz is performing tonight, and there is a heavy gang presence, particularly IOAs. Brown and gold clothing is everywhere, and many of the audience members sport triangle-shaped bandanas that cover the lower halves of their faces. But the IOAs aren't the only gang on hand tonight. As is typical for a Bully Boyz show, members of any number of Chicago street gangs are in the house. Most, but not all, are Folks affiliated, and thus somewhat friendly with the IOAs. The atmosphere splits the difference between alcohol-fueled good cheer and switchblade tension. It's hard to know which way the winds will blow at the VIP Room tonight.

A section of the dance floor is cordoned off for Bully Boyz's performance, allowing virtually no separation between act and audience. As the band members enter this area, the crowd presses forward, jostling for the best sightlines.

The first time I saw Bully Boyz perform at the Capitol Club, the band members and their crew were heavily draped in brown and gold. Tonight, orange is the dominant hue. It's hard not to notice. Almost everyone in the group features the color heavily. For some, orange is displayed overtly, such as the baggy solid orange T-shirt worn by one Bully Boyz associate; in other instances, orange is used in accentuation: over a white T-shirt with orange lettering, Shank sports a white jacket with elaborate orange trim and an orange collar and cuffs. An orange baseball cap is cocked at a right angle atop his dome.

A number of audience members feature the color, too. One patron wears a brown-and-orange-striped golf shirt, another sports a similar shirt with an orange and blue color scheme. Another golf shirt features an orange collar; an otherwise black hoodie is accented by a thin orange string. As always, Phantastic is dressed to impress: the rapper sports an orange hoodie over a white T-shirt that features an elaborate orange, red, and yellow pattern splayed across the front. A red bandana is draped loosely around his neck, and his wrist features a watch with a red band, over which is a tightly wrapped orange bandana. Although it's nearly midnight, he wears bone-white sunglasses. His earlobes are studded with large diamonds, and his facial hair is sheared into a complex zig-zag pattern.

Phantastic grabs a wireless microphone and addresses the crowd. "Put your A's up. No disrespect to nobody, but we sure the hell gonna rep the fuck out the A, nigga." The IOAs in the audience respond by cheering as they hoist their arms in the IOA signature hand gesture, an elaborate twisting of the fingers that resembles the first letter of the alphabet. A bass-heavy heartbeat begins thumping from the sound system, as if the club were suddenly shocked to life via defibrillation. "Put 'em up, put 'em up nigga," Shank intones in time with the music, as the audience chants along at top volume, raising their As to the sky.

Cyberbanging

As with most facets of youth culture, the cultural practices of street gangs have been transformed by new technologies, most recently the Internet and the emergent use of social media as tools for communicative practices. During the Internet's formative period, what some scholars call Web 1.0, it was used primarily as a tool for consumption. Users logged on and consumed content that was created by others. According to sociologist Nathan Jurgenson (2010), the dot-com crash circa 2000, increasing connection speeds, and the shift away from desktop computers to mobile phones and other portable technologies helped usher in Web 2.0, the hallmark of which is user-generated content.

A multicity study of American street gangs and online behavior (Decker and Pyrooz 2012) found that 78 percent of current gang members go online and use the Internet, compared to 81 percent of nongang members. The increased popularity of user-driven sites such as Facebook, Twitter, and YouTube has altered the communicative practices of street gangs, which increasingly utilize user-generated social media technologies. The Internet's accessibility, "ease of use, potential audience size, and reduced risk of user detection has made [it] one of the most prominent methods of gang communication" (Chicago Crime Commission 2012, 298). In a phenomenon known as cyberbanging, "gang members now 'tag' social media sites through posts and pictures, just as they would 'tag,' with graffiti, exposed walls throughout their neighborhood. Gang members instigate conflict from the privacy of a home computer or their mobile phone, adding immediacy and impulsiveness to their conflicts and retaliations" (293). Gang members also use social media to pass information to peers, claim virtual territory, wage disputes, intimidate or make threats, and instigate violence against rival gang members.

There is a growing body of scholarship that examines the role of the Internet in criminal activity. "Cyber-gangs" sometimes collaborate with organized crime syndicates to commit illicit acts that range from money laundering and extortion to human smuggling (Britz 2008). The Chicago Crime Commission (2012) claims that street gangs use social media to commit cyber crimes such as identity theft and fraud, but academic studies have found little evidence to support this. Studies of street gangs and criminal behavior (Decker and Pyrooz 2012), however, have found that current gang members committed cyber crimes such as harassment, drug dealing, and the fencing of stolen goods at about twice the rate of former gang members or those who are not currently in gangs. Law-enforcement agencies increasingly rely on social media technology to track, monitor, and gather evidence against gang members (Chicago Crime Commission 2012; Frank, Cheng, and Pun 2011).

Studies have found no evidence to support the claim that gangs use social media in direct recruitment efforts (Décary-Hétu and Morselli 2011; Womer and Bunker 2010). Rather, social media allows gang members to promote their gang in various ways. In doing so, social networking sites render street gangs "a more accessible phenomenon for a larger portion of the population, increasing the number of favorable impressions that are transmitted about them" (Décary-Hétu and Morselli 2011, 880). In Chicago and elsewhere, gang members now regularly post videos on YouTube and other sites that promote their gang, insult adversaries, and wage war against rival gangs. The videos are steeped in symbolic communicative practices, and are typically accompanied by the invocation of a gang's most powerful symbols: its name, hand sign, colors, number, slogan, creed, and other ephemera.

As with most scholarship on gangs, studies of cyberbanging have failed to consider the relationship between the culture of street gangs and that of gangsta rap. As demonstrated in the online dispute between Chief Keef and Lil JoJo, gangsta-rap music is often the medium by which such exchanges take place. Even less understood is what occurs when online disputes become face-to-face encounters. Studies have found that gang members are about twice as likely to commit physical assault after being provoked online (Decker and Pyrooz 2012). "A single disrespectful comment typed, at a distance, to a rival gang member can escalate into a homicide within hours. Since social networking is instantaneous and mobile, an insult can be posted, read, and responded to in real time; this encourages rashness in communication, which can extend to a gang member's ultimate decision to respond in violence" (Chicago Crime Commission 2012, 294). These behaviors exist at the core of gangsta-rap culture, which is steeped in beef.

Chicago Beef

Beefs, or rivalries between rappers, have a storied history in rap music, and are often waged musically. Perhaps the first well-known beef was the so-called Bridge Wars that began in 1985, taking place between KRS-One (Boogie Down Productions) and Marley Marl and MC Shan (Juice Crew), and debating the true origins of hip-hop culture. The feud began with Marl and Shan's "The Bridge," which implied that rap music was birthed in Queens. KRS-One responded with "South Bronx," which made a similar claim for that borough. This sonic ping-pong match was waged for years, with the songs taking on an increasingly personal nature. It also got a lot of attention from fans and the press, who debated the merits of each side at length. The Bridge Wars laid the foundation for numerous beefs to come, and infamous dis tracks such as Ice Cube's "No Vaseline" and Tupac's "Hit 'Em Up" helped create and cement the legendary status of these artists. It comes as little surprise, then, that these beefs also take place in underground rap circles.

The cyber feud between Xcons and Bully Boyz was launched with the release of "No More Phans," an eight-minute dis track, recorded by Habit and directed at the entire Bully Boyz crew. Habit posted the song on his MySpace page, where it garnered hundreds of listens overnight. In the song, Habit called out Bully Boyz by name, verbally dressing down each member and labeling them, among other things, homosexuals, fake gangstas, and jealous. Habit's song attacked the entire group, but its title was clearly directed toward Bully Boyz frontman, Phantastic.

Habit penned the song following a couple of perceived slights from Bully Boyz. As Habit tells it, he tried to help the group by adding them to some Xcons shows. At one of these concerts, Bully Boyz finished their set with a flourish when Phantastic bought drinks for everyone in the audience. This move, which Habit found outrageously disrespectful, drew attention away from Xcons' subsequent performance. "I brought my people to them, into that whole new crowd at Club Capitol," he recalled. "We sold that motherfucker out and had it packed. We did that. So Habit took it upon himself. Because I'm a Tupac historian, and he said bomb first, so I bombed first![1] I smashed the motherfucker on a eight-minute song. And that's where the beef kicked off."

Bully Boyz responded to "No More Phans" by posting a dis track entitled "Fuck Xcons," in which the rappers called Habit, among other things, a "beautician" who had been raped in prison. "This ain't a MySpace war," barked a Bully Boyz affiliate on the track, who concluded the song with a menacing threat: "I ain't beefing over tracks no more. I'm gonna start catching niggas in the streets, and holla at 'em."

The online beef went back and forth for weeks. New songs were recorded and posted, and fans, associates, and pundits weighed in with opinions ranging from foul-mouthed to articulate. "Locally, that's some shit that fans love to see," said Chilly, an aspiring rapper who followed the online battle from his local high school. "Two groups that are from their city going at it. That's pay-per-view entertainment." In addition to the recorded taunts and insults, the groups began manipulating photos of each other and posting them on MySpace bulletins. One picture posted by Bully Boyz featured Habit's mug on a milk carton. "Habit: Missing," the carton read. "Have u seen me in the hood? Nope!!!!!" Habit threatened retaliation. "Controversy gets more attention than unity," he told me. "I'm not in it for the artistry, I'm in it for the money."

Grafta didn't see any money in the beef and wanted nothing to do with it. "All these egos and shit," he said dismissively. "At the end of the day, the way I look at shit is am I gonna make money on it? Then I don't wanna fuck with it. And I knew that shit wasn't gonna make no motherfuckin' money. Like I told all of them, motherfuckers that's fighting for crowns, why? What is the beef really over? Nothing. No one got richer."

True to form, Shank laughed the whole thing off. "If you don't like us, something fuckin' wrong with you. You got screws loose, you got shot in the head, you a vegetable, you mad 'cause your girl like us. Our MySpace page is on your girl's page. We dropped a comment. Or she dropped twenty [comments] on us. Or she talkin' about she wanting to fuck all kind of niggas. I don't wanna mention names 'cause we got baby mamas and shit. But still, we them niggas. You dig what I'm saying? Don't be mad at us, be mad at yourself."

The online rivalry seemed harmless enough, but when it spilled over into the streets things started to feel dangerous. The beef was complicated by the Bully Boyz's association with the IOAs and Habit's membership in the Spanish Cobras. Both gangs were both part of the Cobras-led Insane Familia alliance, and a dispute between the rappers could lead to problems between the two allied crews. "When it comes to the deeper aspect, I fucks with [Bully Boyz]. I'm affiliated with them," Habit noted, but he was genuinely upset: "Chicago is a gangbanging city. So we can only take it to a certain level. Then I have to turn around and hold the dogs back, because the dogs wanna take it to another level. And it's like, no we can't do that. We tryin' to keep it civilized."

"He came at *us*," Shank countered. "We weren't thinking, 'Let's come at that guy.' But when he threw so much shit into the fire, the fire grew so big that it burned, and we couldn't take it no more. We can't keep going at the same shit. We're gonna actually do something back to you. You go kill three lions, shit you gonna get killed on the fourth one. He fuck around and plot around on you now. You can't keep killing lions. What the fuck you doing? Lions *kill* people!"

Once associates, the two groups were now bitter enemies, and both camps predicted that it would end violently. In December 2006, Xcons booked a show at the Capitol Club and dared Bully Boyz to show up.

A Fight at the Capitol Club

You can practically smell it when a fight is about to begin at a rap concert. The air changes, the mood of the club shifts, and people are on edge. The dance floor clears and the music suddenly sounds forced, until the DJs pull the plug entirely. The house lights flare to life, and a scuffle breaks out somewhere in the distance. Sometimes the fights are quelled by security before they get out of hand, other times they explode into full-blown brawls that resemble old-time Westerns. The fight at the Capitol Club the night of the Xcons show was the latter.

Xcons took the stage with guns blazing. The group was on fire, and put in a performance that crackled with danger. The group openly taunted Bully Boyz from the stage, and though the crowd was close to capacity, Bully Boyz was nowhere to be found. This didn't stop Xcons from doing their own version of Fat Joe's song, "Make It Rain." Habit and Bleek reconfigured the strip-club anthem into a murderous threat:

> We make it rain, we make it rain on the block
> We make it rain, with AKs and Glocks

The Bully Boyz weren't listening. Grafta was holed up in the studio, working late into the night. Hymnal was somewhere taking care of business. And four Bully Boyz members—Shank, Phantastic, Leon, and Escobar—were on the other side of town, cruising around in Leon's lowrider. Escobar picks up the story:

> We riding together in a car, not doing shit, smoking. There was so much beef between Xcons and Bully Boyz, and it was a Xcons event. Phantastic was so thirsty to go over there. So we show up in that place. The DJ stopped the music right when we hit the floor. And everything just paused. It was like a movie. Bully Boyz's in the building. Then the music comes back on, and it's [a Bully Boyz song]. At our competition's show! And there's only four of us. So it's like, there's only four of 'em in here, they gotta be [carrying guns]. Which we were. Why would we go over there four deep when there was over a hundred of 'em? But we didn't go there to start a fight; we went there to make a statement.

"That was around the time that the tension was going on with Bully Boyz," Bleek recalls. "And it just so happened that they had walked in the door right before the fight started. So everybody was thinking, 'Oh there's Bully Boyz, there's Xcons. This is the first time they seen each other since the songs.' And the next thing a fight kicks off."

The Capitol Club is a bad place to be when a fight kicks off. It's a large room whose lone exit leads to a narrow hallway that snakes slowly out to the street. It's hard to get in and out when the venue is not crowded, let alone when 350 people start running towards the door. Chairs flew, tables were splintered, bottles were smashed over heads, women screamed, bartenders ducked, and everyone who wasn't involved in the fight was trying to get outside. I pushed my way to the street and took stock of the situation. People staggered out of the club, bleeding and picking broken glass out of their hair. Police sirens wailed in the background. Bully Boyz stayed inside to watch.

"People are getting beat up," Shank recalled. "We ain't moving for the simple fact that it ain't our problem, our conflict, our drama. Plus the people that they was beating up was some dudes that couldn't do nothing anyway. They was just getting beat up. Dude got hit twice. I seen dude get hit like two times. His hair was all over the place. Jake the Snake hair-ass nigga."

Habit chalked it up to "gang relations. Everybody trying to show support, but everybody don't get along all the time. You can't go to a show without somebody fighting, man. As far as the career I be chasing, that's not a negative. But the personal life is. That shit get out of control."

It took a dozen police officers and three ambulances to quell the situation at the Capitol that night. The club was all but destroyed in the aftermath. Nearly every piece of furniture and glass in the place was broken or smashed. The Capitol stopped hosting gangsta-rap concerts afterwards, a forgotten casualty in the Bully Boyz–Xcons beef.

"It didn't have nothing to do with Bully Boyz and it didn't have nothing to do with Xcons," Bleek insisted. "None of us was even involved, it had to do with some other guys. But we got the blame. We still got the blame for that. Everybody still blame us for that, and blame them. They lost the club for that. That was a big thing. But we didn't have nothing to do with it."

Sissero, a female rapper and Bully Boyz associate, chalked it up to the number of gang members on hand at gangsta-rap shows.

Chicago is a city of gangsters, it's a city of thugs and killers, and everybody's always got their enemy. Gangs are intermixing and it's gonna start some type of chaos, some type of debauchery. So we go to a show and we'll be with a certain group of people, and the other people don't like 'em and it starts a fight. I'm so used to seeing fights at shows. This happens all the time in Chicago; it's an everyday thing. It's really bad. We're killing each other off. I've been around it so much; I've kind of become immune to it. It's very real. Destiny is a motherfucker and it's going to happen however it's going to happen. Sometimes you see death so much that you become immune to death.

The Death of Phantastic

The last time I saw Phantastic alive was at Inclusive, a nightclub on Chicago's West Side that was hosting a weekly showcase for local rap acts. Bully Boyz was performing that evening, and I wanted to be there. I had recently interviewed the group during a late-night studio session. Phantastic never showed up. Nobody knew why he didn't make it.

When I saw Phantastic a couple of weeks later at Inclusive, I made sure to give him some grief about missing the interview, chiding him that he was probably too busy with one of his many lady friends to show up. Phantastic threw his head back and roared with laughter. The striking young woman tucked under his arm giggled, too.

"Oh, man. You got me," he said, clapping me on the back and flashing a warm smile.

"We still need to sit down and talk," I said, pointing to my video camera.

"Tell me when you want to do it," Phantastic said. "Just say the word and I'm there. You cannot finish this thing without putting me in it."

"I won't consider this thing finished until you're in it," I promised, and I meant it. "No worries, we've still got plenty of time. We'll get together soon."

We never got a chance to do the interview. Six days after the Inclusive show, Phantastic was in the hospital with a gunshot wound to the head, hooked up to a life-support system and fighting for every breath.

The phone rang early at Shank's crib that morning, waking him from a deep sleep. It was an acquaintance relaying the news that Phantastic had been shot. Shank didn't believe him. "I was just assuming it was fake," he recalled. "Made a phone call to one of his brothers, and they were crying. I feel chills right now, even talking about it. And it was crazy 'cause right when they told me, crying, that he was really in the hospital, it was reality. It was real. It wasn't a dream. I could feel it in my body, something was wrong. Once I heard my own crying, it was crazy.

It's something that you would never wish on your worst enemy. It's a crazy pain."

Within minutes, word of the shooting was announced on MySpace in a cryptic message, posted anonymously and passed on via a succession of reposts. "I'm on my way to the hospital. Please pray for Phantastic of Bully Boyz who was shot in the head last night. I will not be disclosing the location of the hospital, but please keep him in your prayers. I will be the one to update when I can, and please respect at this time that the Bully Boyz familia might not be in a talking mood as most of us will be in the hospital all day. God Bless."

"I was sleeping," Hymnal recalled. "My sister woke me up with a phone call. I thought it was a dream. But my sister be on MySpace. Quick as hell people put it on MySpace, which I didn't like. That was kind of bogus. When she called me and woke me up, people were already at the hospital."

"So I get there and there's like fifteen people there already," Grafta remembered. "It was already chaos in the hospital. I'm talkin' to people. Nobody really knows what the fuck happened. It was just all fucked up."

As Phantastic lay in the hospital, messages of support flooded MySpace's bulletin boards. Tribute photos were posted, and Chicago's gangsta-rap microscene was on edge. Even Habit showed love to his sworn enemy, posting a heartfelt message on the public bulletin board.

I would never wish this on no man. It didn't really hit me till this mornin and I guess I wish shit woulda went different with us but none the less. . . . Nigga I know u gonna pull through. U have 2. 2 many lil niggas depend on u for hope. I'm praying 4 u nigga!!

With no official word coming from the Bully Boyz camp, MySpace became ground zero for information (and misinformation) about Phantastic. Rumors were circulated, debated, and quashed, only to spring up again later. Two days after the shooting, Sissero posted an update. The situation was improving.

If you don't know yet, Phantastic is in the hospital and is doing better. I wasn't online all day yesterday because I was at the hospital. The doctor informed us that he started doing a little more breathing on his own. I couldn't help but become over-whelmed with emotion as I held his hand and said a prayer. To see a friend in that position is the hardest thing anyone could go through. I swear to God y'all I know he could hear what we were saying. His eyes were closed, but you could see them moving, and that's all the hope we need! If anyone can pull through it's that Tough Boy!

Please, guys, be understanding at this time and not hound for extra information, that will be disbursed in time. Don't count our boy out, he's gonna make it through this! Please don't make assumptions and start spreading rumors. I will be going back to the hospital tonight again after work, if you have any words or wishes feel free to let me know I will pass the messages on to the boys or his family. Take the time to post one of his pictures as your main image, that way people that didn't know him could also say a prayer.

God bless you Phantastic, we're gonna make it through this family!!

Visitors came and went, but Grafta never left the hospital, spending every possible moment at Phantastic's side.

He looked great, it was unbelievable. You would think that if a motherfucker got a blast in the head, they would be all fucked up. But he looked straight. He didn't look like he was shot. I was there for three days. Stank like a motherfucker, same clothes, didn't eat shit. Just waiting for that doctor to come out and be like, 'He's good.' But deep down, I knew. Then they were just like, 'That's it. Ain't nothing we can do.' That's when it hit the fan. Hard.

Sorry to say my Bully Boyz brother Phantastic has passed away today. We are a strong team but keep Phantastic & Bully Boyz in your prayers.—Text message from Grafta.

The universal reaction to Phantastic's death was collective grief. Musical, photographic, and video tributes were posted on MySpace and YouTube, and condolences came from all sides of Chicago. Shorty, a Puerto Rican DJ who was close to Phantastic, created a tribute mix of musical highlights that garnered hundreds of plays. Sissero continued to pour her heart out on MySpace bulletins.

I'm always the one that's supposed to be strong, that's supposed to have all the right words, know exactly what to write and how to make things a little easier. But my heart hurts, and all I can do is speak real talk, because this is a hard and trying moment in my life, and im just so lost and confused and broken. Phantastic I miss that smile, that fly demeanor, those amazing songs, that quick wit, and most of all that shining, beautiful soul. You took the life that was given to you and were a good man, father, artist, person. You were our Malcolm X. You were so strong, and so smart without a college degree, because you taught yourself how to make something out of nothing. This has been a hard and strenuous 3 days, my bank account NSF'd off liquor store purchases of Hennessy, but fuck it g we are going to celebrate the life of Phantastic. He wouldn't want us to mourn, so please think of him in a golden Miskeen outfit flossing in heaven with Biggie and Pac and Pun. The greats get to meet the realest nigga from Chicago!

I'd like to thank the whole Myspace community for your words, messages, dedications, and condolences to us.

Sissero

Bleek was at his sister's house when he received a text from Shank with the news.

I couldn't believe it. I thought somebody was trying to play some type of joke or something. That shocked me. We had our beef with Bully Boyz, but I knew Phantastic way before they even knew dude. He grew up where I grew up, back in the early '80s. And we was shorties playing together. So when I got out of the penitentiary and I reunited with him, he opened up for me at my album release party. So it hurt me, 'cause I never wanted the beef to happen in the first place. It should have never happened.

When Habit heard the news on MySpace, he thought it was a gimmick, a means by which Bully Boyz was promoting its mixtape. "Then after a couple of days it sunk in. It was a little rough on me. I was saddened by it, man, 'cause regardless of all of that, the guy had kids. I wouldn't have wished that to anybody. As far as the loss, Logan Square took a loss as far as the creative geniuses that are there. 'Cause he was part of the movement that we doing right now. All the pieces of the puzzle were there, but when he passed away, it was a piece of the puzzle gone."

Tattoo Tears

Everyone is in mourning at Black Soldier's loft. Usually party central, the mood is somber tonight. Black Soldier is preparing to go on the air to host his weekly Internet radio show. Tonight's program is dedicated to Phantastic, a good friend and compatriot of Black Soldier. Shorty, the local DJ, is on hand, too, here to lend support, co-host, and assist with the technical aspects. Hundreds of listeners are tuned in online, posting shout-outs and words of support on the station's message board. At 8:00 p.m., Black Soldier takes the air.

What up, ya'll? It's ya boy, Black Soldier. Once again, I hate to be the bearer of bad news, but for those that know, Phantastic passed away this afternoon. It's been a long three days. I know there's a lot of questions, there's a lot of unanswered questions, there's a lot of pain. But that's what we here for, we here to help each other get through the pain. Phantastic was the type of nigga to constantly move forward no matter what came his way. So we gotta have that strength and move forward and be there for each other. So tonight's show is dedicated to my nigga Phantastic. We're gonna dedicate the rest of the year to him, man, we gonna dedicate the rest of our movement to him. Chicago stand up, Logan stand up, Humboldt stand up, North, South, East, West, wherever you at, stand the fuck up, man. God bless the dead. It's not a easy situation, but we gonna keep that brother's name alive and we gonna move forward. So on that note, here we go. Phantastic, rest in peace my nigga.

Black Soldier plays the tribute mix of Phantastic's music created by Shorty, and takes a swig from a bottle of Hennessy. His voice is flat and tired, a monotone that expresses the pain of Chicago's gangsta-rap microscene. For the next two hours, Black Soldier and Shorty trade stories and anecdotes about Phantastic, in between Bully Boyz songs and the few Phantastic solo tracks that were released to the public. Still, there's little to celebrate and the mood is grim.

"Chicago, she cryin'," says Ridah, a member of Black Soldier's posse. "You can see the rain outside. She sad as hell. She lost her first son. That nigga was a blessing to the whole world, and it was taken away from the people who didn't get to know him yet. He was such a beautiful soul. It was too easy for him to be smooth and natural and just a beautiful guy. He was just natural and fly. It was like he was holding air all the time."

Sissero shows up with Julie, a friend and former paramour of Phantastic's. Phantastic's brother, Leon, stops by later, drunk and despondent. The radio show continues, but the mourning moves to Ink Town.

A portion of Black Soldier's loft is sectioned off into a room used by Ink Town, an unlicensed tattoo parlor run by an enterprising guy named Salvo. A steady stream of clients stops by, and Salvo inks one body part after the other. Tonight, it's Phantastic tattoos. He does three in a row, including a massive "P" on Shank's and Leon's upper right cheeks. A young woman gets a tribute tattoo on her calf that has Phantastic's name, birth and death dates.

"I been doing a lot of RIP tattoos for close members to the Bully Boyz familia," Salvo tells me. "Tattoos mean so much. It's sacred. To them that's maybe a way of keeping Phantastic close to them. A lot of people get memorial tattoos for the fact that, obviously they know that that's life. But when people get tattoos it means more than just the tattoo. It has a lot of meaning behind it. It's memories, and every time they look at that tattoo, they're gonna think about lyrics they did with him. They're gonna think about the good times, the sad times they had with him."

A few days later, Bully Boyz hosted a party in honor of Phantastic at the loft. The Xcons were invited to attend. As the members of Xcons made their way into the building, Boss Bee recalled feeling a sense of dread:

BOSS BEE: It was uncomfortable to go in that place. It was around a lot of Latinos and a lot of Latinos gangbang a lot. Plus I'm from up north in the pole and the black motherfuckers up there gangbang just as much. His loft was in a building and it looked like when you get in there a motherfucker can leave you in there [makes shooting motion], boom boom boom and throw your ass in a pantry somewhere. You gotta go upstairs in this broke-ass freight elevator. And I'm like what the fuck?

Then we got upstairs to the loft, and I was like, We was just
dissing these motherfuckers and shit.

BLEEK: We knew people would be looking at us. 'Cause it would
be all of his friends and family and fans there. They might look
at us like the bad guys. They may wanna release their anger on
somebody. So when we were invited, all of these things is going
through our head. It was hard to go. It was hard to walk through
that door, go up them stairs, and see all of their friends and
fans and family looking at us. You can imagine the needle on
the record would stop and it'd just be like all eyes on you.
As soon as you walked in the door, you could just feel it.

As soon as Xcons walked in the door, the tensions between the two groups
melted. Shank approached the group and thanked them for coming.
"They was hurting," Boss Bee recalls. "It was like we didn't even matter.
They wasn't upset at us. They missed they friend. They missed they leader. They missed they best rapper. They was playing Phantastic's shit and
throwin' up they Ps. And motherfuckers was hurtin'."

In the weeks that followed Phantastic's death, rumors began to circulate. There was no official word on what happened, and solving the mys-
tery became a much-played game of whodunit. Fingers were pointed in
every direction, and conspiracy theories were abundant. Many blamed
Phantastic's girlfriend, the only other person in the room when he was
shot. The girlfriend swore in an impassioned MySpace post that Phantastic committed suicide and ended his own life, a theory believed by few
who knew Phantastic. Grafta opined that

There's three people that know what happened: God, [his girl-
friend], and him. Motherfuckers say he committed suicide, but
that shit just don't look right. I'm not gonna sit here and say oh, he
shot himself, or oh, she shot him. I wasn't there. But deep down in
my heart, what I feel is that he didn't shoot himself. When you
play with motherfuckin' fire, you get burned. When you play with
guns, motherfuckers get hurt.

Regardless, the suicide rumor gained a fair amount of traction. Others
speculated that it was gang- or drug-related. Some even blamed Phantastic's

family, causing outrage from the MySpace community. In a post entitled
"My Son," Phantastic's mother set the record straight:

> You all want a fact well here is a good one for all of you gossipers.
> I DID NOT KILL MY SON NOR DID HIS BROTHER. So stop treating
> this family as if we did. You will never feel what me as his mother
> and his brother feel. How dare you people treat us like the enemy.
> Last time I checked the only victim was my SON!!!!!

Phantastic's shooting was barely investigated by the Chicago Police
Department. Guns, drugs, and three hundred pairs of shoes were found
at his apartment the night he died, evidence, according to the police, that
Phantastic was up to no good. Grafta thought that the police seemed
happy to have "another motherfucker off the street." Phantastic's death
was ruled a suicide and the case was closed.

Bully Boyz were fracturing without Phantastic. There was infighting,
bickering, and heated discussions that went nowhere. Some of the group
members wanted to persevere, to carry on in Phantastic's name. Others
wanted to quit music altogether and return to the streets full time. Everyone was pissed off, hurting, and barely able to comprehend that their dream
was crumbling at their feet. Some believed that Shank was too quick to step
in and assume leadership of the group. Within two weeks of Phantastic's
death, Shank's MySpace page read: "I am the cap cause a great cap made
me." Keeping the group together and focused would be harder than ever
without Phantastic, the kind of guy who was at ease in any social situation.
Phantastic could sit and comfortably talk business as easily as he could
hang with the most wizened street hood. Shank and Hymnal were strictly
street, more than capable of spinning yarns about their dangerous lifestyles, but less comfortable mingling with straight-laced record executives
and other industry types. "Hymnal is a monster in the making," said a
Bully Boyz insider, "but the streets are going to be the death of him."

Bully Boyz had tons of unreleased material that featured Phantastic, but
it could not be sold to a major record company. After all, the group's lead
rapper was gone and could not be featured in videos, marketed, or go on
tour. No one saw a way for Phantastic's shoes to be filled. There was little
hope for Bully Boyz's future. Phantastic was dead. It was over. Finished.

2

The Blueprint

Social Class and the Rise of the Rap Hustler

No one would ever mistake Phillip Morris for a gangsta. A self-proclaimed "nerd" from Chicago's western suburbs, he sports thick black eyeglasses that would make Clark Kent envious and a neatly pressed button-down shirt that he probably wore earlier that day to the office where he works in electronic medical billing. An army-green messenger bag is slung around his shoulder. A fish out of water in many rap circles, Morris is especially conspicuous at Club Exedus tonight, where the lineup consists entirely of hardcore gangsta rap, and the audience is made up exclusively of hardcore gangsta rap fans.

As usual, Morris is the odd man out. His absurdist, erudite lyrics cover such topics as Chewbacca, naked grandmothers, and decrepit testicles. "I try to rap about off-the-wall stuff," he says.

> I have serious moments, but I also talk about ridiculously silly shit as well, just because I don't want to make music that is normal. I try to be as lighthearted as I possibly can. I'm not hardcore in any sense of the word, except for maybe lyrically, rhyme-wise. I'm not gonna talk about anything I don't have. I'm broke so I'm not gonna talk about money or flashy clothes 'cause I don't have them.

The Exedus crowd is not looking for lighthearted entertainment tonight, but Morris strides to the stage with confidence. Like most of the concertgoers, Morris is black, but the social-class disparity between performer and audience could not be more pronounced: Morris, a white-collar guy from the suburbs, and the crowd, a rowdy throng of urban denizens looking to get their crunk on. "Go back to the suburbs, Humpty!" someone yells from the rear of the club. Morris ignores the taunt; he's been through this before. A beat kicks in and the rapper spins into hyperdrive, spitting a complex jumble of wordplay that sounds like someone reading from a chemistry textbook at ninety miles an hour.

Somehow, it works. The crowd laughs at the punch lines, sings along to the choruses, and cheers wildly at the end of the short set, congratulating Morris with a flurry of back pats and fist bumps. "I have to work a lot harder because I'm not coming with that [gangsta rap], and a lot of the people here are into that type of music," Morris tells me afterwards. "So I really have to come across. When I can wow a crowd like that, I feel like I've achieved more."

Given the difference between Morris and the Exedus crowd, one wonders how the rapper was able to overcome these obstacles and enjoy such a moment, where he was rendered acceptable to an audience that initially viewed him with skepticism. It didn't hurt that Morris—despite his square appearance and outré lyrics—was a dexterous MC who had spent years developing his craft. In his book *Appropriating Blackness* (2003), performance studies scholar E. Patrick Johnson described how a skilled performer can evoke positive responses from even the most dubious spectators. While conducting fieldwork, Johnson witnessed an all-white Australian gospel choir sing before an all-black audience at a Harlem church. Initially, the churchgoers were uncertain, but the Aussies overcame their doubts with a masterful performance. The choir proved it had put in the time and dedication necessary to be competent gospel singers; the churchgoers showed appreciation via thunderous applause. In Chicago, I witnessed similar exchanges; talented white rappers who transformed skeptical nonwhite audiences, skilled female MCs who converted dismissive male spectators.

Performers who lack such skills may not enjoy a positive response. At Club Exedus that night, Morris was followed by K-Pro, a Latino rapper whose entrance was also accompanied by the sound of catcalls. As when Morris took the stage, the audience instantly began to jeer. "Smiley!" someone taunted from the rear of the small club, the nickname taken from a mentally challenged Latino character in Spike Lee's *Do the Right Thing*. K-Pro looked tense and addressed the detractors: "I know y'all didn't expect a Mexican to jump up on the mic. This is talking about the community and what we're going through." The crowd wasn't having it, and chanted, "Smiley, Smiley, Smiley" in time with the beat. K-Pro started rapping tepidly; he stammered and blew the first few lines. This inspired even louder gibes from the audience, and in less than a minute, K-Pro dropped the mic and fled the stage to a hailstorm of laughter and be-mused booing.

The audience's varied responses to these two performances could be attributed to differences in authenticity: Morris wowed the crowd with a florid display of verbal skills, while K-Pro's performance could only be described as mediocre. It's possible that race was a factor: the largely black audience accepted Morris, an African American, but not K-Pro, who is Latino. But race does not explain the audience's initial hostility toward Morris, and I'd seen supposedly authentic rappers get booed before. These commonsense explanations illustrate the shortcomings of race- and authenticity-based theories in understanding present-day rap music culture.

The Declining Significance of Race in Understanding Rap Music

Scholars in a range of disciplines have long associated rap music with blackness and the urban African American experience. This was particularly true for early studies of rap, many of which linked the genre to black history and culture. For example, author William Wimsatt called rap music a black response to "white America's economic and psychological terrorism against black people" (1994, 25). Africana studies scholar Tricia Rose believed that rap music "articulates the pleasures and problems of black urban life in contemporary America" (1994, 2). Sociolinguist Geneva Smitherman (1997, 7) argued that "the language of hip hop is African American language, also known as Black English . . . and Ebonics." And communications theorist Kembrew McLeod reported, "to its core community members, hip hop remains strongly tied to Black cultural expression" (1999, 140).

According to this perspective, even as rap began to diffuse outside the United States, its styles, sensibilities, practices, and attitudes remained rooted in black, American, urban culture. For example, race and ethnicity scholar Anoop Nayak (2003) studied a group of youth in the United Kingdom, where there were few blacks but where the media-fueled notion of cool black Americana had taken hold. Nayak described young people such as Helena, a white woman whose "identification with blackness extended into music, dress and complex forms of body management (engaging in 'black' forms of dancing, invoking stylized gestures or expression, even attempting to 'turn black' through the daily use of a sunbed)" (118). While the perspective that equates rap with blackness has diminished in recent years, it has not been eliminated. For example, in 2009 Marcyliena Morgan, who oversees the Hiphop Archive at Harvard University, opined that hip-hop culture is "part of and a product of African American cultural, political, social, and artistic expression" (14). Responses to this viewpoint include studies that emphasized hip-hop's multicultural roots, offering a partial redress of earlier scholarship. For example, media studies scholar S. Craig Watkins (2005) decried the "false premise" that hip-hop culture is synonymous with blackness. "Not only does the premise disregard hip-hop's rich history and cultural legacy; it also limits its reach and potential impact. Even during its humble beginnings hip-hop was never strictly a black thing. It has always been multiracial, multicultural, and multilingual" (150). Music journalist Nelson George (1998) asserted that without financial backing from whites, rap music "wouldn't have survived its first half decade on vinyl" (57). Latino Studies scholar Juan Flores (2000) wrote of the "amnesia" that served to undervalue or eliminate Latino contributions to the development of rap music and hip-hop culture. Other studies have focused on game changers such as Eminem, whose success and popularity with whites and nonwhites helped diminish the stereotype that whites cannot—or should not—rap.[1] In the estimation of these scholars, Eminem's popularity helped pave the way for credible Caucasian MCs such as Aesop Rock and Atmosphere frontman Slug, skilled musicians who approached the art and craft of rapping with sincerity and respect.

Another more recent body of scholarship has examined rap's propensity for globalization and multicultural adaptation, also helping to alter early perceptions of rap as a strictly "black thing," to its present status as a global culture, adopted by young people around the world and reconfigured or "glocalized" to reflect their language, communities, and cultures. A host of studies have demonstrated how rappers from locations as disparate as Australia (Maxwell 2003), Colombia (Dennis 2012), Japan (Condry 2006), Palestine (Kahf 2007), and South Africa (Hammett 2012) rearranged American rap music into local forms of expression. In the words of Thesis, a Latino rapper from Chicago, "Anybody can get involved in hip-hop. Hip-hop is worldwide, it's everywhere."

Cultural and structural forces that have altered many facets of social life help explain rap's transformation from a Bronx-based subculture to a globalized, multicultural youth phenomenon. These include changing racial demographics in the United States, which has become increasingly racially heterogeneous. Reflecting this trend, rap music has also become more racially inclusive and diverse. This is especially true of present-day rap microscenes, which are often populated by large numbers of non-blacks.[2] The blurring of rap's color line has also been spurred by a more general societal trend towards multiculturalism, and this racial heterogeneity is reflected and reproduced in rap music.

Finally, we live in an era where racial identity is increasingly fluid, calling into question the very notion of a core racial identity. As sociologist Joan Nagel (1994) noted twenty years ago, "people's conceptions of themselves along ethnic lines, especially their ethnic identity, [are] situational and changeable" (154). Writing in 2010, sociologist Tomás Jiménez described a newfound elasticity, freedom, and sense of personal choice vis-à-vis ethnicity:

> Individuals are no longer confined to their own ethnic ancestry in forming an ethnic identity. They are now accessing culture connected to other ethnic ancestries in developing *affiliative ethnic identities*: individual identities rooted in knowledge, regular consumption and deployment of an ethnic culture that is unconnected to an individual's ethnic ancestry until that individual regards herself, and may be regarded by others, as an affiliate of a particular ethnic group. (1757)

To what degree we are on new racial terrain is debatable, but for many practitioners and fans, rap music is no longer exclusively tied to black, American cultural expression. This does not imply that race is less significant than it was in decades past, but that rap's growing propensity for multiculturalism and ethnic heterogeneity, combined with an increasingly racially diverse society and the growing flexibility of racial identity, complicates race-based theories used to explain rap culture. To understand rap music today, we need to expand upon and augment these explanations.

Situational Authenticity

In 1990, a white rapper named Robert Van Winkle sold 12 million copies of his debut album, spurred by the popularity of its smash single, "Ice Ice Baby." When it was discovered that Van Winkle, who went by the stage name Vanilla Ice, had exaggerated the conditions of his formative years in Miami, Vanilla Ice became a national punch line from which Van Winkle's career never fully recovered. A decade later, a white rapper named Marshall Mathers, better known as Eminem, issued his major-label debut and launched one of the most successful rap careers of all time. Eminem's biography was everything that Ice's was not, and his dexterous, profane rhymes were filled with dramatic recreations of his working-class upbringing in urban Detroit. The differences between Vanilla Ice and Eminem are obvious to even casual listeners. Few would dispute that Eminem is the more skilled rapper, but the divergent career trajectories of the two white MCs help illustrate one of rap's most discussed themes, authenticity.

It is difficult to write about rap music in much detail without addressing authenticity. Music scholar Richard Peterson (1997) defined authenticity as a person, place, or object that is perceived to be original, traditional, an authentic reproduction, credible in current context, and real. Peterson asserted that authenticity was not inherent in a cultural object or its creator, but was a social construct. In other words, there was nothing about a person, place, object, or event that made it more "real" or "genuine" than any other; it was a matter of how that person, place, object, or event was perceived by others. To borrow the Thomas theorem, when people define something as authentic, then it is authentic in consequence. If enough people determine that the local hole-in-the-wall Mexican restaurant serves authentic fare and Taco Bell does not, that belief becomes a social reality. According to Peterson's concept, this does not mean there is something inherently inauthentic about Taco Bell, only that this is a widespread perception, a consequence of which is that when most folks want "real" Mexican cuisine, they go elsewhere.

Scholars of music cultures have applied the concept of authenticity to genres such as punk (Hebdige 1979), dance (Thornton 1995), gospel (E. P. Johnson 2003), and blues (Grazian 2003). Peterson (1997) examined the history of country music and illustrated how "hard core" musicians such as Johnny Cash were perceived to be more authentic or genuine than "soft shell" acts such as Shania Twain. Again, this did not mean that Cash was inherently more authentic than Twain, only that he was perceived that way by a majority of fans, music critics, scholars, journalists, and disc jockeys. Over time, this belief concretized into a social reality such that those seeking "authentic" country music gravitated to hardcore artists like Cash rather than soft-shell acts like Twain.

While acknowledging that authenticity is a social construction, some music scholars have attempted to measure authenticity or describe a set of guidelines by which it can be understood. For example, in his study of the Chicago blues scene, sociologist David Grazian (2003) devised a sliding scale of authenticity on which, for example, a white middle-class suburban bluesman was perceived to be less authentic than a black musician from a poor neighborhood but more authentic than a Japanese American player from the city. Grazian also applied the concept to nightclubs, and demonstrated how different Chicago blues venues were believed to be more or less authentic depending on who was doing the perceiving. Grazian's sliding scale illustrated the consequences of these beliefs: those seeking "authentic" Chicago blues wanted to see it performed by blacks, who were thought to be the "real" purveyors of the genre. Tourists from out of town perceived certain clubs on Chicago's relatively wealthy North Side to be utterly authentic, while local denizens thought they were preposterously fake and traveled to Chicago's poor, black neighborhoods in search of a more allegedly authentic blues experience.

The concept of authenticity has also been widely discussed and debated in rap music scholarship. In an influential 1999 article, Kembrew McLeod outlined six dichotomous dimensions of hip-hop authenticity: (1) staying true to yourself versus following mass trends, (2) black versus white, (3) underground versus commercial, (4) masculine versus feminine, (5) street versus suburbs, and (6) old school versus mainstream. McLeod noted that rappers and rap fans invoked these distinctions in an effort to maintain cultural identity, create in-group/out-group boundaries, and thwart mainstream efforts to dilute the "pure" core of hip-hop culture.

McLeod's article has been cited more than 150 times in subsequent studies of authenticity. Rap scholars have applied his concept most often to race and ethnicity.[3] For example, sociologist Edward G. Armstrong (2004) examined how Eminem made rap music safe for whites by constructing an authentic identity that emphasized his impoverished upbringing and familiarity with black, urban culture. In his ethnography of a Bay Area rap microscene, Harrison (2009) devised a rights-based racial hierarchy for underground MCs that classified fourteen ethnic categories into three major clusters (black, nonblack people of color, and white), ranked from high to low. Harrison wrote that "at one time it might have been thought that non-black people were incapable of successfully or convincingly mastering the aesthetics of hip hop performance (i.e., 'white people can't rap'); today, the question is no longer about who is innately or culturally capable but rather what gives someone the right" (106–7).

The drawback to studies that attempt to measure or rank authenticity is that "realness" is an inherently slippery concept. Because authenticity is a social construction based on perceptions, interpretations, and definitions of situations, measuring it becomes problematic in contexts that do not fit normative conditions. For example, while attending a rap concert one night in Chicago, I witnessed an audience's tepid response to a young black rapper named Nexxus. Nexxus resided in a housing project located in a poor South Side neighborhood. He was not a commercial rapper; his lyrics were both socially aware and militant, covering topics such as urban poverty and police brutality. He was a skilled wordsmith and a supremely confident showman. In other words, Nexxus met every one of McLeod and Harrison's criteria for authenticity, yet the audience did not define Nexxus's concert as authentic; his performance was met with muttered jeers and a smattering of polite applause. The explanation for this was contextual: Nexxus was playing to an audience that consisted almost entirely of Puerto Rican rap fans. The audience went crazy whenever a Puerto Rican MC took the stage, regardless of skill level. This scenario illustrates the importance of context in understanding authenticity; what is defined as authentic in one setting can be perceived to be inauthentic in another. Like racial identity, authenticity is not fixed, but a flexible phenomenon that is situationally and contextually dependent (see Harkness 2012b).

As sociologist Dalton Conley submitted in his 2009 book *Elsewhere, U.S.A.,* we currently live in an increasingly multicultural, multitasking, and technologically advanced society, one in which adhering to some sort of fixed, authentic self is not only impractical, it is virtually impossible. Our fragmented, multifarious identities produce a "competing cacophony of multiple selves all jostling for pole position in our mind" (156). Thus, we employ identity situationally, rather than adhering rigidly to a single core self. We talk and behave differently around close friends than we do at grandma's house, at work, or online. Moreover, technology allows us to communicate with others simultaneously, leading to further fragmentation and increasing the pace at which identity switching occurs. We continually make adjustments to suit ever-shifting and overlapping contexts in order to best fit that situation. Social scientists have historically referred to this phenomenon as "code switching," but multitasking, the frenetic pace at which code switching now occurs, and the lack of rules when doing so, render the notion of a singular authentic identity somewhat quaint.

Rap music is not immune to these changes, either. Following (and perhaps, at times, leading) larger societal trends, rap has become more racially heterogeneous, increasingly gender tolerant, more technologically savvy, and, to borrow a phrase from sociologist Zygmunt Bauman (2000), progressively more "liquid." One recent example is rap collective Odd Future, whose sometimes misogynistic and homophobic lyrics can be surprising given that the group features a lesbian female rapper, Syd tha Kyd, and is associated with acclaimed singer-songwriter Frank Ocean, who famously came out in 2012. This type of contradiction is rampant not only in rap music, but in society at large. It represents the new normal. The useful aspect of the authenticity concept is that it illustrates not only how social and cultural boundaries are created and maintained, but also how such barriers can be circumvented or simply ignored. What is lacking are new ways to understand differences in a world where identity is more fluid than ever.

In this book, I move away from the race- and authenticity-based analyses, and seek new ways to understand meaning-making within rap-music culture. That does not mean eliminating these useful concepts altogether, but thinking about them differently. Social class, which remains rap's most enduring dividing line, is often overlooked in theories of race and authenticity. In Chicago's rap underground, symbolic boundaries between different groups of people can be rigid, but they are generally not based on race or notions of authenticity; they are grounded in social class.

Social Class: An Overview

In his 1903 book, *The Souls of Black Folk*, sociologist W. E. B. Du Bois famously wrote, "The problem of the twentieth century is the problem of the color-line" ([1903] 1994, 9). More than one hundred years later, racism and race-based stratification remain critical matters, but the problem of the twenty-first century may well be social class. Social class has become increasingly important to understanding the persistence of the cultural, social, and economic stratifications that continue to create inequalities, in the United States and around the world. As illustrated by the Occupy Wall Street movement, debates over tax cuts for the rich, the transnational flow of industrial labor, and growing income disparities between the wealthy and the poor, social class may be the defining feature of modern life, one that impacts all people to varying degrees. Social class is more salient than ever because in the United States upward mobility—the cornerstone of the American dream—has become increasingly difficult to achieve. On the 2013 Legatum Prosperity Index, which calculates socioeconomic well-being using a number of indicators, the United States ranked eleventh, behind Canada, Australia, and several European countries.[4]

Karl Marx was among the early social scientists to consider the salience of social class. Marx divided society into two groups: the bourgeoisie, a small collective of elites who owned the means of production (factories, farms, land, businesses), and the proletariat, a large group of workers who owned nothing except the ability to sell their labor to the bourgeoisie. Marx believed this was an inherently exploitative relationship, one that created a proletarian workforce forever enslaved to the bourgeoisie. Though he was writing about social class in the wake of the Industrial Revolution, Marx's ideas remain influential, and his overarching concept, whereby the world is divided into the haves and the have-nots, continues to be at the core of current thinking about social class.

The classic sociological measurement of social class combines wealth (income, savings, stocks, property, businesses, and other assets), level of education, and occupational prestige. The calculation of these indicators enables groups of people to be ranked into a hierarchy with three broad divisions—upper, middle, and lower class—as well as more precise categories, such as upper-middle-class, working class, and underclass. High-status individuals such as Bill Gates (a college dropout who is among the world's wealthiest people) exemplify the fuzziness of this measurement; there are individuals who score high on one or more social-class indicators, yet lower on others.

Because a person's income and education are difficult to "see," some afford more weight to the material or behavioral aspects of social class:

the cars people drive, the clothes they wear, the way they carry themselves, the people and organizations with whom they interact. From this perspective, social class is not just a calculation of socioeconomic variables, but a conscious performance used to project a position—real or imagined—on the class hierarchy. We often rely upon these class displays in our evaluations of others. When we opine that a person has "no class," we typically mean this in reference to uncouth, low-status behavior, speech, or appearance. When we judge someone to be "classy," this typically means we esteem her behavior, speech, and appearance to be refined and signaling high status.

Regardless of how social class is defined or measured, what is well documented are the consequences of social class. Members of higher classes enjoy greater outcomes in terms of income, educational opportunities, physical and mental health, and number of years lived. Members of the higher classes are more likely to marry, less likely to divorce, and show greater rates of happiness and personal and professional satisfaction. Members of the lower classes, particularly the underclass, encounter social, economic, and physical woes that are difficult to surmount, and that take a nearly incalculable toll on their lives and well-being.

Scholars, politicians, and pundits have long deliberated the reasons why poverty persists. Marx believed that elites set up society to benefit themselves, essentially creating an economic order that tilts the odds in their favor and makes it difficult for lower classes to achieve prosperity. Conservatives tend to place blame on individuals. From this perspective, America is a meritocracy, and those who fail economically do so because they are lazy and unwilling to put in the work required to succeed. These opposing viewpoints illustrate ongoing debates about social class, and the degree to which cultural and structural forces influence socioeconomic position.

Cultural Explanations of Social Class

Cultural theories of social class examine the socialization that occurs within various social-class groups. According to this line of thinking, the wealthy socialize their offspring and members of their community to be wealthy, and the poor teach their offspring and community members to be poor. Sociologist Oscar Lewis (1968) conceived the culture-of-poverty theory in the 1960s, and his ideas remain controversial. Lewis studied 100 families living in the slums of San Juan, Puerto Rico, and their relatives, who resided in impoverished sections of New York City. Lewis found what he believed was a distinct culture, a way of life in poor communities with the following conditions:

> (1) A cash economy, wage labor, and production for profit; (2) a persistently high rate of unemployment and underemployment for unskilled labor; (3) low wages; (4) the failure to provide social, political, and economic organization, either on a voluntary basis or by government imposition, for the low income population; (5) the existence of a bilateral kinship system rather than a unilateral one; and finally (6) the existence in the dominant class of a set of values that stresses the accumulation of wealth and property, the possibility of upward mobility, and thrift and that explains low economic status as the result of personal inadequacy or inferiority. (4–5)

Lewis argued that these conditions placed powerful stresses on the poor, and the ensuing culture of poverty was created as an adaptation, a behavioral response to larger structural failures. This culture, Lewis asserted, was passed on to new generations, and "by the time slum children are age six or seven they have usually absorbed the basic values and attitudes of their subculture and are not psychologically geared to take full advantage of changing conditions or increased opportunities which may occur in their lifetime" (6).

Lewis's work generated a great deal of disagreement, but his theory illustrated an important feature of social classes; they tend to reproduce themselves. Children born of wealthy parents tend to become wealthy adults, and the offspring of poor parents tend to remain that way. According to recent data, 66 percent of those raised in the bottom quintile of the existing economic structure will not experience upward mobility (Pew Charitable Trusts 2012). Conversely, the same number of children raised in the top quintile will not experience downward mobility. The works of scholars such as Annette Lareau, Jay MacLeod, and Pierre Bourdieu are useful for understanding the "stickiness" of social class.

In her ethnography, *Unequal Childhoods*, sociologist Annette Lareau (2011) describes the different parenting styles found in poor, working-

and middle-class families. Middle-class parents practiced what Lareau called concerted cultivation, which involved the children experiencing an adult-organized schedule filled with activities such as music and language instruction and sports. Parent-child discussions were also central to this parenting style, designed to elicit the feelings, thoughts, and opinions of the children. Lareau believed that this parenting style led to a sense of entitlement in middle-class children, one that played "an especially important role in institutional settings, where middle-class children learn to question adults and address them as relative equals" (2).

By contrast, poor and working-class families raised their children using a model of what Lareau termed accomplishment of natural growth. This entailed children having large swaths of unstructured leisure time and autonomy to do as they pleased. There was a clear boundary between children and adults, and poor and working-class children were often told what to do, rather than having open discussions. As a result, these children (and their parents) were less adept at interacting successfully with institutions.

Lareau found that although poor and working-class children had more "childlike" lives, these differences perpetuated class-based inequalities both during childhood and later. With greater aptitude for navigating institutions, the middle-class children reaped advantages that were even more apparent when Lareau caught up with her study participants ten years later. Now young adults, the contrasts between poor and middle class were more pronounced. Children raised in middle-class families were more likely to graduate from high school and gain admission to four-year colleges, while poor and working-class children were generally unable to attain these goals. These findings were true regardless of race, illustrating the dramatic impact of social class. Lareau conduced that "social class origins have effects that are powerful and long lasting" (311).

MacLeod (1995) spent several years living in a low-income neighborhood, where he befriended and followed two disparate groups of high-school-aged males. One group—delinquent, pessimistic whites whom MacLeod dubbed the Hallway Hangers—had few career aspirations, fared poorly in school, and used drugs and alcohol frequently. The second group—optimistic, high-achieving blacks MacLeod called the Brothers—had ambitious career goals, worked hard in school, and eschewed the antisocial behaviors exhibited by the Hallway Hangers. The Brothers believed in the American dream; that through hard work one could achieve upward social-class mobility. MacLeod's stunning revelation occurred in the latter part of the book, in which he revisited these two groups several years later only to discover that their differences in ambition and effort produced nearly indistinguishable socioeconomic outcomes. Both groups were impoverished, dispirited, and stuck in low-wage jobs or ensnared in the criminal justice system. Both groups failed to achieve hallmarks of adulthood, such as stable jobs and home ownership. Strikingly, both groups blamed themselves for their failure to achieve upward mobility, rather than considering larger structural inequalities that may have hindered them. The Hallway Hangers remained pessimistic, but the Brothers still believed in the American dream.

MacLeod drew upon the work of French scholar Pierre Bourdieu (1984) in explaining these outcomes, including Bourdieu's concept of cultural capital. Cultural capital is the capacity to reproduce collectively agreed upon symbols of elite status for conversion into economic capital. Cultural capital creates class distinctions by dividing people into in-groups and out-groups, based upon highbrow pursuits such as attending the opera or speaking French. Bourdieu proffered a scheme of three types of cultural capital: embodied (personal attributes such as knowledge, skills, and disposition), objectified (material goods), and institutionalized (credentials such as academic degrees). Applying this concept to social class, upper-class children inherit cultural capital from their upper-class parents. They learn to think, speak, and behave in ways that signal to others that they are wealthy, elite, educated, and understand the rules of "appropriate" behavior. Conversely, the poor and working classes inherit cultural capital that signals them as members of these groups. Members of the upper and lower classes are then treated in kind by institutions, teachers, and authority figures. Regardless of class position, cultural capital has innumerable consequences, and helps explain why an allegedly level playing field such as education may not be so equal after all. MacLeod's Brothers believed that education was the path to upward mobility. "They care about school, accept its norms and standards, and conform to its rules. As black lower-class students, however, the Brothers are lacking in the cultural capital rewarded by the school system—hence their poor academic achievement and placement into lower tracks" (1995, 102).

Scholars have criticized Bourdieu for the class bias inherent in his theory of cultural capital—who decides what constitutes highbrow culture, after all? People are increasingly omnivorous in their cultural consumption and few limit themselves to one "class" of cultural pursuit (see Peterson and Kern 1996). Furthermore, it stands to reason that if members of the upper classes create symbolic boundaries based on a culturally valued knowledge, cultural consumption, and credentials, members of the lower classes must do this also.

Sarah Thornton (1995) proffered a theory of subcultural capital to explain distinctions at dance clubs in the United Kingdom. In this setting, highbrow cultural pursuits were not valued in the same way as was, for example, being a DJ at a top nightclub. This led to Thornton's great insight: "subcultural capital confers status on its owner in the eyes of the relevant beholder" (11). In other words, cultural capital is situational—what is valued in one context may not be esteemed in others, and the knowledge or abilities required to attain social distinction within a particular setting vary.[5] This does not do away with Bourdieu's classic theory, but acknowledges the contextual nature of defining cultural value.

Structural Explanations of Social Class

Numerous scholars have criticized culture-based theories of social class, and instead look to structural factors that help create and maintain rich and poor. Structural theories of social class point to large-scale social forces such as the economy to explain social-class categories. For example, during the recent economic crisis, millions of people lost their jobs or homes and experienced downward mobility. Structural theories of social class also point to large-scale changes in technology and employment that have created vast numbers of new poor in the United States. This includes the shift from solid blue-collar jobs to low-wage service work, the reduced demand for labor caused by automation, and the suburbanization of employment.

These trends have been exacerbated by structural forces that include reductions in welfare, increased immigration, and the exportation of American manufacturing jobs to other countries. "Our elected leaders have made major cuts in the safety net including welfare and other social supports [and] poor people must compete more fiercely for low-paying jobs and scarce resources with new immigrants to the United States as well as with poor working people around the globe" (Anderson 2008,

8–9). These trends are tied to a dual system of education, in which those with little or no schooling are pushed into the lowest segment of the service sector, while college graduates are able to move into high-tech (and high-paying) fields.

Social stratification has also been worsened by the growth of the criminal justice system, which has focused the bulk of its attention on young ethnic-minority males, blacks in particular. While blacks represent about 12 percent of the U.S. population, this group currently makes up over 40 percent of America's prison population. Sociologist Devah Pager has conducted a number of experimental studies to assess the impact of incarceration on various social and economic outcomes. In one such experiment, trained student testers applied for entry-level jobs in Milwaukee to measure how incarceration affects hiring practices. Whites who stated that they been incarcerated received half as many callbacks as whites who had not; only 14 percent of incarcerated black testers received callbacks, compared to 34 percent for blacks with no stated criminal history. Pager concluded that "criminal records close doors in employment situations. Many employers seem to use the information as a screening mechanism, without attempting to probe deeper into the possible context or complexities of the situation" (2003, 956).

Even ex-convicts who find jobs earn less than those without criminal histories. The income of ex-inmates is 10 to 20 percent lower than those who have not served time, and wage growth is diminished by about 30 percent (Western 2002). For ethnic minority males, the financial consequences of incarceration are even more pronounced.[6] Finally, incarceration has been found to impact long-term physical health and to have devastating effects on families.[7]

Research in this area also reveals an important facet of the criminal justice system: it exacerbates already existent social inequalities. By focusing its attention on those at the lowest rungs of the socioeconomic ladder—young, poor ethnic minorities with low rates of education—the criminal justice system "deepens disadvantage and forecloses mobility for the most marginal in society" (Western and Pettit 2010, 8). These effects are cumulative and intergenerational, passed on from parents to children, creating long-standing cycles of disadvantage.

The Connection between Social Class and Race

Both cultural and structural explanations of social class illustrate one of its most salient features: the connection between social class and race. It is nearly impossible to separate the two because existent social-class stratifications align with hierarchies of race. The wealthiest Americans tend to be whites and members of some Asian ethnic groups, while people of color are overrepresented in the working- and underclasses. Longitudinal data collected in Houston, Texas (Shelton and Greene 2012), found 33.7 percent of blacks earned less than $25,000 a year, compared to 14.5 percent of whites. While 12.5 percent of whites were paid over $100,000 annually, only 4.7 percent of blacks earned this amount. These trends extend well beyond Houston. The authors wrote, "more than 80% of African Americans report an income in the lowest 60% of the total U.S. income distribution" (1488).

W. E. B. Du Bois hypothesized that slavery and its legacy of structural, institutionalized racism created different social classes based on race: "It was the policy of the state to keep the Negro laborer poor, to confine him as far as possible to menial occupation, to make him a surplus labor reservoir and to force him into peonage and unpaid toil" (1935, 696). Building on the work of Du Bois, sociologist William Julius Wilson (1987) asserted that postslavery population shifts resulted in vast numbers of poor blacks, concentrated in large central cities, who are especially vulnerable to structural changes in the economy.

Elijah Anderson (1999) conducted ethnographic research in the poor enclaves of Philadelphia and posited two distinct social types of families, "decent" and "street." Anderson characterized the former as sharing many of the middle-class values and behaviors exhibited by mainstream white society (38). These included hard work, self-reliance, personal responsibility, sacrifice, saving money, respect for authority, politeness, cooperation, strict child-rearing practices, and alignment with community-based institutions such as schools and churches. Conversely, street families demonstrated a lack of consideration for others, disorganization, anger, alienation, frustration, and immorality. The extreme end of the street families consisted of criminals. "People in this class are profound casualties of the social and economic system," Anderson wrote. "Many pride themselves on living the 'thug life,' actively defying not simply the wider social conventions but the law itself. They sometimes model themselves after successful local drug dealers and rap artists like Tupac Shakur and Snoop Doggy Dogg" (36). Anderson concluded that these behaviors were a response to both structural forces and cultural conditions in poor neighborhoods. For members of the lower classes, particularly people of color, there are great risks. These risks are both structural (unstable employment, institutionalized racism, and discrimination) and cultural (the ongoing threat of violence in low-income neighborhoods, exposure to drugs, and other health hazards). With the deck stacked against them and little to lose, their response to these woes can be even more perilous: risk-taking behavior such as joining street gangs or taking part in underground economies.

People of Color and the Rise of the Middle Class

Anderson's work is both complicated and enhanced by that of scholars who have examined the black middle class in the United States. Sociologist Mary Pattillo-McCoy attributed the enlargement of the black middle class, which began in the 1950s, to structural features: "unprecedented economic growth and prosperity after World War II, along with the social and political pressures of the civil rights movement" (1999, 17–18). Using standard sociological metrics to calculate the size of the black middle class, Marsh et al. (2007) examined census data and discovered that 13 percent of blacks held at least a bachelor's degree, 46 percent lived in an owner-occupied home (as opposed to renting), and 25 percent were employed as managers or other professionals. While these figures were lower than comparable numbers for whites, the authors concluded that the black middle class is growing, both in total number and as a percentage of the black population. Analyzing data from the General Social Survey, Hunt and Ray (2012) found that concurrent with the growing socioeconomic status of black Americans from 1974 to 2010, there was an increase among the same population in middle-class self-identification and a decline in those who described their social class as belonging to any other category. In other words, as the black middle class has expanded, blacks increasingly define themselves as middle class.

Despite some measurable similarities, the black middle class differs from its white counterpart. Economically, the black middle class "remains a vulnerable group clustered in lower-middle-class occupations and, because of its recency, lacking any substantial wealth. . . . They also experience some of the economic pressure, and recognize the stigma of being African American" (Pattillo-McCoy 1999, 122–23). Additionally, the recent economic crisis has hit the black middle class especially hard. Studies forecast that 68 percent of today's middle-class blacks will earn less than their parents, compared to 30 percent of whites (Pew Charitable Trusts 2012).[8] Growing disparities in social class have bifurcated America's black population in a manner that echoes larger societal trends. Here, as elsewhere, there is division between the haves and the have-nots. Sociologists Cherise Harris and Nikki Khanna point out that "because of the conflation of race and class in America, middle-class culture is often understood as whiteness and blackness is understood as the behavior and experiences associated with the urban ghetto" (2010, 644).

From a cultural perspective, some elements of the black middle class mirror those of the white middle class, emphasizing "academic excellence, conservative styles of hair and dress, proficiency in Standard English, and the values of sacrifice and delayed gratification" (653). There are calculable benefits for adopting these types of behaviors. For example, a recent study of racial speech patterns (Grogger 2011) found that people who speak in voices identified by others as "black" earn about 12 percent less than similarly skilled whites. For those whose voices are not identified this way, the earnings gap is eliminated.

Such behaviors, however, do not come without some cost. Blacks who do not dress, talk, behave, and consume culture that signals them as "black" can face accusations of selling out from some members of the black community: "Both physical appearance and social class are yardsticks used to measure whether or not one is 'black enough.' Anyone who falls outside these racially and culturally prescribed norms is potentially subject to ridicule and exclusion" (Harris and Khanna 2010, 655). A recent study of 90,000 junior high and high-school students confirmed the social toll that comes with what the authors called "acting white": high-achieving whites were among the most popular students in school, while the popularity of black and Latino students who earned straight A's decreased with peers of the same race (Freyer and Torrelli 2010). For these and other reasons, the black middle class holds an "ambiguous position within the racial hierarchy [and] may resist assimilating fully into the mainstream" (Lacy 2004, 913).

The notion that there are two "types" of blacks, rooted in behavioral and ideological differences associated with variant social classes, illustrates the increasing cultural, social, and economic disparities described by scholars of the black middle class. Michael Eric Dyson (2005) wrote of an "Afristocracy: upper-middle-class blacks and the black elite who rain down fire and brimstone upon poor blacks for their deviance and pathology, and for their lack of couth and culture" (xiii–xiv). He contrasted this with a "Ghettocracy," the black underclass and working poor. Dyson's Ghettocracy concept also included rappers "whose values and habits are alleged to be negatively influenced by their poor origins" (xiv) and who romanticized a mythical black ghetto in their lyrics and lifestyles.

The bifurcation of an ethnoracial group into class-based collectives has occurred outside of the black population as well. The fastest-growing ethnoracial group in the United States today is Latinos, including Mexicans and Central Americans, and the percentage of Latinos in white-collar occupations has grown substantially (see Alba and Nee 2003). A 1996 Pepperdine University study of the Latino middle class found that the mainstream media stereotyped Latinos as gangbangers or irate political activists. As in the black community, working-class Latinos accused their middle-class counterparts of being sellouts and white wannabes. Middle-class Latinos "were often seen as cultural traitors. Apparently, retaining one's 'authentic' Latino ethnicity requires remaining in place both socioeconomically and geographically. Even the accomplished have often felt a need to feign 'street-wise' mannerisms and humble roots" (Rodriguez 1996, 2).

The dichotomies described in studies of the black and Latino middle classes, along with Anderson's theory of "decent" and "street" families, add nuance to race-based explanations of culture, revealing class-based distinctions that occur within ethnoracial groups. These class-based divisions, disparities, and tensions are reflected in rap culture, mirrored in the split between backpackers and gangstas. According to Robin Kelley, gangsta rap was partially a black underclass response to the growth of the black middle class. Gangsta rappers "remind listeners that they are still second-class citizens—'Niggaz'—whose collective lived experiences suggest that nothing has changed *for them* as opposed to the black middle class" (1996, 137). The resentment described by Kelley reflects a black underclass that feels left behind. Recent studies find, however, that one's social class position influences one's beliefs about what causes socioeconomic stratification. As the black middle class has grown in size and stature, there has been an attendant decline in this group's belief that structural factors are to blame for inequality (Shelton and Greene 2012; Hunt 2007). A growing number of middle-class blacks and Latinos place responsibility on individual factors such as motivation and personal effort, an ideology at the core of the American dream.

The American Dream

The United States was built on the premise that upward mobility is available to all. Fundamental to this American dream is the conviction that through hard work, motivation, and sacrifice, anyone can achieve greater social status and financial prosperity. According to this perspective, America is the "land of opportunity," a level playing field where those who work hard enough can "make it." Factors such as social class, gender, race, ethnicity, country of origin, family name, background, age, physical appearance or ability, religion, and sexual orientation have no bearing on a person's capacity to rise up. Furthermore, striving for the American dream implies virtue because it is aligned with the country's most cherished ideals: individualism, effort, inspiration, thrift, sacrifice, and success.

One reason for the dream's endurance is its sheer pervasiveness. This rags-to-riches narrative—in which an average person achieves greatness—has been a central feature of popular culture for eons. It is contained in ancient fairy tales such as "Cinderella," the Arthurian fable of Sir Gareth, the story of the Roman emperor Diocletian, the writings of Benjamin Franklin, and Horatio Alger's tales. Today, the rags-to-riches narrative is found in any number of pop culture offerings, including movies (*Slumdog Millionaire*), music (Sugarland's "Baby Girl"), video games (*Grand Theft Auto*), game shows (*Who Wants to be a Millionaire?*), and reality TV programs (*Joe Millionaire*). And anyone who has ever purchased a lottery ticket or put a coin into a slot machine knows the allure of instant wealth.

The rags-to-riches narrative is also featured in the sports arena, where superstars such as Kobe Bryant and LeBron James—both drafted by the NBA out of high school—seemingly came from nowhere to play for professional teams and earn millions. Yet few aspiring athletes go on to play professionally. Currently, about 3 of every 10,000 male high-school senior basketball players will eventually play for the NBA (National Collegiate Athletic Association 2012). Thus, while many people subscribe to the

American dream ideology, achieving upward mobility is less common than believed.

Opinion polls attest to the widespread and enduring faith in the American dream ideology in the United States, even in light of evidence to the contrary. Using longitudinal survey data, Jennifer Hochschild (1995) found that Americans are virtually unanimous in their support of the ideology, but there was variation between and among blacks and whites, particularly when measures such as social class and gender were taken into account. Overall, blacks had less faith in the American dream than whites, women were more likely to endorse it than men, and the ideology was strongly supported by immigrants and their descendants.

It was Hochschild's findings about social class, however, that were most surprising. Despite measurable gains in the post–civil rights era, middle class and well-off blacks were increasingly skeptical about the American dream compared to low-status blacks. Hochschild described the former as "succeeding more and enjoying it less" and believed that poor blacks were "under the spell" of the American dream. Hochschild asserted that the dissatisfaction of middle-class blacks was due to a confluence of factors: "relative deprivation—caused by a mix of unfulfilled (and occasionally unwarranted) rising expectations, gender competition, and the frustrations of living with white racial bias" as well as aggravation that came from within the collective black community (121, 140). In other words, with apologies to The Notorious B.I.G., the more money blacks earned, the more problems they encountered. Hochschild left no stone unturned in attempting to answer the question why poor blacks professed a strong belief in the American dream despite having little chance of achieving it. One set of factors was interpersonal and historical: poor blacks viewed work as a primary path to achieving the dream, and described themselves as hard working more than any other racial or class group. With a strong psychological need to maintain a sense of control over their lives, poor blacks denied disadvantage, focused on how far blacks had come compared to previous eras, and viewed themselves as better off than others at the lowest rungs of the class ladder. A second set of factors was institutional: churches, community groups, schools, families, and the media collectively reinforced the notion that the American dream remained available to anyone willing to work hard.

A metastudy of opinion polls from 1978 to 2008 (Hanson and Zogby 2010) demonstrated the resilience of the American dream ideology: the majority of Americans continue to believe that "most people who want to get ahead can make it if they're willing to work hard" (573). In fact, during this period, while there was an uptick in pessimism about opportunities for the working class, there was rising optimism about the chances of the impoverished. The authors concluded that there was a "resistance to questioning the American Dream, regardless of inequalities" (581). America's changing demographics have done nothing to quell the belief in the dream, either. Blacks, Latinos, and Asians accounted for 83 percent of America's population growth from 2000 to 2008, yet "members of all racial and ethnic groups are equally optimistic that they will achieve the American dream in the future" (Cohen-Marks and Stout 2011, 842). Furthermore, immigrants—who tend to be lower on the social class ladder—are generally more optimistic than native-born Americans about their chances of making it.

If anything could dampen enthusiasm for the American dream, surely it would be the recent economic crisis. The Great Recession has taken a devastating toll on the economic condition of many Americans, and has hit the black population particularly hard. From 2005 to 2009 black wealth plunged by 53 percent, wiping out a generation of economic gains (Pew Charitable Trusts 2012). In the wake of the economic downturn, rates of unemployment for blacks were twice as high as for whites, and blacks were significantly more likely to lose their homes due to foreclosure (Stout and Le 2012, 1339). Yet black belief in the American dream has never been higher. Political scientists attribute this optimism to the election of Barack Obama, asserting that positive symbols of black success have more explanatory power than do empirical economic data in the changing attitudes about the American dream among the black population (1350). Research has demonstrated that symbols of black success like Obama can transform how blacks perceive their own socioeconomic opportunities. For example, a study of *The Cosby Show*—a sitcom about an affluent black family that ran from 1984 to 1992—found that viewers' belief that the American dream was achievable for blacks rose after watching the program (Jhally and Lewis 1992).

The Come Up

Studies that connect powerful symbols of success and media consumption to endorsement of the American dream help answer one of the questions raised in my class-based analysis of Chicago's rap microscenes: Why do gangsta rappers, a relatively lower-class group whose members have objectively fewer chances of achieving upward mobility, profess a greater belief in the American dream than their backpacker counterparts? Two classic communications theories—identification and distinctiveness—are useful in unpacking these processes.

Identification theory (Kelman 1961) suggests that during interactions, people are more likely to identify with members of in-groups—those with physical or behavioral traits perceived to be similar. Based on this perceived similarity, they will then begin to identify with (and emulate) other characteristics of these individuals or groups. According to the theory, when, for example, a Japanese viewer watches a Japanese character depicted on television, she will identify with the character based on their shared ethnicity and then begin to see herself as similar in other ways. If the Japanese TV character is portrayed as intelligent, the viewer may believe that she, as a Japanese person, is also intelligent.

Distinctiveness theory (McGuire 1984) suggests that people with physical or behavioral traits that are rare within a given population tend to identify with others who possess the same traits. According to the theory, if a Japanese viewer watches an American TV station where Japanese people are underrepresented, she will become more aware of her race than she would were she watching a program of Japanese origin, where her ethnicity would not stand out.

Identification and distinctiveness theories have been used to explain racial preferences and media consumption, among other things. Studies have found that viewers rated television characters of the same group more positively and perceived themselves as having similar behavioral characteristics (Hoplamazian and Appiah 2013; Fujioka 2005; Appiah 2002). The theories have also been used to consider the potentially harmful impact of media. For example, a content analysis of TV advertisements found that when blacks were depicted in occupations, they were portrayed as having little authority. Latinos were so infrequently depicted in occupations that their degree of job authority could not be analyzed (Mastro and Stern 2003). In addition to creating and maintaining stereotypes, such media may encourage members of these groups who consume them to internalize their implicit messages.

To connect these studies to gangsta rap and the American dream, symbols of success alter people's perceptions that the American dream is achievable. When those symbols of success—powerful figures such as Bill Cosby, Barack Obama, or Jay-Z—possess traits that consumers perceive they share, consumers identify with the successful figures and emulate their other behaviors. Yet positive symbols of blackness in the media often frame blackness in particular ways. For example, a longitudinal study of advertisements in magazines found that blacks were most likely to be depicted as musicians or athletes (Bowen and Schmid 1997). Because blacks tend to pay more attention to blacks depicted in the media, identify with them, view themselves as similar, and emulate their behaviors, the media-fueled image of the gangsta rapper has become one of the most resonant figures in black popular culture today. Politicians and pundits decry gangsta rap as amoral, but celebrity gangstas represent positive symbols of achievement to the young black men who pay attention to gangstas, identity with gangstas, see themselves as similar to gangstas, and begin to emulate gangsta behaviors.

Mary Pattillo-McCoy (1999) wrote of a similar phenomenon in her ethnography of black middle-class youth in Chicago, whom she described as mesmerized by a "ghetto trance." Drawing upon iconic gangsta-rap figures from pop culture, as well as gang members and drug dealers in the neighborhood, the teens "play gangsta verbal games, buy the emblems of ghetto fashion, and swagger like the main characters in a black shoot-'em-up movie" (123). Much of this was harmless and fun—youth who were "thrilled" by gangsta rap because it was cool. But a smaller portion of the teens became "consumed" through their engagement with gangsta rap, crossing the line from playful simulation into criminal activity. Pattillo-McCoy eschewed the popularized explanation that this criminality stemmed from a lack of legitimate opportunities. Rather, for the middle-class youth in Chicago, being a gangsta criminal—like those glorified on the big screen and in the neighborhood—was exciting.

I met plenty of "thrilled" gangsta rappers in Chicago, too—young men who emulated gangsta rap because it was cool, fun, and titillating. I also met those who were consumed by gangsta rap, and crossed over into criminality. Some of the latter were middle-class youth who took things too far. But there were also working- and lower-class men with limited opportunities, low levels of education, and histories of incarceration. These were not young people whose evenings were spent playing gangsta-rap games at the local church, as described in Pattillo-McCoy's study. These young men mimicked the gangsta style, swagger, and material emblems, but also emulated a "gangsta" approach to capitalism and achieving the American dream. Drawing on the same pop-culture myths that produced the other facets of gangsta, these young men perceived music as their only ticket out. "This is our crack and basketball, this is all we have," said Joka, who dealt drugs to fund his musical ambitions.

This is the only opportunity an uneducated motherfucker like me from the West Side of Chicago has. Nobody's gonna rescue us. It's about scraping whatever you can scrape together right now to stay alive to keep working tomorrow to get what's gonna lay the foundation for us to rescue ourselves. You bust your ass, eventually it'll come. I'm gonna make a million in this business.

Gangsta rap's mediated history is brimming with rags-to-riches narratives of rap hustlers who combined criminal behavior with the American dream ideology and achieved enormous upward mobility. Legendary gangstas such as Eazy-E, The Notorious B.I.G., Snoop Dogg, Big Pun, Jay-Z, and 50 Cent went from streets to stages, mapping out a rap-hustler blueprint for others to follow. The appeal of this blueprint is not difficult to understand for those at the bottom of the hegemonic structures of race and social class. Those who subscribe to the rap-hustler tenets, writes Todd Boyd (2003), redefine an American dream on their own terms: "Making money off of their immense talents, gaining leverage and visibility because of it, and then telling a hostile and often racist America to collectively kiss their 'young, Black, rich and famous' asses in no uncertain terms" (7). To understand the rap hustler blueprint, and the consequences of those who are consumed by it, one must return to where it all began—South Central Los Angeles.

The Ongoing Cultural Influence of LA Gangsta Rap

In September 2012, *Forbes* magazine published "Cash Kings," its annual roundup of rap's top earners (Greenburg 2012). Pioneering gangsta-rap producer Dr. Dre topped the list, raking in an estimated $110 million, despite his not having released an album of solo material since 2001. The majority of this fortune came not from music, but from his popular line of Beats By Dr. Dre headphones. A series of awestruck online articles accompanied the printed piece, including features about celebrity rappers such as Ludacris ("A Rap Mogul Diversifies His Empire") and Jay-Z ("A Lesson on the Power of Entrepreneurial Capitalism"). Online viewers could read the stories accompanied by the strains of "I Get Money (Forbes 1,2,3 Remix)," a collaboration between 50 Cent, Jay-Z, and Sean "Diddy" Combs.

As with Dr. Dre, music was rarely the sole source of income for these branded rap moguls. Most of them were shilling products such as liquor (Bryan "Birdman" Williams), soda (Lil Wayne), and signature clothing lines (Young Jeezy) to fatten the coffers. Ludacris—who ranked tenth on the list, despite not having issued a solo album since 2010—had his own brand of headphones, a cognac label, a voiceover deal with RadioShack, and various film and music endeavors. Attaching his name to corporate brands was crucial according to Luda, who also emphasized the importance of maintaining a strong work ethic: "We work so hard that we never get a real chance to stop and reflect on what we've done sometimes. So the *Forbes* list is a great representation of, 'You know what, wow, we *are* out here working as hard as hell!' "

We're a long way from South Central, but that's really where the story of branded rap moguls begins. It is impossible to comprehend the relationship between gangs and gangsta-rap music without considering the ongoing cultural influence of gangsta rap in Los Angeles in the late 1980s and early 1990s. Three authors (Chang 2005, chapter 14; Cross 1993; Quinn 2005) described the development of the gangsta-rap microscene in Los Angeles, including—to varying degrees—the influence of street gangs.[9] Combined, these works demonstrate how Los Angeles's gangsta-rap microscene was the product of large-scale social forces combined with cultural exchanges between key players. Within a few years of its inception, the iconic gangsta rap created there was a worldwide phenomenon that informs rap music to this day.

Gangsta-rap music was not birthed in Los Angeles, although LA resident Toddy Tee's 1985 song "Batterram" detailed the violent tactics of the Los Angeles Police Department (LAPD) during this era. Credit for the gangsta-rap genre is typically afforded to Philadelphia denizen Schoolly D, whose 1986 song "P.S.K." is widely considered the first commercially released gangsta-rap track.[10] P.S.K. stood for Park Side Killers, the name of Schoolly D's street gang. A song that borrowed Schoolly's cadence and subject matter quickly followed: "6 in the Mornin" by LA-based rapper Ice-T. In the song, Ice-T "managed to outline the events that made up the life of many LA street youth: police harassment, the arrival of rock cocaine and abusive stories about women. And T had found a meter that worked for the slow and stealthy pace of LA cruisin'" (Cross 1993, 26).

"6 in the Mornin'" was a direct outgrowth of the socioeconomic conditions that plagued Los Angeles during this period. These included deindustrialization, the outsourcing of factory labor to foreign countries, the bifurcation of service labor into low-wage McJobs and lucrative knowledge-based employment, white flight to the suburbs, the first-ever decline in Los Angeles's black population, the rise of the black middle class, and budget reductions for public services, education, job training, and affordable housing. Statistics from the Los Angeles Unified School District show 1987–88 high school dropout rates reaching 79 percent in some South Central neighborhoods, with junior-high rates reaching 25 percent (Johnson, Farrell, and Oliver 1993, 118). These phenomena created a substantial number of newly impoverished residents, particularly people of color, who resided in communities increasingly characterized by large concentrations of jobless and working poor. "The deteriorated socioeconomic conditions of neglected inner cities have led scholars to compare ghettos like South Central Los Angeles . . . to South African 'bantustans'" (Cho 1995, 463).

Though LA street gangs date to the 1920s and began to proliferate in the 1940s and 1950s, gang membership in the city increased by 500 percent during the 1980s (Hagedorn 1988; Quinn 2005). The abundance of cheap and increasingly powerful guns aided an increase in deadly gang-related violence in urban areas; from 1984 to 1992, gang-related murders in Los Angeles rose by nearly 400 percent. Exacerbating these trends was the one area the state seemed willing to spend money: locking up young, inner-city men of color for drug-related crimes, with especially harsh sentences for crack. Perhaps it is no surprise that "the most intense growth period for drug incarceration rates, from 1989 to 1993, coincided with the 'classic gangsta rap' years," and that in 1990, one-third of young black males in California were prison, on parole, or on probation (Quinn 2005, 47). Adding fuel to this was an extended history of corruption and brutality on behalf of the LAPD, whose tech-heavy surveillance of black youth had reached new heights. The totality of these trends resulted in a profound alienation, coupled with the creation of a "survival culture" (see Glasgow 1980) on the part of inner city youth in Los Angeles, whose responses—at least those related to gangsta rap—included joining gangs, selling drugs, and attempting to make it in the music business (47).[11]

Los Angeles's primordial gangsta rappers employed these deteriorating socioeconomic circumstances as a resource: The city's socioeconomic plight and chaotic milieu became primary fodder for songs and music videos that both dramatized and critiqued these circumstances (42). These conditions were the central lyrical concern of what remains gangsta rap's signature group, Niggaz Wit Attitudes or N.W.A. The popularity of Ice-T's "6 in the Mornin" inspired a 1986 soundalike from N.W.A, its debut single "Boyz-N-The Hood." Drawing on a long history of African American folklore and pop culture figures, N.W.A rapped in a "participatory style of narrative," lending their music an aura of insider authenticity that encapsulated the "aggression and anger of the streets of South Central in their intonation and timbre" (Cross 1993, 37). What made N.W.A distinct from gangsta-rap forefathers such as Grandmaster Flash and Ice-T was that the group did not purport to merely narrate the conditions of the inner city; they claimed to offer first-person accounts from the front lines. Some critics decried the group's image and lyrics as a marketing ploy, but it succeeded beyond anyone's imagination. N.W.A's 1988 opus *Straight Outta Compton* placed West Coast gangsta rap permanently on the musical map, drawing the attention of the FBI and selling millions of copies with virtually no radio airplay. The group's outlaw image and controversial lyrics cemented a prototype for gangsta rappers that is largely unchanged today; all subsequent gangsta-rap artists owe a debt to N.W.A's self-proclaimed "reality rap."

The success of N.W.A and its LA peers can be attributed, in part, to their perceived authenticity. Kubrin asserted that "since its early pioneers were gang members, gangsta rap relates to the life experiences of the rappers themselves, and its lyrics portray gang and ghetto life from a criminal's perspective" (2005, 361). This popular perception is only partially accurate. Many of Los Angeles's pioneering gangsta rappers were not gang members or had only peripheral associations to street gangs (Chang 2005; Quinn 2005). Most of these fledgling gangsta rappers, however, grew up in communities where gang activity was common, and used this proximity to craft cinematic soundscapes steeped in gang minutiae: "the nuanced hand signs, vocabulary, and gestures, the special clothing and color-coding, and the territorial graffiti" (Quinn 2005, 53). Thus was born a "formula" whereby the subgenre's architects appropriated, interpreted, packaged, and sold the hidden world of street gangs through what appeared to be inside knowledge (Charnas 2010, 221). Indeed, "part of the significance of N.W.A was that they realized that rebellious street norms could be exploited for economic gain" (Watts 1997, 46).

If their gang-related yarns were based more on proximity than firsthand experience, the early LA gangsta rappers' familiarity with the narcotics trade was more direct. For example, N.W.A's Eazy-E reportedly started the band's independent label, Ruthless Records, using proceeds from drug dealing (Quinn 2005).[12] Eazy-E played up his unlawful past to the press and on wax, lending him an air of street-level authenticity that helped to cement his iconic status.[13] Regardless of its veracity, Eazy-E's criminal twist on the American dream was good for business; it generated controversy and media attention. In doing so, Eazy-E and his ilk contrived a "rap hustler" archetype that resonated with mainstream audiences, and provided a script that has been mimicked by celebrity and aspiring gangsta rappers ever since.[14]

Dimitriadis pointed out that the rap hustler "holds a very special place in the American popular imagination. He embodies such capitalist values as rugged individualism, rampant materialism, strength through physical force, and male domination, while he rejects the very legal structures which define that culture. He is both deeply inside and outside of mainstream American culture" (1996, 188). Eazy-E and N.W.A's popularization of the rap hustler archetype was so successful that the formula was immediately replicated by artists and promoted by record companies looking to cash in on its appeal, spawning subsequent generations of rap hustlers.

Rap Hustlers in the Era of Bling

Gangsta rap gained notoriety in the early and mid-1990s, and effectively became the popular face of all rap music. According to sociologist Margaret Hunter (2011), the newfound popularity of gangsta rap during this era was attributable to a change in hip-hop culture, from an emphasis on cultural practices to conspicuous consumption. During this period key gangsta-rap artists such as Dr. Dre, Snoop Dogg, Tupac Shakur, and The Notorious B.I.G. rose to prominence. These artists represented a significant development for gangsta rap because they removed much of the subgenre's anger and sense of systemic injustice, and replaced it with an emphasis on wealth and materialism.[15] The members of this cohort gave a facelift to Eazy-E's rap-hustler blueprint, replacing his gritty urban warrior with a relatively upscale variety of gangsta that took cues from films about Latino drug lords (*Scarface*) and Italian mafia dons (*The Godfather*, *Goodfellas*). These movies "had specific ties with hip hop culture, where they were—contrary to the white film press's perception of them as classical, cautionary tragedies—commonly perceived as inspirational rags-to-riches tales" (Reinikainen 2005, 39–40).

Embodying late-millennial capitalist impulses, the songs and music videos produced by gangsta rappers during this era preached hyperconsumerism and wanton materialism with a twist, what media studies scholar Roopali Mukherjee (2006) called the "ghetto fabulous aesthetic." This aesthetic, Mukherjee wrote, contained a "particular class trajectory, often a meteoric rise from rages to riches," and paired lavish symbols of the postmodern American dream—expensive cars, diamond jewelry, and luxury clothing—with "emphatic affirmations of working class, urban, black life" (600). With cooperation from the media and the corporate music industry and drawing upon iconic black American pop-culture figures such as the pimp and the street hustler, the celebrity gangsta rappers of this period repeatedly reminded audiences of their wealth, business acumen, and criminal misdeeds. "At the height of [gangsta rap's] appeal, record labels had even resorted to marketing the criminal background of rappers as a way to ensure 'street cred'" (Watkins 2005, 103).

The formative years of rap music featured a division of labor between businessmen and artists, but as the genre grew from a tiny subculture into a multibillion-dollar global industry, some of the most prominent rappers aspired to greater ownership over the means of production. These included new-millennium rap hustlers such as Jay-Z, 50 Cent, and Rick Ross, all of whom were lauded as much for their financial and marketing acumen as they were for their music. These modern-day gangsta rappers were not content merely to own their own record labels, but rather aspired to be one-man brands, shilling everything from autobiographies to signature clothing lines to bottled water. Jay-Z personified this "spirit of rapitalism" (see Harkness 2012b) on a 2005 Kanye West song where he famously rapped, "I'm not a businessman, I'm a business, man." Greg Dimitradis called Jay-Z the "ultimate corporate hip hop 'hustler'" because he embraced the duality of this role: "Jay-Z raps in intricate ways about his 'big balling' lifestyle and former (alleged) past as a drug dealer, [and] he has also embraced his role as an aggressive capitalist entrepreneur who can move across social circles and classes" (2009, 42). Indeed, today's rap hustlers pitch more than products, they sell a complete lifestyle (Hunter 2011).

The notion of entrepreneurship is central to the American dream ideology. Communications scholar Christopher Holmes Smith (2003) used the term "hip-hop mogul" to describe the high-rolling gangsta/entrepreneur who clawed his way out of an urban war zone to superstardom. Smith pointed out that the rap mogul "bears the stamp of American tradition, since the figure is typically male, entrepreneurial, and prestigious both in cultural influence and personal wealth" (69). Those who achieved this elite status often did so as a means of transcending the confines of a hegemonic socioeconomic structure that places young black men at the bottom. The social and cultural prominence of such moguls, Smith wrote, was not lost on the average young black rapper from a poor inner-city neighborhood: Were he "savvy enough to leverage his gains within and against his immediate surroundings, then he can graduate from relative obscurity and move up to the more elevated plane occupied by the moguls and their handpicked superstars" (83).

It was this class-based trajectory from gritty ghetto mise-en-scène to corporate boardroom that characterized the rap hustler. He embodied the liminality of this role because he was both street and smart. He rose to the top, but kept his feet planted in the 'hood, never forgetting where he came from because he did not have to abandon those roots. In doing so, the rap hustler "espoused capitalist ascent and loyalty to a culturally distinct community—a way of achieving American success without entirely assimilating" (Kenna 2008, 266). Or as Todd Boyd phrased it, "this hip hop generation has decided that though they want the money and power offered by mainstream society, they do not want to have to change in order to get it. They want to be *of* the mainstream without being *in* the mainstream" (2003, 15–16).

Significantly, the rap-hustler archetype did not eliminate or obscure race. On the contrary, the rap-hustler archetype foregrounded racial identity. The rap hustler combined the American dream ideology with an undeniable, albeit caricatured, sense of blackness. Like Eazy-E and the cavalcade of rap hustlers who followed, adhering to the rap-hustler script was a means by which to transcend not race, but rather social class. It is for this reason that social class is paramount to understanding the relationship between street gangs and gangsta rap.

Hagedorn (2008) noted that the media-fueled image of the rap hustler, combined with gangsta rap's exploding appeal, "had an influence on gang members themselves. This new, studio-produced gangsta or nigga identity now influences how actual gang members, and other youth, see themselves: Life imitating art imitating life in a manner that would make Jean Baudrillard proud" (100). Of course, young people enthralled by gangsta rap are not mechanical pop-culture receptacles; youth culture also informs the culture industry. The rap-hustler archetype—informed by gang and prison culture and promoted by the culture industry—had considerable influence on the rapping gang members I met in Chicago, all of whom aspired to achieve enormous success in the music industry. In light of their adverse socioeconomic conditions, these young men's adherence to the rap-hustler script was perceived as a path to achieving the American dream. To subscribe to the American dream ideology is to believe in the transformative power of work, the focus of the next chapter.

3

Bangin' on Wax

Recording Studios as Symbolic Spaces

Less than two weeks after Phantastic's death, Grafta received a call from a local radio station that wanted to broadcast one of the fallen rapper's unreleased songs. Phantastic appeared on most of the tracks on Bully Boyz's debut mixtape, and had been hard at work in the months since its release, recording as much new material as possible. At the time of his passing, Phantastic had recorded almost fifty songs that had never been heard by the public. Many of these were tunes that Grafta and Bully Boyz were working on in preparation for the group's sophomore release. Grafta knew that some of Phantastic's most powerful material remained in the vaults, and wanted one of those songs to be heard on the radio.

He was still in mourning when he returned to the group's recording studio, located a few blocks south of Chicago's downtown Loop. It was 3:00 a.m. and he was alone. Numb. Grafta entered the studio and switched on the lights. The room was usually loud and full of life, the boys in the band cracking jokes as they tried out new verses on each other. Tonight the room was still and quiet. Grafta was overcome by the history of the space, the memories attached to it: "I walked in, and this weird thing came over me," he recalled. "The reality really struck hard. Like man, this is where we spent most of our time. He used to sit right there and write his lyrics. I was getting all these vibes."

The recording studio was the place where Grafta, Phantastic, and the other members of Bully Boyz had spent nearly every evening for the past two years. The studio was a workspace, a clubhouse, and a party spot. It was a dream factory, the place where the group's ambitions took flight. The studio wasn't a home away from home for Bully Boyz; it was home. These memories, and the emotions Grafta associated with them, made his return to the studio difficult. "I was mentally fucked up," he remembered. "Who ain't? You're gonna be fucked up after a situation

like that, doing music with someone that you consider a brother, someone that you go to work with every day. You spend more time with motherfuckers you work with than you do with your family. We *was* a family.
It was like we worked, and then after work we partied, we chilled."

Grafta sat down in front of a vast recording console that consisted of a
multichannel mixing board, two king-sized computer monitors, assorted
drum machines and keyboards, and a variety of digital gadgets. He
poured himself a glass of Hennessy, the blue light of the computer screens
illuminating the space in a soft glow. He fiddled with a few knobs on the
mixing board and peered through the plate-glass window that overlooked the vocal booth. A lone microphone protected by a mesh wind-
screen stood at attention, poised and ready. But there would be no vocals
recorded tonight. Grafta pulled up Pro Tools on the computer and began
sifting through more than seventy songs in various states of completion.
He clicked the mouse, closed his eyes, leaned back in his chair, and listened. The producer steadied himself as Phantastic's vocals reverberated
from the studio speakers, enveloping the room with sound. The MC was
gone, but his voice was still alive. That *voice*, Grafta thought to himself. In
the wake of his passing, Phantastic's lyrics assumed a haunted, almost
prophetic quality, with the fallen rapper detailing his criminal exploits,
gang affiliation, commitment to hustling, and his repeated prediction that
he would meet with an early demise.

The amount of music Phantastic left behind was not surprising to anyone who knew him. Of the nine original members of Bully Boyz, Phantastic was the most diligent worker, the one who pushed everyone else as
hard as possible. This work ethic produced hours of unreleased material—
Phantastic recorded new songs constantly, right up to his passing. With
Phantastic gone, only the music remained. His tireless work ethic is what
Grafta remembered most about Phantastic.

He was motivated. That was one thing I loved about him. Like,
dude, take a rest. Fuck music right now. We've been in the studio
for a whole week. We can't kill ourselves over this shit. Let's chill
back for a second. But he was always like music music music.
From the day I met him, he was like, "This is what I'm on. That's
it. I ain't got nothing else. Music and my kids. The way I can feed
my kids properly is through music." He loved his kids just like he

loved music, in a different way, though. The kids are always gonna come first, but he was one to put music first.

In selecting a song for the radio show, Grafta had plenty of material to choose from, but one track stood out. The song was an earnest, soulful number where Phantastic spoke directly to the eldest of his two sons. The lyrics detailed how a teenage Phantastic, still a high-school student, first heard the news that one of his girlfriends was pregnant. Abortion was considered but ruled out; Phantastic made the decision to be the best possible father to his child, the dad he never had growing up. In the song's second verse, Phantastic expressed concern that his son would follow in his footsteps, that the boy would pick up the bad habits of his father. He urged his son to seek a legitimate path to success through education, rather than running in the streets like his old man. As the music faded to a close, Phantastic told his son how much he loved him. It was a poignant parting statement, Phantastic's final message to the world. Grafta knew he had found the perfect song.

> If there's any record that he ever wanted to be heard, it's this one. He had really held that record to the chest. So I started mixing, and it was crazy, listening to a record that he had dedicated to his kids. It was real emotional for me. Me sitting in the studio mixing it, you can only take so much. Even though he's not physically here, that music is forever.

Symbolic Spaces of Musical Activity

The image that comes to mind when one thinks of musicians—rappers or otherwise—generally involves spaces of musical activity: the MC hammering out verses in the vocal booth or prowling the concert stage as the audience cheers. Spaces such as these are central to music cultures because they are the places where the bulk of musical activity takes place. They are where musicians "do" music.

Recording studios are ubiquitous in popular music history and lore. The names spill from the tongue. Abbey Road, the Record Plant, and Electric Ladyland are as iconic as the celebrated works recorded there. Pop-music writers produce book-length treatments that detail the recording of critically lauded chartbusters such as *Rumours, Thriller,* and *Dark Side of the Moon.* VH-1's *Classic Albums* series applied the technique to the small screen, and it is hard to think of a movie about twentieth-century musicians that does not centralize such spaces. Biopics lionize the studio in films such as *Walk the Line,* where Johnny Cash reinvents country music during his first recording session, and *La Bamba,* where Ritchie Valens endures take after take to perfect a vocal. Documentaries centralize the studio as integral not only to the songs recorded in them, but to the identity of musicians who record them. In *Rattle and Hum,* U2 makes a pilgrimage to Memphis's Sun Studios to bask in its ambiance, hiring "Cowboy" Jack Clement to produce tracks, as he once did for Elvis Presley and Jerry Lee Lewis. (In the film, Bono marvels that "the exact same studio exists, even the same tiles.") *Let it Be* and *I Am Trying to Break Your Heart* detail the creative and personal tensions that plagued the Beatles and Wilco as they recorded new albums. Even fictional films highlight the importance of recording studios. In *Hustle and Flow,* a pimp discovers the joys of the creative process after installing a claptrap bedroom studio. All of this mythmaking renders the recording studio, as a symbolic space, fundamental to understanding music cultures.

Early hip-hop culture was rooted in overlapping performative practices that occurred at the community level. The primordial rap-music scenes of New York City were "entirely dependent upon face-to-face social contact and interaction" (Dimitriadis 1996, 179). As rap gained popularity and home-recording technology became increasingly ubiquitous, the genre moved away from its performative roots and shifted to a culture centered on recorded music. This changed the meaning and interpretation of rap music, in part because "the recording studio facilitates and demands certain musical production practices that render it distinct from live performance mode" (Forman 2002, 79). Today, a good portion of rap culture takes place in recording studios, yet they are somewhat understudied. I argue that recording studios are crucial to the genre, and essential sites for the qualitative study of rap music culture.

Hip-hop scholars have considered the role of recording studios in studies of digital sampling, the spatialization of production styles, live instrumentation, and musical aesthetics (Forman 2002; Marshall 2006; Nielson 2010; Schloss 2004; Shusterman 1992). Others have used the cultural objects created in studios—songs, CDs, and mixtapes—as fodder for textual and content analysis (Harrison 2006; Hunnicutt and Andrews 2009; Kubrin 2005). I take an alternative approach and examine recording studios as symbolic spaces: culturally specific locations in which identity and meaning are shaped by social exchanges. From a symbolic perspective, what musicians do in studios is less important than what these spaces do for musicians.

Functionally, studios allow rappers to record songs, which involves mastering various techniques specific to these spaces and the practices that take place within them. This entails breath control, pitch, delivery, and assorted mechanical skills, all while minimizing bodily movements lest they be audible to the microphone. Studios also serve as gathering places where artists collaborate, network, educate, and learn. Furthermore, studios enable enterprising musicians, producers, engineers, and beat makers to earn additional income, which can subsidize the cost of equipment and other capital purchases.

Studios have symbolic properties as well. They serve as sites of legitimization and personal transformation for aspiring rappers. Mastering the art of recording, be it through producing music or rapping over music created by others, serves as a means of identity construction and development. After all, "recordings are the auditory inscription of a [musician's] performed identity" (Shank 1994, 172). Studios enable MCs to develop a style and aesthetic distinctiveness that are key to their voice, image, and identities as musicians. Music, lyrics, songs, samples, and CDs contain declarations of an MC's character, proclaiming who a rapper "is" or at least aspires to be. In part, this identity construction is achieved musically through a combination of style, production value, aesthetics, song selection, lyrics, and the ideologies embedded within all of these. Cultural objects such as an individual track or a collection of songs are part of a total package that declares a rapper's identity.

If this sounds like a lot of work, that's because it is. Most musicians in Chicago's rap underground envision studios not as sites of leisure, but as workplaces. The relationship between these locations and work render them spaces steeped in social class—they offer platforms upon which displays of occupational identity are enacted. In other words, studios are symbolic spaces that have meaning beyond their intrinsic use value.

Technology and the Proliferation of Home Recording Studios

Sociologist Edward Kealy (1982) asserted that the "real" rock revolution of the 1960s occurred when revenues generated by superstar musicians allowed them to seize control of the recording process, in some cases building their own studios and overseeing every aspect of their music. Under the traditional system, record companies exerted almost complete control of the recording process, but during rock's early period, musicians and producers took control. This control was not limited to music. Traditional recording studios were impersonal spaces whose assembly-line functions were almost clinical in nature. Rock musicians of the 1960s and 1970s yearned for a more intimate "home workshop" experience, with aesthetics that emphasized comfort and atmosphere. "The 'back to nature' movement in popular culture in the early seventies led to a number of real barns being converted into studios. . . . By the late seventies it was not unusual for affluent superstars to record in mansions and castles, on yachts or ranches, to fly to Jamaica or Nigeria for some extra musical atmosphere, or to have their own mobile studio follow them from concert to concert" (110).

In this era, recorded works were the "dominant industrialized commercial medium of popular music," and the principal aim of musicians interested in success was to create studio recordings that could be sold in record stores and broadcast on the radio (Shank 1994, 172–73). Recording technology was expensive and aspiring musicians had to invest large sums to book time at professional studios that were run by trained sound engineers.

In addition to their economic role, recording studios were equally important for their ability to capture a musician's identity on tape. Upon entering a studio,

> musicians find themselves in an environment very different from the distracted heterogeneity of the nightclubs. The physical arrangement of the machines and the furniture, the changes in a band's sound as a result of the technology, and a corresponding set of practices and beliefs that accommodate this technology, all produce specific constraints on the process of inscribing a band's identity on tape. (175)

The high cost of studios, the relative rarity of the studio experience, and the key function of recorded works in both constructing a musical identity and "making it" helped inspire a reverence for recording studios that remains intact. The expense of recording and the scarcity of the studio experience, however, have been dramatically altered by technology. Advances in technology lead to modifications in communication that alter social life and allow for new possibilities within art and culture (Peterson and Anand 2004). Prototypical examples include the cultural changes that occurred in the wake of inventions such as the printing press and the personal computer. Writing about music, Peterson (1997) described the shift in singing styles that developed after the invention of the microphone. Instead of shouting and overenunciating to compensate for lack of volume, as singers did in the premicrophone era, small-voiced vocalists could "croon" softly into a microphone, which led to the development and popularity of more intimate forms of singing. "At a stroke the vocal skills of a generation of performers were made redundant as their style became defined as forced, corny, and distinctly old-fashioned" (107). The careers of crooners such as Frank Sinatra, Bing Crosby, and Elvis Presley were fueled by this technological innovation. The popularity of those crooners in turn revolutionized the recording and radio industries.

Technological developments have also altered the style and substance of rap music. The genre's pioneers appropriated technology as a means by which to attach two turntables to a mixing apparatus that enabled DJs to create uninterrupted audio loops. This novel use of technology "refocused crowd attention on the rappers, whose spoken exhortations became more elaborate. . . . Thus rap was importantly shaped by the increasingly standardized electronic equipment used by artists" (Lena 2012, 35). The drum machines and digital samplers that became ubiquitous elements of rap-music production "offered increased control over the recording process and enhanced cost efficiency by circumventing the need for extra studio musicians" (Forman 2002, 80). Rap musicians took immediate advantage of these technologies and used them to create aural collages that simultaneously broadened rap music's sonic landscape, defied copyright laws, and redefined the concept of the postmodern musician.

Economics has also played a role in technology-driven cultural change in music. Beginning in the 1980s and 1990s, media-creation tools became cheaper, faster, and easier to use, and sales of personal computers and recording software soared. The inflated costs associated with studio recordings traditionally served as a gatekeeper of sorts. Today pure audiences have dwindled with the advent of "prosumers," those who both produce and consume media products. Rather than simply listening to music, anyone can create songs in home studios and make them available online for others to hear. Furthermore, the increasing accessibility of broadband Internet and the rising use of this technology for social-media purposes have made it cheaper and easier for independent artists to share their works. Today, local musicians can circulate their material "beyond the immediate physical audience, in effect allowing musicians a form of distribution previously reserved for mainstream products, but without the connection to the major record labels or the demands to compromise associated with such a union" (Price 2006, 50).

The widespread dissemination of music online has drastically diminished the size, scope, economic power, and influence of major music corporations (Condry 2004). This has resulted in the slashing of major-label recording budgets, leading to "the closings of hundreds of commercial studios and the commensurate rise in the number of records being made in people's bedrooms, basements, and converted garages. . . . The universal acceptance of digital recording—mostly in the form of the ubiquitous computer-based Pro Tools system—is another huge change" (Massey 2009, xi).[1]

In 1990, Avid Technologies, a small Massachusetts company that designs audio and video recording equipment and software, earned $7.4 million in gross revenue. The following year, Avid issued the first version of Pro Tools, a high-end audio recording system that garnered acclaim from musicians for its ability to produce professional-quality sound recordings without the expense of a professional-quality recording studio. Avid's annual sales leapt to $32.3 million that year, and by 2007 Avid products grossed nearly a billion dollars annually. Pro Tools remains among the company's top-selling products.

The success of Pro Tools is attributable to musicians and audio enthusiasts of all stripes, but the software has gained particular currency among those working out of home studios. In rap music, "the proliferation of home-based studios by self-acclaimed, technically skilled MCs and producers has revolutionized the music industry" (Price 2006, 17). In Chicago, affordable digital recording software such as Pro Tools helped spawn countless home studios, which increased participation and altered the content and character of the city's underground rap music. Today, instead of rap microscenes that are dominated by a handful of corporate and independent acts who record in professional studios, the bulk of Chicago's rap music is being produced in thousands of home studios. "Technology and cheap technology has made it a lot easier," said Mr. Grimm, a Chicagoan who uses Pro Tools to produce rap records from his apartment. "You used to have to go out and buy a four track [cassette recorder], and they were $500 when I bought one. And not a lot of people have $500 to spend on a piece of audio equipment. Nowadays you can download freeware off the Internet to make beats all you want. You can buy $50 programs. Even $300 programs are more affordable for a lot of kids."

Get on the Mic

When setting up interviews for this book, I asked the musicians if we could talk in a place where they created music. More often than not, this resulted in us meeting at their home studios. Some recorded their music exclusively at home; a few booked sessions at professional studios and laid down tracks there. Others employed a combination of these strategies, crafting basic tracks in home studios, but recording vocals or mixing and mastering tracks in professional settings.

Having access to high-quality recording equipment, even at home, was perceived to give musicians an edge over the competition. Barry Shank (1994) wrote that in recording studios, "a romance of technology dominates. . . . The more expensive the studio and the fancier the machines, the 'better' the sound quality and the greater chance the finished recording will have of successfully competing for listeners with the thousand other recordings finished that day" (175–76). In this sense, recording studios were symbolically important because they allowed rappers to make status claims. As Jean-Pascal Daloz (2010) noted, "among all of the attributes of social eminence, the possession of prestigious commodities is perhaps the most obvious. . . . [They] function as badges of social rank, denoting the superior status of elites against the groups below or vis-à-vis outsiders" (61).

Most of the musicians I interviewed had some form of studio; therefore the type of equipment housed in the studio was a means by which rappers differentiated themselves from others. For example, Bully Boyz rented a space that they stocked with pricey gear. "All these other motherfuckers in they little home studios thinking they making platinum hits," Grafta said. "No, you better get your sound up, get that shit thick." Here Grafta used his separate studio space, expensive equipment, and ability to generate a "thick" sound as a symbolic means by which to distinguish himself as a professional. He contrasted this with amateurs whose home studios featured smaller, less costly recording setups.

The majority of underground rappers, however, did not rent separate recording spaces. Instead, studios were constructed in bedrooms, basements, garages, attics, living rooms, and just about anywhere with enough room to house them. Nearly all of the home studios received some sort of spatial primacy—musicians dedicated one of the central areas of their living quarters to a site for recording. For example, Gutta J cleared out most of the furniture from what would typically be a living room and converted the space into a recording studio. Upon entering his apartment, it was the first thing one saw and was where Gutta J spent nearly all of his time at home.

A typical studio was controlled by a computer mainframe, connected to a mixing board, which was attached to assorted instruments, microphones, and electronic gadgets. This was where instrumental tracks—the sonic foundation for songs—were created. A second feature common to every studio I visited appeared to be the most important: the isolation booth, where vocals were recorded. Some isolation booths were fairly large. For example, Mr. Grimm transformed the master bedroom of his apartment into a recording studio and converted its walk-in closet into an isolation booth. Others made do with whatever space was available. This could entail the appropriation of smaller spaces, such as kitchen pantries or linen closets.

The isolation booths ranged from impressively high-tech to comically cut rate. Some booths were aesthetically pleasing, with soft light flitting overhead and soundproof padding strategically affixed to the walls and ceilings to improve the clarity of the recorded sound. The symbolic properties of home studios, however, were revealed more clearly when touring those that did not feature professional-grade equipment or pleasing aesthetics. For example, Jae Lee converted his kitchen's broom closet into an isolation booth. Chunks of cheap foam-rubber mattress padding were attached to the closet's interior walls and a "little ten-dollar microphone" ran from the recording console in the living room. Jae Lee noted that the isolation booth featured no interior lighting, and when the doors were closed to record, "it's dark as hell so if you ain't got your [lyrics] memorized, it ain't gonna work. We can't afford no big studio or nothing like that." Sir Krazy, who housed his studio in a low-ceilinged basement and converted its tiny bathroom into an isolation booth, beamed as he gave me a tour, insisting, "It don't get more 'hood than this." Here the professional-amateur distinction was made in the opposite direction from pros like Grafta; Sir Krazy aligned his toilet/booth with "'hood" authenticity. Similarly, J Problem, whose isolation booth consisted of a utility closet with no interior lighting, asserted that illumination was nonessential. "Rapping with the paper" was not necessary, he said, for MCs who had their lyrics memorized. In doing so, J Problem reversed this hindrance to distinguish himself from amateurs who had not committed their lyrics to memory.

Daloz (2010) reported that one hallmark of elite distinction was the "vicarious display" of social capital: members of elite groups make status claims based upon their associations with prestigious social actors. In addition to their aesthetic qualities, studios were also emblematic of who was recording in them. For example, Gumbo converted a large walk-in closet in his apartment into an isolation booth, and described the rappers who stopped by to record: "Come through my crib, you gonna see there's *real* gangstas rapping. I ain't talking about studio gangstas. Motherfuckers come into my crib, pulling all they [crack] rocks out of they socks, putting them all on the table while we doing tracks. They ain't fakin' that shit."

These discursive and cultural practices illustrated one of rap's fundamental uses of cultural capital vis-à-vis social class: the inversion of elite and non-elite status indicators. Whether it was Sir Krazy's "'hood" toilet/isolation booth or the "real" crack-toting rappers who recorded at Gumbo's, the symbols of elite status that were deemed culturally valuable were those that would typically be associated with non-elites outside of rap culture. This situational reconfiguration of social class reversed existing hierarchies and reframed those with non-elite indicators as elites. Conversely, those who possessed expensive equipment, rented separate spaces, or booked time at professional studios touted these as signifiers of elite status and in doing so upheld the hegemonic class order.

Regardless of size, aesthetic qualities, or technical attributes, the isolation booths functioned as key sites for "doing" rap music. Stepping into this symbolic space was described as transformative by the rappers. "I get in my own world," Bleek told me. "I like to be in a small booth, I like to feel confined. I don't need all that space. I just wanna do me. I close my eyes and I envision like I'm onstage. And that's when I do what I do."

Recording studios were also important because they served as many an MC's port of entry into rap music. The Chicago MCs recalled how they learned to rhyme by freestyling with peers on street corners and in school lunchrooms, but most described a sense of legitimization they felt upon recording for the first time. Recording sessions demarcated the point at which rappers advanced from freestyling hobbyists to serious MCs, at least in their own minds. It was only when they had recorded their first song that they became true musicians. For example, Boss Bee recorded for the first time on the day he was released from prison. Upon arriving home, he received a call from Habit, who invited Boss Bee to record a track at his home studio.

> I remember it like it was yesterday. First day out the joint. As far as rapping, I was fresh. I had just wrote a rap the night before I paroled out. I went in the booth and I was so excited, man. This was my first time *ever* in a studio. *Ever.* Wasn't no big million-dollar studio, it was what we could work with. And I got in there and did it in one take. That was the first thing I ever recorded in a booth for the first time. And I won't never forget that.

The symbolic properties of studios were illustrated in Boss Bee's recollection. The aesthetics of the studio did not diminish the experience for him. Being in a studio—any studio—was what mattered. Boss Bee demonstrated professionalism by nailing his verse in a single take. In this manner, recording studios served as symbolic spaces in which identity was socially constructed through cultural practices. More than any other location, recording studios were spaces that gave musicians an identity that could then be performed and projected in settings beyond the studio.

In writing about the development of the musician identity, ethnomusicologist Mavis Bayton (1990) found that assuming this status proved to be transformative. Becoming a musician meant that a person would "listen to music differently, discuss it differently, engage in technical talk with other musicians" (253). For example, instead of attending gigs as spectators, Bayton wrote, those who had taken on the musician identity now went to nightclubs to watch closely, generate new ideas, and interact with peers. In other words, assuming the musician identity meant that music-related activities ceased to be social events or leisure pursuits; they were now construed as work.

Midnight Oil

In a small home studio, located on the Northwest Side of Chicago, Habit worked late into the night. He spent most of his evenings here, writing lyrics and recording songs. "I write at night, when it's quiet like this," he told me. "Sometimes I just get into myself, try to get as deep as I can get. I write a lot. I think of shit all day long. By the time it's time to sit down, one, two, three o'clock in the morning, I already got so much shit in my head that I already tapped into ways to express it. It comes out pretty fast. I record it even quicker. I got the shit down to a science."

Like most musicians in Chicago's rap underground, Habit described his home studio as a space where work took place. Live performances give him a chance to cut loose, have fun, and entertain the audience. The studio was all about labor.

> Recording is harder than performing. Performing is a treat. You can enjoy a performance; you don't necessarily enjoy recording. But being in the studio, I love it. I don't know what I would do without this fuckin' studio. I'd rather be in the studio all the time. There's just you and a room and a microphone, and somehow, some way, you have to—with words—get a picture across to somebody when they hear it. And to be able to hear a song ten years later and still visualize things, that's talent.

My encounters with Habit have always had a certain edge to them, a feeling of not quite knowing which way the winds were blowing. A cloud of mayhem seemed to trail the rapper everywhere he went, and it was hard to not get caught up in it. Late at night, in his home studio, Habit exuded a quiet calm, revealing a reflective side that I had glimpsed only on occasion.

It may have been part of larger changes that had recently taken place. A few months earlier, Habit quit Xcons to pursue a new direction with a group of young rappers he dubbed Bomb First. It struck me as an abrupt move, given that Xcons had formed in prison and spent years making plans. Habit was typically vague in explaining the change:

> What happened with Xcons was just it wasn't the direction I felt I was trying to go with my career. I was moving one way and I felt they was moving another way. And I was just trying to get more

into what I was trying to do with people that was more into my mentality and my actual lifestyle. I'm still cool with Xcons, everything's all right, but I'm just trying to do me. So I put the pieces together, from the guys that I know—from the guys that I been knowing since before jail, in jail, or after jail. It wasn't just a prison thing. [Bomb First] got together about four months ago, and since then it's just been nonstop grinding, hustling man.

Around time of Bomb First's formation, Habit issued a solo effort that contained some of his most personal material to date, including "Reflections," which he released online to a modicum of acclaim from the gangsta-rap microscene. Others found it soft. Regardless, "Reflections" was the most honest song he had ever issued to the public, a far cry from Xcons' lurid criminology. Recording the song marked a shift for Habit, a new direction, not only musically but personally. He still wasn't sure what it all meant. He just knew things had changed and "Reflections" seemed to symbolize this turn of tides.

I think it was the first time I stepped out my box, the box I put myself in. In jail, there was no boxes; I wrote that when I was in jail. In jail, we didn't limit ourselves at all 'cause everybody was in the same situation. So if you speak that real shit, everybody really felt that shit. 'Cause you in jail. Motherfuckers ain't there for nothing. So putting out a song like "Reflections," that was a risk for me, a big risk. But I put it out, and that was the beginning of me finding where I wanted to be in this rap shit, the message I was trying to portray.

To mark the occasion, in another symbolic move, Habit shaved his head, cropping off the long braids that he had been growing for more than a decade. "That was a process in my life," he said. "Walking away from Xcons, that wasn't easy. Cutting the hair was an extension of that, just starting over. I'm gonna do me to the fullest extent. There was a lot of baggage in that hair. When I cut that off, I cut off a lot. I cut off prison. I grew it in prison, and it was like let go of all that shit already and move the fuck on. It had an immediate effect. Creatively and personally, I felt different."

Habit's current creative output was higher than ever, reaching as many as four completed songs written and recorded in a single night. "Right now, I'm in the zone like that," he said. "For about the last month, I been doing three songs a day. Trying to do four, sometimes I do two. But a good average is three songs a day. Sweat. It *is* work." Habit wasn't sure what would become of these efforts. "I don't know," he shrugged. "I ain't got no solo joints scheduled to come out. So I'm just working, recording about a trillion songs. Just to listen to 'em, I guess. I give 'em to my mom." I wonder if Habit might pull a Lil Wayne, start releasing as much music as possible, flood the streets with material.

I think deep down inside, I might be already plotting that—like a mixtape every week. But the want is greater than the money. If I had the money to do it, I'd do it. But ain't everybody got money. One thing you're gonna keep hearing in this interview is *broke*. Motherfuckers ain't balling, man. We ain't on the track with outrageous numbers, outrageous cars. No, we keep it true to life. Some people got outrageous cars and all that shit—they already rich and famous. But it's a lot more gutter down here.

I asked Habit if being a millionaire would change the type of music he made. "Probably," he nodded. "I don't know. I ain't got a million dollars, so I can't really say how hungry I would stay. But the hungry music is always better to me."

Recording Studios as Work Spaces

In Chicago's rap underground, recording studios were spaces where work took place: music was produced, lyrics were written, vocals were recorded, and songs were mixed and mastered. Most musicians portrayed the recording process as tedious and repetitive. "There's take after take and you have to constantly be in there 'til you get it right," a rapper named Slimdakon explained. "So it's a challenge sometimes. You have to really work at it. It's time and commitment and dedication." This did not mean that Chicago rappers disliked the recording process—many seemed to derive more pleasure from recording than any other musical activity. But in describing the recording process, nearly everyone used a discourse that emphasized the amount of labor involved.

According to the participants, the amount of time "grinding" in the studio offered empirical evidence of legitimate work. Live gigs could be hard to secure and were somewhat infrequent, but recording was labor that could be done every day of the week, if desired. The results of studio labor were tangible—songs were written, recorded, mixed, and disseminated online. CDs were released and distributed. Income was occasionally earned, and the recorded music garnered exposure that sometimes led to paying gigs, merchandise sales, or opportunities to network. This imbued the rappers with an occupational identity that legitimized their pursuit of careers in the music industry. By gaining that identity they reversed the existing social-class hierarchies and aligned their musical aspirations with the American-dream ideology. Without the symbolic space of the recording studio, describing rap music as a job would have been far less convincing.

The mythical image of musicians in recording studios involves the capturing of a single inspired performance. In Chicago's rap underground, the reality was more mundane. Rarely were there artistic conceits such as "creating a vibe" or trying to get into a particular headspace for recording. There was just work. Vocals were recorded one slice at a time. A single verse of a song generally consisted of sixteen lines of rhymed text. Similar to the structure of pop songs, a finished rap track consists of two, three, or more verses typically broken up by a chorus (known as the hook), with additional musical or vocal flourishes, bridges, or breaks placed throughout for variety.[2] During one recording session, I observed an MC named O-mega lay down vocals for a song called "Ohh No." Using a process known as "stacking," for each verse and chorus O-mega recorded three separate vocal tracks: (1) a main track where he rapped all the words, (2) a backing track that closely followed the main vocal, with emphasis on particular words or lines, and (3) a "hype" track, where he added quick rebuttals, laughs, taunts, and echoes that gave the song more of a group feel. Placed or "stacked" together, the three vocal tracks had a fullness that the song might not otherwise enjoy. With three verses and a hook, often captured one sentence at a time, O-mega had to record twelve successful vocal takes to complete "Ohh No." Given time for mistakes, retries, and other holdups, O-mega recorded more than 120 takes to perfect the track's vocal portion. All part of the job, he explained:

> The studio is all about perfecting your craft. It's to be sounding professional. When I record, you gotta have your ad-libs and your

standouts and your shouts. I'm a perfectionist for this; I'm not gonna stop until that shit's perfect. I'm thinking to myself, every time I'm in the studio, I wanna do something better and better and better than the last time I was in the studio. That's my job.

In addition to the hands-on tasks, recording also required what sociologist Arlie Hochschild (1983) called emotional labor. Hochschild defined emotional labor as "the management of feeling to create a publicly observable facial and body display" (7). Hochschild described two types of emotional labor: surface acting, where workers faked positive or negative emotions, and deep acting, where workers accessed genuine emotions and used them during client interactions, similar to how method actors supposedly access real feelings and project them into performances. Hochschild studied flight attendants and bill collectors, and discovered that emotional labor was part of the workday for both. Flight attendants had to suppress their true emotions in order to display the sunny dispositions mandated by the job. Bill collectors had to suppress their true emotions and present harsh and threatening dispositions that would frighten clients into paying their debts. This led to feelings of alienation on the part of both sets of workers, because both believed that "faking it" was part of the job. Over time, Hochschild argued, this led to the workers feeling alienated, not only from their jobs but also from themselves.

Chicago's underground rap musicians told me that their job required the deeper form of emotional labor. They claimed to access and express their core emotions and display them through cultural objects such as recorded songs. Participants insisted that rapping required more than merely reciting a series of words that rhymed, it was to put one's very self into the act of doing so. An MC named Visual described the importance of emotion in the recording process, and the sometimes ephemeral nature of this type of work:

> I'm trying to get that emotion, man. Sometimes I'll go in there, the first take, it's already there, 'cause I was waiting to let that out. Sometimes I lose it 'cause you can't really pull emotion just out of nowhere, it's gotta build up. So I may have to take a little break and sit down, relax, drink some water, have a conversation with somebody, put on some CNN. Whatever will get my head off the song. With me it's emotion that I gotta get in that song. People

gotta feel like this dude's sincere, he's serious, he's really trying to tell me something. He's not just feeding me some lines. I gotta go in there and give people that feeling. You gotta hear it in my voice. That's my main focus when I'm in the studio.

Bully Boyz producer Grafta emphasized the importance of avoiding conflict during studio sessions. "Some artists are hardheaded, you can't tell 'em shit," he said. "They think they the producer, the engineer, everything. But somehow you gotta find a way to communicate with them. You never in the middle of making music wanna try to create a conflict. 'Cause it just makes motherfuckers lose momentum, motherfuckers start arguing. That's not the way. Everybody's gotta be open and creative." When conflict arose in the studio, surface acting was required. Grafta had to maintain a cool façade when discussions got heated. Doing so, he said, was all part of the job.

In addition to loci of emotional labor, recording studios were crucial sites for networking, another form of labor. In Chicago's rap underground, recording studios were used for collaboration, with musicians making guest appearances or "features" on each other's songs. Some rappers were members of more than one musical group, doubling or tripling the amount of work involved, but potentially offering higher dividends in terms of exposure and income. For example, Wes Restless recorded and performed as a solo artist and also as a member of three local groups. Additionally, Restless made guest appearances on dozens of CDs and collaborated on a number of one-off projects, including CD-length pairings with fellow artists. This sometimes led to paid production gigs at his home studio. Through persistent networking and collaboration, Restless became a prominent member of the backpack microscene.

Finally, recording studios required a substantial amount of what a trio of social scientists (Neff, Wissinger, and Zukin 2005) termed entrepreneurial labor, the upfront investment of time and/or money required to gain employment in competitive culture industries. The authors studied fashion models and new media workers, those with "cool" jobs in fields that demanded entrepreneurial labor such as a model's headshots and the self-created websites that advertised the Internet worker's prowess. Models and dot-commers were drawn to these occupations because "cool" jobs were perceived to offer autonomy, creativity, excitement, wealth, and status. Because of this, workers accepted the risk and instability associated with employment in these pyramid-shaped, "winner take all" fields, and performed a good deal of entrepreneurial labor in attempting to gain entry. Such risks, the authors wrote, were "justified by the expectation of high rewards—the million-dollar-a-year Revlon contract or the million-dollar share of an IPO. But the number of workers who actually get such rewards is small" (329–30). This did not dissuade their subjects from spending time and money for the privilege of working; the models and dot-commers believed they were on the verge of being "discovered" at any moment. The culture industries, the authors asserted, were "built upon workers being motivated by the promise of one Big Job being right around the corner" (319).

Similarly, the underground rappers in Chicago invested substantial amounts of money to furnish their home recording studios, and spent significant amounts of time working in them. This entrepreneurial labor was performed with the anticipation that these investments would reap music-industry fortune and fame. Though many of the backpackers had day jobs to support their rap ambitions, many of the gangstas forwent traditional paid labor in order to focus on music. For example, I asked Chilly if he had a job and he shook his head. "This *is* my job. This is gonna be my job. This is gonna be what's gonna help me provide for everybody." The belief that rapping was their primary job was particularly true for those at the lowest end of the socioeconomic strata, whose lack of education and training gave them few opportunities for paid labor, other than the most menial employment. Their investment of entrepreneurial labor was not in dollars, but in time.

Most of the gang members in Chicago's rap underground supported their music-industry ambitions through criminal activity, particularly low-level drug dealing. "I'm a medical supplier," Hymnal told me with a wink. "I just do it just to help pay the bills or pay for studio shit or shit I need to perform."[3] Similarly, Joka funded his music ambitions through small-time drug dealing, an emulation, he claimed, of Eazy-E's rap-hustler blueprint:

> Street money is street money. When you see me with a job? I sold drugs my whole life. People who got jobs, I respect 'em. But for some of us, you wanna go as hard as we go, you gonna have to get some hustle money to create some machines in your studio and some shit you can charge for. It's what Eazy-E did. Eazy-E wrote

that formula. He took his hustle money, he turned it into rap money. Today, I gotta sell twenty dime bags so that tomorrow I can write another fuckin' song.

The rhetoric of work used to describe the cultural practices that took place in recording studios underscored the symbolic properties of the space. Using discourses of labor, rappers aligned themselves with the American-dream ideology that through individual effort one can achieve upward social mobility. Hard work conveyed responsibility, skill, seriousness, entrepreneurship, and alliance with middle-class values. As Jeanita Richardson and Kim Scott (2002) pointed out, "In an economic sense, what rap and hip-hop artists have done is apply the capitalistic skills and networks valued by society" (184). In doing so, the rappers took a low-status and oft-maligned cultural practice (rapping) and reframed it as high-status and culturally valued (hard work).

The relationship between social class and ideologies of work was examined by Michèle Lamont (2000), who found that blue-collar factory workers created a moral order centered on the work ethic to keep economic, physical, and other uncertainties at bay. Lamont's factory workers stressed the importance of perseverance in the face of adversity, discipline, long-term planning, delayed gratification, and industriousness. These behaviors and attitudes, they believed, were part and parcel of being a "decent" person. Workers deemed lazy were scorned. The factory workers' daily routine was "often painful and time-consuming, yet underpaid, physically demanding, or psychologically challenging" (26). Moreover, because the factory workers could not easily escape the crime, drugs, and poverty of their neighborhoods, labor was the "only" means by which they might acquire upward mobility. All of this served to build up a collective identity for the workers, one that eliminated the hierarchy of class-based stratification and leveled the moral playing field.

When Chicago's underground rappers talked about rap as a form of labor, many used the term "grinding," which referred to the all-consuming nature of being an MC—the number of hours required, the sheer effort involved. For example, QT advised rap aspirants to "grind hard, man. You got to just make it your life. If you don't stop, and you keep going harder, and you keep getting better and better, you gonna make it." The word "grind" invoked images of labor, sweat, and the blue-collar ephemera of the factory. In Chicago, the notion of grinding was sometimes embedded directly into the cultural objects created in recording studios. For example, Marz released a CD entitled *Grind Music: The Movement* that emphasized perseverance, effort, and delayed gratification. Songs such as "Let's Get Rich," "Get Bread," and "On the Grind" promised vast wealth in return for hard work and motivation.

Writing near the turn of the twentieth century, pioneering economic sociologist Thorstein Veblen opined that conspicuous leisure was the ultimate form of elite status display because it implied freedom from labor. Today, this notion is somewhat quaint. Working around the clock is not only the reality of labor in the knowledge economy, it is a sign that one is winning the game. As Dalton Conley (2009) put it, "success in today's professional world doesn't mean retiring at fifty to play golf in Florida, it means working more and more hours as you move up a towering ladder of economic opportunity (and inequality)" (xiii). The MCs in Chicago took this notion to heart, inverting Veblen's concept of conspicuous leisure into what might be termed "conspicuous labor," whereby hard work was intentionally displayed as a claim to elite status. The labor that took place in recording studios signified this work and was distinguished from leisure activities. For example, Urban Spexx told me, "I think it was a hobby when we were beat-boxing in tunnels. That was doing it just to do it. Now, we do it day in, day out. This is a job. If we weren't taking this seriously, we wouldn't keep making music and putting it out there. I think those are the steps that we're doing to try to make it a career."

By discursively situating the studio as a workspace, rappers were able to counter the stigma that many felt about their chosen vocation. While those who aspire to enter pyramid-shaped industries such as sports enjoy social and cultural approval, some Chicago rappers were met with ambivalence from friends and family members over their pursuit of rap careers. For example, an MC named Urban Po told me, "My folks, they church people. So they think I'm going to hell. Sex, drugs, and rock n' roll. They see it all going down in a crash of glory. But they cool. At the end of the day, they hear the little stuff that happened and they like, 'Well that's good. You stayed with it.' They wasn't like standing up [cheering], but at the same time, it's cool." Family members and friends might believe that the rappers should set aside rapping and get "real" jobs, but by framing rap as work, these concerns were easier to dismiss. The recording studio functioned as one means by which to attain this.

The premium placed upon hard work also helped to deflect anxieties about achieving success in the face of the nearly insurmountable odds of making it in the music business. Hard work gave one an edge that supposedly lazy rappers did not enjoy, and lent a sense of order and control to an unpredictable occupation; hard work provided a means by which the financially struggling rapper might someday realize upward mobility. Black Soldier linked this ideology of hard work to cultural legitimacy. Talk was cheap, he said, but through hard work, one could prove that one was serious about what one was doing. "I don't even look at [rappers] like they real or they fake," he said. "I look at it like do they work hard. To me, you fake if you don't put in your hustle."

There was, however, a point at which clocking hours in the studio could be perceived as a form of laziness. Rappers who spent too much time in the studio might be accused of being "studio MCs" or "Facebook rappers," those whose musical activities took place entirely at home and/or online. These rappers were labeled inauthentic because they were always in the studio, and lacked the experience necessary to perform credibly in concert. Gangsta rappers who spent too much time recording might be labeled "studio gangstas," whose lyrics bragged of criminal exploits, but who never left the house. QT described one such studio gangsta, who worked out of a home studio in the suburbs. "He rap about how he got guns, he move crack. The nigga wasn't real, man. He'd sit in the crib all day and be in the studio. Staying in Evanston, lying about the shit he do."

Debates over which MCs are telling the truth and which are lying have existed from rap's inception. No subgenre of rap, however, is more scrutinized for cultural legitimacy than the gangsta variety. Recording studios were symbolic spaces in which rappers constructed occupational identities, but the cultural objects produced in studios also carried symbolic significance. Audio recordings provided a crucial platform upon which rappers made public claims to cultural legitimacy and were a locus for the social construction of authenticity.

Criminal Records

Given the multitude of gangs in Chicago and the number of gang members who rapped, it follows that vivid descriptions of gang life were prevalent in their song lyrics. According to T-Bird, the shared qualities of gangs and rap music made them mutually compatible: "Hip hop comes from the streets; gangbanging is in the streets. It's obviously gonna be mixed. They coincide with each other. You got somebody from every set out there spitting, so that's gonna find its way into the music."

The gang members who produced this type of lyrical content described it as organic—they were rapping about their lives, surroundings, and everyday experiences. The lyrical content of rap music has been criticized as violent (Kubrin 2005; Richardson and Scott 2002) and misogynistic (Rose 2008; Dyson 2007; Armstrong 2001; Keyes 2000), but the rapping gang members in Chicago insisted that their lyrics delivered a message. According to Hymnal,

> It's very important to have a message. If you ain't got a message, what you rappin' for? My message is for the young nigga that's growing up in the 'hood. Just keep doing his thing, live life. Pop bottles, fuck bitches, get money, nigga. Help your mom out with the rent. Pay her phone bill one day. Do something with yourself. That's what I rap about. Be a strong ass nigga. If you ain't strong, you weak, and only the strong survive. If you ain't strong, you a bitch.

Bleek insisted that his lyrics, which detailed his criminal exploits and time behind bars, were cautionary tales. "I speak about prison a lot. And they may get tired of it or whatever, but that's who I am, that's what I been through. So I try to show guys living my life, this is what I been through. You don't want to make the same decisions I made. I'm not trying to glorify it."

Given the mass appeal of the gangsta-rap subgenre, it made good business sense for Chicago's rapping gang members to pen lyrics that described their firsthand experiences in gangs. There was real money to be made, which was among the primary goals. "I'm from the streets and gangs and shit," Boss Bee said. "I don't think I can get rich rapping gospel music, you feel me? I rap what the people wanna hear. And the streets is where I'm from so I'm always gonna do that best."

When Pierre Bourdieu described institutional cultural capital, he was referring to high-status credentials granted by institutions, particularly academic certificates and degrees. However, in Chicago's gangsta-rap microscene, the prized cultural institutions were not universities, but gangs, prisons, and housing projects. Having direct experience with one or more of these institutions functioned as subcultural capital in Chicago's gangsta-rap microscene. These symbolic status indicators were embedded into cultural objects in attempts to build subcultural capital and enhance career outcomes.

In writing lyrics, the gangsta-rap musicians in Chicago drew upon the city's checkered history of gangs, criminal activity, and political corruption. This included references to Prohibition-era mobsters such as Al Capone and Frank Nitti as well as street-gang figureheads such as Larry Hoover, Jeff Fort, and David Barksdale. Also referenced were similarly themed pop-culture ephemera, such as the 1987 movie *The Untouchables*, and Chicago's history of crooked cops and political scandal. For example, a rapper named Count (not part of my research) released a song entitled "For the Gangstaz" that mentioned "Larry" and "Jeff" and the difficulties they encountered.

By incorporating Larry Hoover and Jeff Fort into his lyrics, Count aligned himself with iconic gang-related figures from Chicago's past. This was a claim to authenticity and an evocation of a space and place unique to Chicago. Such references "both anchor rap acts to their immediate environments and set them apart from other environments and other 'hoods as well as from other rap acts that inhabit similarly demarcated spaces" (Forman 2002, 179). "We've always been a gangbanging city," Rayzor noted. "This goes all the way back to the Al Capone days. Different organizations, the mobs that we had to GDs, the Vice Lords, and the Latin Kings. This what our city has been notoriously known for."

Naming Al Capone or a Chicago street gang in rap lyrics was hardly unique to the gangsta microscene; backpackers, independent acts, and even corporate rappers from Chicago made similar references. Gangsta rap's mass appeal meant that the subgenre's lyrical tropes were adopted by plenty of rappers who had nothing to do with gangs. For example, Rusty Chains, a white MC who described his music as gangsta rap, told me:

There's a lot of Black Stones, and GDs, and Vice Lords, and Latin Kings. Chicago is definitely a city filled with gang culture and it rubs off in my music. I'm not trying to say that I gangbang, 'cause I'm not a gangbanger, I never wanna be a gangbanger. My escape is to talk about it really, because you get fed up with it sometimes, being around it. It's rough. I've had a lot of messed up shit happen with gangs in the city. So it's part of me, it's happening, it's around me, so I gotta talk about it.

To Chains, the number of gangs in Chicago, the city's gang culture, and his alleged proximity to and frustration with gangs made them a topic that warranted his lyrical attention. This practice was not unlike those of the middle-class teens described by Mary Pattillo-McCoy (1999). The youths' esteem for pop-culture gangsta rappers, combined with their proximity to neighborhood gangs and drug dealers, led them to describe their own surroundings as a "ghetto."

To enhance the believability of their claims, gang members who rapped wrote lyrics with high degrees of specificity. This included hyperlocal references, gang-specific minutiae, and other forms of insider knowledge: descriptions of gang-related hand signs, gestures, clothing, slang, logos, slogans, creeds, colors, tattoos, left-right body alignment, numbers, and graffiti. The more precise the claim, so the thinking seemed to go, the greater its chances of being perceived as firsthand knowledge. Casual listeners might miss these references, but those familiar with Chicago gang minutiae would comprehend them immediately. Dwight Conquergood (1994) observed a similar phenomenon when studying gang graffiti in Chicago:

> Gang graffiti is inscrutable to outsiders because it draws on an elaborate system of underground symbols, icons, and logos, the nuanced meanings of which can be keyed according to certain semiotic manipulations: inversions, reversals, and fractures. Middle-class citizens driving through the so-called "inner city" look at a graffiti-covered wall as meaningless gibberish and a sign of social disorder, whereas the local homeboys look at the same graffiti mural and appreciate the complex meanings and messages it artfully conveys. (26)

While this strategy was somewhat successful as applied to rap lyrics, it remained difficult to distinguish those who were writing about personal experiences from those who were penning fiction. There was skepticism throughout Chicago's rap underground that gangsta-rap lyrics contained true-to-life accounts. "Anybody can read a book about guns and know about guns, anybody can read a book about how to mix drugs,"

Blaze said. "You can hang out with some people and learn some slang language. When you get a CD of somebody you ain't never heard, and he's talking all this grimy, thug, gangsta, gutta, poor, penitentiary shit, I don't think you can tell the difference."

Most of the rappers who were gang members insisted that they could distinguish firsthand accounts from those that were invented. "I came from the 'hood," Gravel said. "Lived it. Came from the projects. Madison and Western. Lived it. Rockwell Gardens. So if you came from the Rockwell, you would know when a rapper's real and when he ain't real." Others asserted that because they were gang members, they were likely to know personally or at least be acquainted with fellow gang members who were part of the gangsta-rap microscene. For example, Bleek said,

> I get around a lot of Chicago, every side of the city. You can't go nowhere in the city and say you don't know Bleek or somebody from Xcons, somebody that knows us. I got a lot of friends and affiliates throughout the whole Chicago. So if somebody comes out and he's rapping, some new cat, I'll check his history. If he's speaking and he lived what he say, I probably know some of his people. I'll do my history on a artist real fast.

Another strategy calculated to enhance claims to authenticity was to incorporate minutiae related to criminal activity, weapons, violence, and institutions such as housing projects and prisons. In mainstream society, contact with the criminal justice system can have dire consequences. A felony conviction impacts a person's life opportunities in any number of ways, diminishing everything from employment prospects to long-term health. Reflecting the corporate tier of the rap industry, in Chicago's gangsta-rap microscene the stigma of incarceration was eliminated. Rather than being viewed as hindrances, criminal behaviors became valuable forms of subcultural capital that were perceived as being convertible into fortune and fame. This explains why nearly every Chicago rapper with any proximity to the criminal justice system emphasized it. This included backpackers with no direct prison experience. These rappers claimed to be storytellers, whose fictional accounts of criminal behavior, they insisted, were as legitimate as the lyrics of those who had personally committed crimes. For example, Pipemouth, a twenty-one-year-old white rapper from suburban Evanston wrote a song about a drug dealer who was sentenced to life in prison. He explained,

> I like telling stories. Obviously, I didn't get taken away to prison forever, but when I was writing, that was the shit that was going through my head, so I had to put it down . . . I come from a relatively wealthy family. I'm not out of the ghetto, I'm not out of the projects, nothing like that, but I still am real and I fuckin' rap about what I see and what I want to rap about and what I want to talk about.

Again, the situational use of authenticity came to the fore (see Harkness 2012a). Pipemouth did not claim to come from the "ghetto." Instead, he downplayed the relevance of his socioeconomic status (an objective category) and emphasized his commitment to writing "real" lyrics (an interpretive category). Doing so enabled him to craft a fictional account of drug dealing and prison, invoking powerful forms of "street" authenticity, while maintaining his belief that he was being true to self.

Firsthand encounters with the penal system were among the most valued forms of subcultural capital because they provided government-certified evidence of one's "realness," irrefutable proof of one's position on the societal ladder. Direct knowledge of the penal system was prominently signified in song titles, lyrics, CD artwork, and music videos. Some gang members who had served time posted their prison mug shots or official Illinois Department of Corrections records on social networking sites. As with references to gangs, the thinking seemed to be that the more detail provided, the better the chances that the claim would be accepted as legitimate. For example, Rayzor, who had served several years in the penitentiary, described the lyrics to one of his prison-themed songs:

> It gives you an inside look at what it's really like. It takes you from the beginning of the song, going down the hallway, this is the famous tunnel, where they strip you naked, you gotta spread your ass. There's about a hundred motherfuckers in the hallway and it's like, "Get on the yellow line! Strip search, open your mouth." You're right next to people you don't know, and the guards whup you if you look the wrong way or ask the wrong question. They just beat on you; it's like modern-day slavery.

In crafting works that demarcated them as "real," the MCs employed situational authenticity, emphasizing the objective or interpretive schema that matched their backgrounds and experiences. Those who had served time in prison upheld this experience as a paradigm of legitimacy. As Habit put it,

> You ain't a part of this lifestyle if you ain't got felony fuckin' convictions and you ain't been in prison for some-odd years. That's what this lifestyle's about. So if you don't know that a motherfucker is official in the street—if that's the quota, if that's the standard of being real, being in prison and still being a rapper—if that's the standard of being real, then you know I'm as real as it gets.

Gang members who had not served time, however, did not view themselves as less authentic than Habit. Like him, they employed situational authenticity, but emphasized interpretive categories of cultural legitimacy rather than objective criteria. For example, Grafta told me that drug dealers who have never been imprisoned are better criminals than those who have. "Never knock another man's hustle. If that motherfucker's a good ass drug dealer, he a good ass drug dealer. Don't talk shit: 'Oh, that nigga never been to jail.' That nigga was smarter than you! That nigga moving right. He was switching his phone [number] every day, got plastic surgery, switched his face up." In Grafta's estimation, not serving time implied street smarts (an interpretive category), rendering one a better criminal than those who had been jailed (an objective category).

In these cultural practices, rap's obsession with cultural legitimacy is laid bare, as gang members wage authenticity debates over the types of crimes committed or the number of years spent behind bars. This illustrates how even rappers with powerful claims to so-called street authenticity, such as gang membership or prison records, still bicker over who is or is not "keeping it real." Jennifer Hochschild (1995) called such debates "finding someone to be better than" and linked it to endorsement of the American-dream ideology: "Poor African Americans spend a lot of time persuading themselves and others that they are better than someone else because their discipline, energy, or virtue has raised them above their circumstances" (167). While mainstream society finds little virtue in gang membership or prison records, gangsta rap's upending of traditional class hierarchies esteems such statuses as desirable. I am not suggesting that young people seek out prison sentences to enhance their street credibility, but once they achieve this status, rappers employ situational authenticity to claim insider standing.

Symbiotic Resources

Scholars, politicians, and pundits have lambasted gangsta rap in particular for its lyrical content and allegedly negative impact on youth. Others have defended gangsta rap for its ability to report on living conditions in poor urban communities. Generally overlooked in these discussions is gangsta rap's utility and functional value for its practitioners. I argue that for street gangs, rap music is not only symbolically significant, but has empirical worth. Simply, gangsta rap is a resource for both rappers and street gangs.

In Chicago, gang membership served as a valuable resource, used by members of the gangsta-rap microscene who were gang members to accrue tangible benefits.[4] The relationship between gangs and gang members who rapped was symbiotic. Rappers who were gang members used this affiliation to generate revenue, promote and market their music, and recruit band members. The gangs relied on rap music as a source of income, for promotion and marketing, as a recruitment tool, and as a means by which to wage rivalries and settle disputes.

The symbiotic relationship between street gangs and street artists is not without precedent. For example, sociologist Richard Lachmann (1988) found that New York City gangs recruited young graffiti writers to make territorial claims, carry out disputes, and boost the gang's reputation. In return, the gangs provided valuable material and social resources to the artists, funding equipment purchases (spray paint) and providing payment via cash, narcotics, and protection. The graffiti artists did not become full-fledged gang members, but their association with gangs enhanced their reputations as "deviant" artists. Moreover, the taggers enjoyed "the rewards, prestige, and protection afforded by their gang affiliation and were aware that tagging allowed them to reap those benefits without the dangers faced by full gang members involved in felonies and in warfare with rival gangs" (239).

The relationship between gangs and economic activity has been widely studied (Padilla 1992; Jankowski 1991; Moore 1990; Skolnick et al. 1990;

Levitt and Venkatesh 2000). A study of street gangs in Massachusetts and California (Pih et al. 2008) found that gangs were "primarily economic entities in the illegitimate economy instead of strictly delinquent groups, and consequently, gang membership has also taken on an economic character" (474). Similarly, rappers in Chicago who were gang members used gang membership as an economic resource for their music aspirations. Some gangs offered direct funding and other support, including material acquisitions such as musical equipment and clothing, as well as the purchase of services such as recording studio time or music-video production. Rappers also used money netted in gangs to fund their music careers. For example, Rayzor dealt crack from the housing project where he resided and used the profits to finance his rap aspirations:

> I grew up in a predominantly organized area. You partake in what you see your peers do. Coming up in Cabrini Green, just like any other projects, when you're in the drug game, you gotta go for yours. You only live once. Some people are happy punching the nine-to-five with a job; there's nothing wrong with that. But I'm in a situation in a project where the fast money is put to use, whether it be studio time or whatever.

Furthermore, gangs were economically crucial because they supplied an important consumer base. "They may be the majority of our fans," Bleek told me. "If I'm about to put my mixtape in the streets, they probably gonna be my number one target market. They gonna buy my music, I'm gonna give 'em something to listen to, something to trap [i.e., sell drugs/ make money] to." Hymnal concurred: "We got straight 'hood songs. There's people out there that stay in their cars hustling all day and night. Say you got a dude that hustles in his car eight hours out the day, selling crack, dope, whatever the fuck he's selling. We make music that the dude will play that CD in that car while he's hustling."

Rappers who were gang members sometimes drew upon lessons they learned from the gang and applied them to the business of music, evoking Eazy-E's rap-hustler blueprint. When Bully Boyz released its debut mixtape, the group enlisted members of the IOAs to stand on busy street corners and hawk the disc to passersby. "We had a plan: let's get the streets, let's make this money. We flooded everybody's 'hood," Grafta recalls. "We was everywhere selling that shit. We were on Fullerton and

Cicero, we were on the West Side, we were out there in Kedzie. It started off with 1,000 CDs to like I need to re-up, almost like the street business with drugs. And that started building [our reputation]." These revenues flowed in both directions: some rap acts consisting of gang members used revenues earned from music and merchandise sales to assist members of the gang. "You ain't real niggas if you have an establishment and a commission, and only certain niggas get money," Hymnal proclaimed. "Certain niggas is gonna stamp that shit so everybody can eat right. We are family."

In addition to the economic resources, gangs in Chicago also used rap songs to increase their presence in the city. Songs were distributed via CD and MP3, and videos were uploaded to websites such as YouTube and Vimeo. These works were then made available to social networking sites and passed on by others. Some gangs even set up pirate radio stations and broadcast their music to local or Internet audiences. All of this was a sort of sonic graffiti, a means by which gangs could market their name or People/Folk Nation affiliation, and enhance the gang's reputation. Embedding the gang's key emblems into cultural objects was a means by which to represent, celebrate, demonstrate allegiance to, and promote the gang by invoking its most powerful symbols.

The songs and music videos were also a means by which gangs could recruit new members. These recruiting efforts were not direct, but posting gang-related music and videos online increased a gang's presence, and the most popular sets enjoyed a status not unlike that of brand-name clothing or high-end cars. In a consumer marketplace rife with competition, gangs vied with one another for members. Having popular songs and videos online helped to solidify brand image and attract new recruits.

Like street gangs, which swell their ranks in order to increase potential revenues, there was a perceived economic benefit to recruiting as many rappers as possible into the fold. Rap groups sometimes consisted of dozens of gang members, and popular rappers garnered the most spotlight time. According to Smokey, "It's all affiliated, it's whole crews doing they [live] sets and letting whoever's the hottest get up front. The hot dudes get up front, and everybody else play they role, get in line, set that chess board up, and move forward together. That's how we do it." Deciding which rappers were going to be showcased was determined internally by the groups as well as by audience response. This did not produce internal tensions because rappers who were not selected for prime time were still able to participate and assist, similar, as Shank described it, to bench players on a basketball squad:

> We can't feed everybody at once. The industry's not gonna take twenty artists at once. As far as the rest of the team, they still branded. They just know that right now, the bigger picture is us stamping the name to make this grow. But they're still loyal. They're in the circle with us; we're breaking bread. There ain't no way we leaving anybody behind. This is a brotherhood.

The mainstream media often portrays gangs as violent, but many gang members go out of their way to avoid physical altercations (Garot 2010). In addition to serving as tools for marketing and recruitment, the songs and music videos were utilized as nonviolent means by which a gang could wage battles with or disrespect adversaries, and sometimes settle disputes. These songs threatened enemies or called for bodily harm, but their overarching purpose was to show contempt and provoke. For example, Infamous D (not part of my research) released a song entitled "Throw the Crown Down (King Killa)" that urged listeners to "throw the fork up and throw the crown down." The accompanying video, which was posted on YouTube, consisted of a lone visual—the Latin King "crown" hand sign inverted and held not upward, but aimed towards the ground. To "throw down" the hand sign of a rival gang is a gesture of impertinence, intended to insult or provoke.

Another means by which gang members used songs to provoke or disrespect was by appropriating the instrumental track of the target of one's acrimony and rapping insults over it. Lil JoJo did this when he took the music for Chief Keef's song "Everyday" and added new lyrics over the top. The Xcons swiped the backing track for one of Bully Boyz's most popular songs and recorded new lyrics over it that insulted the group. This practice was similar to the inversion of a gang's hand sign—taking a culturally significant symbol and reversing its meaning to form an insult. There is a long history of this type of sonic appropriation in rap music, and the practice is not unique to gang members. For gang members who rapped, however, the consequences could be more severe.

These "dis" songs and music videos were posted online and circulated throughout the gangsta-rap microscene via social networking sites. Audiences—many of whom claimed to be gang members—debated the

BANGIN' ON WAX · **137**

merits of these works on message and bulletin boards, with winners and losers declared by the number of plays and comments, or via online voting polls. The "dis" songs and videos brimmed with symbolic violence, but were largely a web-based phenomenon that enabled gang members to cyberbang without the threat of physical violence or arrest. "We try to keep it on a wax level, and not a street level," Trilogy explained. "Once it gets pushed to a certain point where you need to put a kid in his place, that's when you speak out. You do it with the music. A lot of people talk a lot of stuff on the record, beefwise, and they get to the violent point where they're gonna do this or that. Threats."

These online threats, however, sometimes led to problems offline. Primarily this involved the threat of physical violence if the rappers—or their affiliates or even fans—eventually interacted. "Wax beefs lead to street beefs," Bleek told me. "I battle rap, but I battle with gats. If you gonna say something to me on record, then you better be willing to say something to my face." In many instances, these face-to-face exchanges occurred during live performances, the topic of the next chapter.

4

In Da Club

How Social Class Shapes the Performative Context

Nearly six months passed before I saw Bully Boyz again. Although I ran into some of the guys from time to time, and attended a birthday party held in Phantastic's honor, the group mostly kept its distance from the gangsta-rap microscene. There were no shows, no new songs, and only the occasional online rumor that a Phantastic mixtape was in the works.

"The last year has been the bumpiest year in our fuckin' lives," Shank told me when I finally caught up with the group at its recording studio. "We lost our brother, our best friend, our backbone. It's like every time we get close to doing something, something happen, you know. It's just weird. We're about to get a deal, Phantastic dies. What the fuck? It don't make sense. That's what the whole year felt like."

Phantastic was irreplaceable, but if Bully Boyz was going to recover, it would have to find someone to fill the vacancy. At its peak of popularity, the group consisted of nine members. In the wake of Phantastic's passing, most of them had moved on to other things. Some were pursing careers as solo artists, some were in jail, others dropped out of music altogether. Only Shank and Hymnal remained, with Grafta still handling production. "It's like having to start all over," Grafta said. "All right, we just gonna start from scratch, fuck it."

Bully Boyz auditioned a number of MCs and weighed its options. Shank was pushing the group to recruit Chilly, an eighteen-year-old wunderkind who built a reputation through a series of mixtapes when he was still in high school. Chilly had been hanging out on the periphery of Bully Boyz for a while. Though he was a gang member in his early teens, music was now his full-time pursuit, another advantage. Everyone respected his work ethic, his rhyming skills were sharp, and he lived right down the street from the three remaining Bully Boyz. "We tried other people, but a lot of 'em were not ready," Shank recalled. "Chilly was already doing productive music; his movement was moving. He was making tracks every day. He was doing what he needed to do."

Any group of musicians can form a band, but the best ones have chemistry, an indefinable quality that makes them stand out. The original Bully Boyz had a perfect blend of personalities and styles. Each character was unique and added something to the whole. Collectively the balance was just right. "Everybody was different," Shank agreed. "I was the hyper dude, Phantastic was the swagtastical dude, Hymnal was the raunchy, punch-you-in-the-head type of dude." Finding a replacement for Phantastic was tricky because his character—the smooth, cool cat at center stage—was essential to Bully Boyz's chemistry. Chilly was undeniably talented and hard working, but his persona, stage presence, and musical identity were nothing like Phantastic's.

Shank continued to advocate for the up-and-coming kid rapper, but Grafta wasn't convinced the fit was right. "I was always hearing about Chilly," the producer remembered. "So I go into the crates of Chicago mixtapes that I got, and I was like let me take another listen to this shit. And I started listening to it, and I was like man, you know what? I want to make him the third. He's young as fuck, they're a little older, but I think this motherfucker will really add what we're missing."

With Chilly on board, the retooled Bully Boyz started over, recording new material in search of the elusive chemistry that came so naturally the first time around. It was grind time. "We'd sit in here and knock out like forty-two hooks, like forty, fifty tracks," Grafta recalled. "Hook knocked out, next one, next one. Once we had the hooks, we knew the record was really gonna be something, we knew where the fuck we were going."

The success of Bully Boyz's debut had made them kings of Chicago's gangsta-rap microscene. But the debut was only a mixtape. The sophomore release was to be a full-blown album of all-original material, set to Grafta's signature instrumental tracks. Recording an album would position Bully Boyz to reach their ultimate goal: a major-label contract.

Through the process of recording night after night, the group began to regain confidence. "We ain't just throwing 16s on tracks, we sittin' down and making classic records," Chilly told me. "We're making our *Thriller* right now, shit that they gonna play later on. We gonna sweep up the industry." Shank agreed: "This album is gonna make the world know who Bully Boyz is. Once they listen to it, it's gonna be over."

As usual, the cool-headed Grafta kept things in perspective. His focus remained where it had always been: on the money. "Right now what we're doing is trying to get that check," he said. "Even though it's been awhile, people still know us, people are still waiting for what we got. It ain't nothing to make it all happen again. But now we're doing it on a bigger level." Getting to that next level, however, was going to require more than recording a hot album. To rebuild its fan base and recreate the street buzz that made them underground heroes, Bully Boyz needed to extract itself from the studio and return to the stage.

Step in the Arena

Scholars sometimes bemoan the loss of live performance in hip-hop culture, describing its historical shift from collective, community-based cultural practices to passive, technology-centric activities that take place in private spaces. As hip-hop culture became more popular in the 1980s, corporations seized upon its most profitable element, rap music, to the detriment of breakdancing, graffiti, "and other face-to-face community building practices" (Dimitriadis 1996, 191). Rap thrived under corporate rule, but it became a more self-contained pursuit, created in recording studios and increasingly consumed in automobiles or through headphones.[1]

Those who have written the obituary for live rap performance, however, may have done so prematurely. At rap's corporate tier, where recorded music has become effectively free, touring acts (and the merchandise sold at concerts) continue to be lucrative. While live shows at small, local venues don't generate millions of dollars, microscenes remain rooted in and characterized by these events. A recent body of ethnographic research has explored the presence of face-to-face performance in rap microscenes, including studies of concerts, open-mic nights, freestyle sessions, battles, and ciphers. These varied performance types and the venues where they take place have been used to consider topics that include collective agency, racial politics, identity, authenticity, rituals, and cultural production (Alim, Lee, and Carris 2011; Condry 2006; Cutler 2007; Dowdy 2007; Harrison 2009; Lee 2009a; Lee 2009b; Packman 2009; Smith 2005; Stahl and Dale 2012). In this chapter, I take an alternative approach by examining nightclubs as workplaces, and considering how social class shapes the performative context. Recording studios represent the back stage of Chicago's rap underground; nightclubs symbolize its front stage.

Collectively, these two spaces are the central locations where MCs "do" most rap-music culture, but they are used differently and have distinct functions and symbolic significance. Like recording studios and the cultural objects created in them, concerts present benefits and challenges unique to gang members, topics I also consider.

When asked about the first time they performed live, most of the Chicago MCs did not discuss nightclubs or even rap music. Many began earlier, performing in primary school orchestras, choirs, and churches. Long before stepping onto a stage, they learned to rap on playgrounds, in classes, in school lunchrooms, and during freestyle ciphers.

In rap microscenes, gaining experience as a live performer is seen as a critical stepping-stone in the career trajectory from novice to professional (Condry 2006; Lee 2009c). The Chicago MCs described their entry into performing as a series of nonlinear steps, beginning at the fringes and inching toward the core. For example, O-mega served as a hype man for a rap group several months before taking center stage. Others started out as DJs before abandoning turntables and picking up microphones. High-school talent shows, open-mic nights, and poetry slams served as transitional events that enabled rappers to learn the craft, develop skills, and gain confidence as performers. These events served as ports of entry, and eventually led aspiring musicians to the microscene's signature performance space, the nightclub.

Most participants recalled their first time performing at a nightclub in detail. For example, Chilly started out rapping with friends, and then recorded some tracks at a buddy's home studio and posted them online. A local rap group heard the material and offered the fledgling MC a chance to open for them. "I showed up like thirty minutes early, trying to be real professional," he recalled. "I was super nervous right before it started, but as soon as the beat dropped, it was go time. I did my thing. The crowd loved it. My first show was a good show, which is rare."

A large portion of the research for this book took place in nightclubs. In six years of fieldwork, I observed performances at fifty-seven venues in the Chicagoland area, returning to several repeatedly. At these locations, I witnessed more than 500 live performances, often numerous artists on the same night. This was useful because I could better gauge how different musicians were received in the same setting. One of the benefits of studying live rap performances was an immediacy of feedback; audiences were not subtle about their likes and dislikes.

Some participants were seasoned performers who had been playing live for years. Others were new to the practice, and had only appeared in public a handful of times. A few had never played a nightclub or similar venue. Rappers were rarely paid—or were paid very little—to perform. The exposure and potential income from merchandise was considered payment enough. "Look at comedians, those guys make twenty dollars a night, fifteen dollars a night doing sets at these fuckin' clubs," Black Soldier said. "It's the same as us doing these fuckin' shows for free or this pay-to-play shit in Chicago. A rapper's a dime a dozen." Touring musicians earned modest sums, but most of those dollars went back into the costs associated with traveling. No one I met was making much money from performances, but live shows were perceived to be important for career building. "Do as many open mics, as many shows as you can," Wes Restless urged. "Even if you're not gonna get paid, even if five, ten, fifteen people are there. Get your live show up, learn how to perform."

In Chicago, the majority of the larger and more prominent venues were located on the city's North Side, but I also attended shows on the South and West Sides, and a few in the far western and southern suburbs. Performances took place in sports bars, hole-in-the-wall dives, dance venues, nightclubs devoted primarily or exclusively to live music, and larger concert halls and theaters that seated several thousand. I also watched performances at parks, retail stores, restaurants, coffee shops, art galleries, community centers, schools, universities, warehouses, lofts, house parties, and street festivals.

Audiences ranged in age from early teens at all-ages shows (which were uncommon) to mid-thirties. The average age of spectators, by my estimate, was similar to the rappers, about twenty-five years old. The ethnoracial makeup of audiences was contextually dependent on such factors as venue type, location, and the subgenre of rap being showcased.

The subgenre of rap featured at venues also reflected the geographically bounded race- and class-based stratification of Chicago. Venues on the city's North Side largely catered to backpack rap. Nightclubs that showcased gangsta rap were scarcer, and tended to be located on the South and West Sides and in the less wealthy, less white North Side neighborhoods. Audiences in these venues tended to reflect local demographics. North Side venues catered to a mixture of blacks, Latinos, and whites; South Side venues featured mostly black audiences, and venues in neighborhoods such as Humboldt Park, home to large Latino populations, were filled with Latino patrons. These differences illustrated the intersectionality of race and social class, as well as the microscenes perspective. Chicago is best understood as an assortment of neighborhoods rather than a holistic entity (Sampson 2012), and its rap underground is better appreciated as a collection of microscenes whose symbolic boundaries are demarcated by social class (backpacker/gangsta) and race (neighborhood). In Chicago's rap microscenes, there were four primary types of live performance: ciphers, open-mic nights, battles, and concerts.

Ciphers were informal, spontaneous performances that occurred when a group of MCs formed a circle and each one freestyled for some amount of time before passing the "spotlight" to another rapper, who then took over with his or her own improvised rhymes.[2] Ciphers did not take place on stages, but groups of MCs regularly ciphered outside performance venues or between acts. For most MCs, the cipher was their first public rap performance, an initiation sometimes fraught with anxiety. However, ciphers tended to be less competitive than battles, and enabled players to develop skills, network, seek employment opportunities, and vie for in-group status among peers. Once burgeoning rappers had mastered the art of ciphering, they often graduated to other forms of live performance, usually open-mic nights or battles.

Open-mic nights typically took place in clubs on weeknights as a way for the venue to attract patrons during off-peak hours. The Subterranean, a Wicker Park nightclub that featured live bands from a variety of genres, hosted a weekly free open-mic night that was popular with backpackers. At an open-mic night, rappers typically signed up for five or ten minutes of stage time. One by one, they were called to perform—it was not unusual to see twenty or thirty rappers appear at these events. Open-mic nights were scarcely attended by those who were not rap musicians, but these settings allowed newcomers to network and develop skills alongside sympathetic peers.[3]

Battles were verbal duels that took place at large and small venues, and also in less formal settings. Such contests are an important element of rap culture, a tradition that recalls other forms of "combative/playful African American oral practices—the dozens, signifyin', toasting, boasting, vouting, talkin' shit" (Maxwell 2003, 23).[4] A battle consisted of several rounds in which two rappers faced off in competition, insulting each other with improvised rhymes for a predetermined amount of time, generally thirty to ninety seconds. Based on audience response, the winners of each round advanced to the next round, where they competed again. The winners of the second round advanced once again, until only two rappers remained. The final two MCs battled each other verbally until one forfeited or the audience declared a winner. The winners of rap battles stood to gain status and occasionally money or other rewards, such as hip-hop-themed clothing, studio time, or a similar career-related product or service. Most of the rappers I met had battled at some point, but it was not nearly as common as live concerts. This was due to a perception that battling did little to advance one's career beyond the microscene.

Concerts were live performances that took place in front of an audience, one that typically paid to attend. Chicago has hundreds of live music venues, although few showcased rap exclusively. Instead, venues that hosted rap concerts generally held them on a weekly, biweekly, or monthly basis. Acts were booked in advance, and most artists heavily promoted these gigs online and in person. Because concerts were the province of rappers who were career building, I focused on this performance type in the field.

The structure of concerts varied. Some featured four to seven acts, each performing for a predetermined amount of time, usually fifteen to thirty minutes. Other concerts were revue style, in which two or three dozen acts took the stage, one after the other, sometimes for just a single song. Other concerts consisted of a single act, often performing a brief set at a venue not exclusively dedicated to live music, such as a dance club or a coffee shop. Other concerts consisted of scheduled performers preceded or followed by an open-mic in which audience members could get onstage and rap for a few minutes. Rappers were sometimes interspersed with singers, poets, spoken-word artists, comedians, political speakers, and break-dance troupes. At most concerts, a DJ played transitional music between performances, and an emcee oversaw the proceedings—announcing the acts and bantering with the audience.

Among rappers, there was a status hierarchy for the different types of live performance. Ciphers were the least prestigious, probably because they were the least formal and anyone could participate, regardless of skill level. Because they took place at venues and featured equipment such as microphones, open-mic nights were more prestigious than ciphers, but not by much. Like ciphers, open-mic nights featured unrestricted participation, rappers of varying skill levels, and performers who were not paid. Ciphers and open-mic nights were also weighed down with novices, which may have reduced their status. Battles were considered more prestigious than ciphers and open-mic nights, and adept battle rappers were viewed with reverence. The winner of a battle was typically awarded some form of prize, an external validation of skill that enhanced the event's status. Concerts were the most prestigious performance type, in part because they usually took place in formal or semiformal venues with paying audiences. The larger, more formal, and more popular the venue, the more prestigious it was to perform there. Atop the hierarchy were concerts held in large venues such as the House of Blues, the Metro, and the Congress Theater. Underground MCs who played these sites did so as opening acts for nationally and internationally recognized rap artists. Gigs of this nature were infrequent, hard to secure, usually garnered some form of payment, and were the most exalted. The majority of concerts I attended, however, took place in small venues before audiences that ranged from enthralled to indifferent.

MC Sazon at Aquarius

For MC Sazon, turning twenty-one meant more than being able to buy booze in bars, it meant being able to perform in them. Having celebrated that landmark last week, that's why he's here tonight at Aquarius Club and Restaurant, located on a busy artery in Logan Square.

As restaurant-cum-nightclubs go, Aquarius is about average—a couple of pool tables, an ancient pinball machine, a horseshoe-shaped bar surrounded by red leather stools, a handful of table-and-chair sets, and a small dance floor illuminated by overhead lights. The modest surroundings aren't keeping the crowds away—a steady stream of patrons enters through Aquarius's lone doorway.

Tonight is "industry night" at Aquarius, which amounts to a DJ spinning dance tracks, punctuated by a couple of short performances from local rap artists. MC Sazon is slated to play first, followed by two gangsta-rap acts. The crowd at Aquarius is almost exclusively Puerto Rican, augmented by small clusters of blacks.

Sazon, who lives with his mother in Humboldt Park, is also Puerto Rican. He got into rap when he was ten years old after watching a music video for "The Crossroads" by Bone Thugs-N Harmony. "I was ten years old coming in from school," Sazon remembers. "I went to my mom's house. We used to have this station out there called the Box—it was a music video station. And I turned it on and that was the first song I heard that day. Ever since I heard that song, I been into the hip-hop scene. It just flipped on me."

Tonight Sazon wears a relatively demure variation of hip-hop fashion—baggy jeans, a loose tan T-shirt with an illustration of a boom box on the chest, close-cropped military haircut, glasses, and a small diamond in each ear. From a distance, he comes across as a quietly confident young man, but Sazon is shy by nature, humble and self-deprecating. His cousin came with him tonight to help get the crowd into it. "It's family," the cousin tells me. "Gotta support."

Sazon's musical oeuvre consists mostly of socially progressive backpack rap with an earnest message and a positive worldview. Tonight he's planning to switch it up; he's crafted a two-song set of Latin-tinged "club bangers" designed to encourage dancing.

"We're Latino and our people love to dance," Sazon explains. "So you wanna keep 'em moving."

I ask Sazon if he gets nervous before a show like this and he answers in the affirmative.

"My mom told me that if you're not nervous before a performance, then you don't really care," he says. "But I'm only nervous until the first few lines of the first song. After that, I'm fine."

I buy Sazon and his cousin a drink. The cousin borrows a couple of smokes from one of the bartenders and purchases a cherry-colored Jello shot. Sazon barely touches the alcohol—he wants to stay sharp for the show, plus he's got to work tomorrow morning at Pep Boys, an auto parts chain where he works as an assistant manager. We sit at the bar and wait, watching as incoming patrons are patted down and frisked by a pair of security guards. Music thumps from a couple of speakers located near the DJ, who hovers over a pair of CD players and a mixer, laid out on a folding table set up at one end of the dance floor.

An older woman, perhaps in her fifties, plays matchmaker, approaching Sazon and pointing out her friend, a striking twenty-something Latino woman sitting across the bar from us. The friend is shy, turning in embarrassment when we look her way. Sazon is shy, too, and doesn't approach her or say anything. Tonight is not about flirtation; he's lost in thought, focused on the performance.

"You gotta be dedicated to what you're doing," Sazon tells me. "You can't just be like, 'I need a way out the 'hood, I'm gonna try to rap.' You gotta love this, man. You gotta love what you're doing. You gotta be able to put your heart into it, and put your mind into it and put your talent into it."

The DJ alternates between gangsta rap and reggaeton, rap music of Latin and Caribbean origin that has grown in popularity in the United States. Early on, the balance leans toward current and classic gangsta rap, but this gives way to exclusively reggaeton songs, many of which are well known by the patrons. They sing along in Spanish and crowd the dance floor.

After an hour of music, a young black announcer calls for a dance contest, offering the best hoofer tickets to an upcoming concert. Seven young women take the floor, gyrating as the spectators surround them, hooting and hollering in approval. The patrons—male and female alike—go nuts during the contest, crowding the dance floor to the point where it's hard to see the dancers. The lights are turned off, too, further reducing visibility. Based on audience response, three women are selected as finalists, and compete in a second round, with the tickets going to the dancer who garners the biggest reaction. The winner appears to have a lot of friends on hand, all of whom go crazy applauding her moves. During the contest, Sazon stands off to the side, saying nothing, waiting his turn at the microphone.

The competition ends and the house lights are turned on. Everyone retreats to the bar and the tables, leaving the dance floor empty, save for the announcer, who introduces Sazon:

All right, check one two. Like I said, we'd like to thank everybody for coming out to support our Chicago artists. Get ready, Aquarius. This is how we do it every Thursday. Reggaeton and hip-hop industry night. Brought to you by Four Fantastic Events—make sure you go to the website and check out the pictures. I go by the name DJ Two Step. This is my man DJ Neurotic on the ones and twos. We got a performance coming up next. Go 'head and introduce yourself, papi.

He hands a cordless microphone to Sazon, who looks skinny and nervous, alone on the dance floor.

"Ay yo, I go by the name MC Sazon, man. Can I get a few people closer to the stage, people who gonna dance?"

The patrons remain planted in their seats.

"He wants y'all to move in a little closer," the announcer implores.

No one moves an inch. The beat to Sazon's first song begins.

"I know y'all like salsa, right man?" Sazon asks the crowd, in time with the music. "Mixed with a little reggaeton and shit. I had my boy make this beat for me. It's nice, man."

The twenty-something woman from the bar begins rocking back and forth slowly on her stool. No one else moves.

"She dancin'," Sazon points out helplessly.

Crickets.

He begins rapping, sinking tepidly into the first few bars of his verse before stopping.

"Can I get some crowd participation in this motherfucker?"

The audience just sits there, staring at him, arms folded, unimpressed.

Nightclubs as Workspaces

Like recording studios, nightclubs were symbolic spaces in which work took place. The number of concerts played in a given time period served as evidence of an MC's willingness to grind. The more concerts a rapper played per week, month, or year, the harder they claimed to be working.

Rappers described the labor related to concerts in different ways. For some, it involved the technical skills required to produce a confident performance: eye contact, gestures, timing, enunciation, having lyrics memorized, interacting with the audience. Others stressed physicality and the corporal demands of performing. Some emphasized emotional labor, the expectation to deliver an energetic, passionate show regardless of circumstances. Nightclubs provided prime opportunities for labor such as promotion and networking because they brought together the various microscene members in a single location. "Artists, fans, promoters, writers, industry executives, club owners, bartenders, the regulars, and the first timers. The dynamic interaction among all these actors is what brings a club scene to life" (Condry 2006, 87). Nightclubs often buzzed with promotion and networking activity: people handing out flyers and posters, giving away or selling CDs and other merchandise, and engaging in small talk with microscene peers.

MC Sazon's experience at Aquarius exemplified how, as in all vocational spaces, there were work-related challenges. Concerts were not dictated by formal rules, but followed a system of conventions—agreed-upon ways of doing things understood by members of the microscene. "Conventions regulate the relations between artists and audience, specifying the rights and obligations of both" (Becker 1974, 771). At times there were unforeseen circumstances that disrupted what Erving Goffman (1974) called the performance frame—the sum total of structural and behavioral conventions and obligations related to a performance.[5] The difficulties encountered by rappers during concerts illustrated how social class shaped the performative context. To explicate this, I classify these challenges along three categorical schemata: structural issues, technical difficulties, and interactive conflicts.[6]

Structural Issues

Concerts were sometimes impacted by structural issues beyond the control of the rappers that disrupted the performance frame. For example, most of the shows I attended had small turnouts, but there was variation, including some that were patronized by only a handful of spectators. Reasons for low turnout included lack of promotion, a lineup consisting of unknown artists, poor weather, and competing concerts that drew fans elsewhere. These structural issues impacted both the backpacker and gangsta-rap shows, and could be difficult to foresee. There were also, however, structural challenges related to social class that impacted turnout that were easier to predict.

Venues principally dedicated to backpacker rap tended to be situated in central neighborhoods with lower crime rates that were closer to public transportation. These locations appealed to fans because they were safer, easier to find, and simpler to access without a car. Venues that regularly hosted gangsta-rap concerts tended to be situated in peripheral neighborhoods with higher crime rates that were further from public transportation. These locations were less appealing to fans because they were more dangerous, harder to find, and more difficult to access without private transportation. Due to these structural differences, gangsta-rap performances tended to draw fewer patrons than backpacker shows.

Backpacker concerts were also more likely to be held in venues specifically designed for live music. These venues were more closely aligned with a "pure" performance frame (Goffman 1974). In pure performances, such as a plays held in theaters, there are clear demarcations between audience and artist, bounded by physical and symbolic conventions such as raised stages, backstage areas, formal seating, and curtains that signal the start and end of the show (Mullen 1985). Nightclubs that catered to backpacker rap were generally less "pure" than theaters, but featured some of the same elements. For example, they were more likely to have raised stages that separated audience from performer and directed the audience's attention toward the show. These venues were more likely to feature PA and lighting systems designed for live music, seating that faced the stage, and backstage areas that separated performer and audience.

Relative to backpacker shows, gangsta concerts were more likely to be held in nontraditional venues or semitraditional venues, such as dance clubs and sports bars, that were not designed for live music. These venues were less likely to have raised stages; those that did had stages that were lower and closer to the audience. If there was no stage, the venue was converted in various ways, such as clearing an area of the dance floor. These venues were less likely to have PA and lighting systems devoted to live music, less likely to have seating that directed the audience's attention toward the performance, and less likely to have backstage areas that separated artists and audiences.

The further the venue strayed from the pure performance frame, the more likely there were to be disruptions to the conventions of live music performance. Semi- or nontraditional venues, such as sports bars and dance clubs, might be packed with patrons who ignored the concert and focused on other activities. Venues like Aquarius—where MC Sazon failed to ignite the crowd—attracted regulars who were there to dance, flirt, and hang out with friends. Because Aquarius was primarily a restaurant, some patrons were there to eat. A rap concert could be an interruption, rather than an enhancement.

At nontraditional or semitraditional venues, artists had to work harder to procure and maintain the audience's attention. For example, at the Capitol Club—the strip joint turned dance venue where I first saw Bully Boyz perform—musicians sometimes had a hard time getting patrons to watch the show. One night, I witnessed a talented group called Lab Rats struggle to get a bar-bound audience to move closer to the stage. There was a sizable crowd, but the patrons were content to sit and chat at the bar, and mostly ignored the vigorous concert taking place at the other end of the room. Between songs, the Rats' lead rapper, Thesis, tried to lure the audience with humor:

> Yo, real quick, I know your ass cheeks gettin' all sweaty sittin' over there. Please, do us a favor, show some love, come up here. Come up front, we ain't gonna bite—or at least a couple of us won't. [Nobody moves.] All right, man. We gonna do what we can. Fuck it.

Lab Rats continued its energetic set to no avail; the audience remained planted at the bar, snubbing the band. After a couple of numbers, a frustrated Thesis made a direct appeal:

> Is Chicago in the house or is Chicago *not* in the motherfuckin' house? If we don't show love for each other how the fuck are we gonna expect anybody else to show love for us? Come on, y'all. Make some *fuckin'* noise for everybody that blessed the stage. Yo, I know it looks like mad fun and shit, but we pour our blood, sweat, and tears into this shit. And all we ask is for a little bit of energy, and we promise you we'll give you that shit right back. So let's set the shit off right here, and let's bump that shit up. All the way the fuck up. [Nobody moves.]

There were also structural challenges related to the running order of the acts. Those who performed early or at the end of the night sometimes did so in nearly empty venues because the crowd had not arrived or had already left. It was not unusual to see headliners play for audiences that were smaller than those watching the acts that preceded them. At other times, headliners would demand to go on when attendance was at its peak, with the opening acts being forced to follow as the crowd thinned. Again, there were differences between backpacker and gangsta concerts. At semitraditional venues such as dance clubs, the arrival and exit of patrons was not aligned to live performance, but to the temporal conventions of dance clubs. Gangsta shows held in these settings tended to start and end later, which reduced the potential audience base. Gangsta concerts were also more likely to be structured revue style, and tended to feature more acts than backpacker shows. This increased competition, gave the artists less stage time, and made it more difficult for an act to stand out.

Technical Difficulties

Concerts were sometimes plagued by technical difficulties that disrupted the performance frame—CDs skipped, microphones died, computers crashed, speakers blew, and power failed. Technical difficulties were more frequent in venues that were not dedicated to live music, where the equipment could be substandard or not as well maintained. "These hole-in-the-wall bars, [the audience] can't even hear," an MC named Doctor Who said. "The sound systems are so terrible." Because gangsta-rap shows were more likely to take place in nontraditional or semitraditional venues, they were fraught with more technical challenges. These issues occurred at backpacker concerts, too, but they were more likely to be smoothed over by sound engineers, and were less disruptive to the performance frame.

The venues owned and controlled the sound equipment, and staff sometimes used this gear in ways that compromised performances. Nontraditional and semitraditional venues were less likely to have dedicated sound engineers, and tended to rely on staff members, such as bartenders or in-house DJs, to operate the sound equipment. For example, one night I attended a gangsta-rap concert at a Mexican eatery that did not normally feature live music. The tables and chairs in one of the restaurant's rooms were removed, and the rappers performed in the center of the floor, surrounded by a small audience of friends.

There were three opening acts, each of which played two songs each. Twenty minutes into the show, the headliner, a group called Hood Rich, began its set. Hood Rich completed one song, and then launched into a number about "niggas" selling rocks and shooting guns. A few bars into the tune, the DJ—a staff member who was operating the soundboard—shut down the sound system. The song clanged to a halt, sucking the wind out of the performance. No explanation was offered, and everyone looked quizzically at the DJ, who avoided eye contact.

The audience began booing and shouting obscenities at the DJ. "Ay, run that shit back you soft-ass nigga," one spectator yelled.

"The soundman fucked us up," one of the Hood Rich rappers said to the grumbling crowd. "Do y'all want another song?" The attendees responded affirmatively, but the power was not restored. Angered, a member of Hood Rich intentionally dropped his microphone on the floor, and the group and its entourage stormed toward the exit en masse.

"I'm taking this salt shaker with me," one concertgoer told her friend. "'Cause these motherfuckers shouldn'ta turned that shit off."

As the crowd streamed out of the restaurant, Hood Rich and the DJ nearly came to blows. "What's up with the performance right now, dog?" a band member demanded, inches from the DJ's face. The rapper clapped his hands together, emphasizing his words with fierce smacks. "Ay, *listen* dog, don't call Hood Rich no more, dog, if you're gonna fuckin' end shows like this. Real talk, nigga. 'Cause we got credibility!"

Interactive Conflicts

Concerts put rappers in face-to-face contact with various microscene members, which could lead to interpersonal conflicts and other challenges that disrupt the performance frame. These challenges were born of temporal and social demands from the venue personnel, microscene peers, and audience members that placed constraints on the musicians and also shaped the meaning and interpretation of the performance. Furthermore, the varied structures and technical setups of venues affected the dynamic interactions between these groups, as illustrated by Lab Rats' unresponsive audience at the Capitol Club and Hood Rich's run-in with the DJ at the Mexican restaurant.

Concert audiences are often depicted as starry-eyed fans worshipping larger-than-life performers, yet this idyllic image is less common than believed. "Those who have attended numerous clubs and concerts for years will be familiar with instances of mixed reaction to performances, tensions amongst listeners/dancers, and a detectable lack of unity amongst those involved" (Negus and Velazquez 2002, 142). This ambivalence is exacerbated in underground microscenes, where the symbolic power differential between performer and spectator is more evenly weighted.

At concerts held in an arena, there is a purer performance frame with conventions that encourage a power dynamic between artist and audience member that includes considerable distance. Jay-Z sits backstage at Madison Square Garden, while the audience awaits his arrival. A plethora of physical barriers and gatekeepers ensures total separation between artist and attendees. The house lights dim, the curtain drops, and the rap star appears, towering over the audience from a tall stage. The crowd's attention is directed, physically and symbolically, toward Jay-Z, who is illuminated with elaborate spotlights and whose voice is pumped through a state-of-the-art sound system. After conventions such as a main set of songs, one or more encores, and final bows, Jay-Z exits the arena via limo. The house lights are turned back on and prerecorded music is played through the sound system, signaling the concert's end. A spectator at this event would have a difficult time disrupting the performance frame. Even those brave souls who hop on stage at arena concerts are whisked away by security, and anyone too disruptive is escorted out. The larger the venue and the more conventions in place, the less power a spectator has to impact the performance frame. As venues get smaller, however, the performance frame weakens, the conventions diminish or disappear, and the symbolic relationship between artist and audience member is altered. The weakened performance frame can decrease audience engagement. As MC Sazon and the Lab Rats discovered, the lack of conventions at a venue can reduce spectator obligation to acknowledge or appreciate the concert. Conversely, the lack of conventions can increase interaction between audience and performer. Engaged audiences in small venues tend to interact more frequently with performers, both physically and verbally. The weaker performance frame is among the primary appeals of concerts held in nightclubs, which are perceived to be more intimate than arena shows.

In his ethnography of Chicago's folk music microscene, sociologist Clinton Sanders (1974) reported that disruptive crowds were a common complaint among musicians. In the small venues he studied, spectators regularly interrupted performances with everything from song requests to heckles. Musicologist Mark Duffett (2002) pointed out that heckling is a common element of concerts, serving as a form of resistance that intentionally questions or even renounces the symbolic power differential between artist and audience. Even uncritical comments from audiences, such as song requests, momentarily interrupt the performance frame and divert attention from center stage. When heckling is critical or hostile it can signal ideological opposition or a rejection of the performance as substandard.

In Chicago's rap underground, concertgoers were sometimes vocal in their displeasure; most rappers had been booed, jeered, teased, or taunted at some point. Social class impacted these dynamics. Because backpacker venues tended to have stronger performance frames, the symbolic artist-audience power was more highly skewed in favor of musicians. As a result, audiences at backpacker venues were more likely to be attentive to the performance and less likely to interrupt rappers during a performance or interact with them offstage. Conversely, gangsta venues tended to have weaker performance frames, reducing the symbolic power dynamic. Audience members were likely to perceive less distance between themselves and musicians at gangsta-rap venues. They felt greater freedom to either tune out the concerts altogether or interact with the rappers on and off stage. In other words, relative to backpacker shows, the structural arrangement and social dynamics of gangsta shows reduced the symbolic distance between audience and performer, and encouraged both audience indifference and greater interaction between performer and spectator.

Throwing Coconuts

To counter in-concert disturbances and preserve the performance frame, musicians generate strategic response repertoires designed to save face and restore the flow of the routine (Mullen 1985; Sanders 1974; Scarborough 2012). In Chicago these strategies included everything from the humorous and direct pleas utilized by Thesis to abandoning the performance frame altogether, as Hood Rich did. As performers gained experience, they developed broad repertoires that enabled them to strategically respond to changing contexts.

The promise of the American dream is that through hard work, anyone can achieve his or her goals. Those who do not succeed only have themselves to blame—they were lazy, didn't work hard enough, or lacked motivation. Although differences such as venue type or location affected audience behavior, the Chicago MCs did not perceive structural variation as impactful. Because they endorsed the American dream ideology and framed live performance as work, inability to achieve desired results was attributed to individual failings, rather than structural factors. O-mega illustrated this point:

> O-MEGA: It's really up to you. If you're onstage and you're just
> kind of [dead], not really moving, if it seems like you don't
> care, then the audience won't care. You have to have that
> energy. You have to hype up the crowd, you gotta move
> around, jump around, act stupid, throw CDs, pour water on

yourself, whatever it takes for the crowd to be like, Wow!
[Claps.] That's what you gotta do.
GH: What do you do if the crowd won't get into it—if they're dead
even though you're putting on a great show?
O-MEGA: What can you do? Still give it your all, if there's like two
people standing in front of you or a hundred people standing
in front of you. If they not feeling it, why are they not feeling
it? Because maybe you're not giving it your all. I really do think
that a performer can make that crowd go crazy. It's your job.
That's why they pay you to get onstage, to get that crowd hype.
Don't get me wrong, we've all been through it. But you can't
stop. You can't shut down. You can't be like, "If they're not
gonna feel it, fuck you." No. I gotta still give it my all. If I gotta
do a back flip, do a somersault, climb a fuckin' coconut tree
and throw coconuts at you, you gonna feel that shit.

A final class-based distinction between these performative contexts of
backpacker/gangsta concerts was that gangsta shows attracted more gang
members. In part this was attributable to gangsta rap's appeal among
gang members, but there was also a structural element. Because Chicago
gangs are bounded by neighborhoods and territories, gang members
were more likely to attend shows closer to their home turf. For the same
reason, gang members who rapped were more likely to perform in these
venues. The relatively weaker performance frames found in these venues
also meant that gang members in the audience were more likely to interact with musicians. This dynamic created distinct cultural practices and
challenges that warrant further explication.

The Performance of Gang Identity at Rap Concerts

The symbiotic relationship between gangs and gangsta rap was apparent
at live performances because rap concerts sometimes doubled as public
meeting spaces for gangs. Sudhir Venkatesh (2008) described the difficulty of assembling large numbers of gang members for meetings without being detected by the police. The gang he studied held summits at
youth centers, churches, street corners, and parks. In Chicago's gangsta-
rap microscene, concerts provided a perfect cover for such gatherings, and

gangs regularly amassed at nightclubs to conduct business without police interference. In some instances, gang members booked shows themselves, including private events such as birthday parties held at nightclubs, as a way to amass the gang in the least conspicuous manner. In addition to functioning as a location for conducting business, these spaces hosted gatherings that were crucial for building loyalty and gang unity. Amassing the gang at a nightclub also provided a built-in audience for the rappers, who were assured of at least some sort of turnout.

A study conducted in Massachusetts and California (Pih et al. 2008) found that gangs were an important source of social capital for members because gangs provided personal protection and security. In Chicago's gangsta-rap microscene, rappers who were gang members relied on their gang for security, especially at live shows. According to Hyper, "You catch me at a show, I'm probably going to be represented by most of my block. I travel no lighter than two or three cars with my guys."

At times, the distinction between gang members and gangsta rappers was blurred during performances; large entourages of gang members often accompanied gangsta rappers on stage. These crewmembers did not rap, but served as "hype men" for the artists—emphasizing certain lyrics, encouraging the performers, displaying artist-related banners, signs, T-shirts, and CDs, and pumping up the crowd. Of course, this practice was not limited to gangsta rap or to gang members, but it occurred more frequently at gangsta shows, and the number of nonmusicians onstage was typically larger. In part, this was because the weaker performance frames at nontraditional and semitraditional venues diminished the boundaries between audiences and artists. The lack of structural devices such as raised stages encouraged the commingling of artists, entourages, and concertgoers during gangsta-rap shows. While a stage can only support a finite number of people, an area cleared for the purpose of performing, such as a dance floor, can accommodate a much larger group.

Symbolically, having one's entourage participate in the concert lent a larger-than-life appearance to the performance. Visually and aurally, being backed by a posse commanded more audience attention than a lone MC or group. Ultimately, this practice occurred at the intersection of street gang and rap music cultures because it was a means by which to physically and symbolically control space. As Erik Nielson (2012) wrote, "the posse tradition grew out of the pervasive New York gang culture that immediately preceded (and helped give rise to) hip hop, and so the inherently territorial nature of gangs predictably affected the preoccupation with demarcating and controlling spaces that we see throughout hip hop" (357).

Because most of those involved in Chicago's gangsta-rap microscene were not gang members, discerning who was or was not affiliated presented an initial challenge in my research. At the onset of my fieldwork, deciphering the gangs' symbolic codes was difficult. Dwight Conquergood (1994), who conducted ethnographic research on Chicago street gangs, believed that the communicative practices of street gangs were deliberately complex and obscure:

> The need to mobilize and heighten group consciousness by creating a strong boundary against the outside world accounts for the densely coded and deliberately opaque nature of gang communication. Gangs rely heavily on nonverbal channels of communication: hand signs, color of clothing, tilt of a baseball cap, brand of tennis shoes and style of lacing, whistles, visual icons (both in graffiti murals and body tattoos), mode of crossing arms, and earrings. These nonverbal channels of communication are incomprehensible to outsiders. (26–27)

As I became more attuned to the nuances of this coded communication, displays of gang membership at live performances were more recognizable. Over time, I came to understand how these communicative practices were not only symbolically significant but functionally imperative.

In some instances displays of gang membership were overt, such as rappers who would state the name of their gang or People/Folks affiliation in lyrics or when addressing the audience between songs. For example, upon introducing a number at a concert, Focus, an IOA-affiliated rapper, told the crowd, "This song is called 'Straight A's.' It's a lot of Aces in the motherfuckin' house, nigga. A's up, nigga!" The IOAs in attendance responded by cheering and "throwing" (i.e., hoisting) their "A" hand signs.

Gang members who rapped regularly threw their gang's hand sign during songs as a means of representing or signifying the gang. This typically occurred in conjunction with lyrics that invoked the gang's symbols. For example, Dustup, a Spanish Cobra, would throw the Cobras' hand sign during lyrical references to the gang, such as its name, number, or colors. Others gripped the microphone in such a way that any time they rapped they were effectively signifying their gang via hand gesture.

When concertgoers from the same gang responded in kind, throwing the gang's sign back at the rappers, the exchange fostered inner-gang unity and solidarity. A variation of this occurred when a rapper or entourage member would fist bump their hand signs with audience members. These symbolic exchanges between artist and audience have roots in black performative practices and ancient religious rituals; their history predates their adoption by rap musicians or street gangs.[7] According to some participants, these ritualistic interactions were the mark of a superior performance. For example, after a well-received concert at a gang-packed show on the South Side, T-Bird told me, "I had motherfuckers throwin' they hands up, throwin' they gang signs. I had motherfuckers *feelin'* that shit."

Hand signs were also used during live performances to insult enemy gangs. Rappers were generally cautious not to invert or "throw down" another gang's hand sign during performances, although it happened on occasion. Entourage members and those in the audience, however, threw down the signs of rival gangs with some regularity. As I discuss later in the chapter, such actions were not always inconsequential.

Of course, rappers with no gang affiliation also employed hand gestures while performing, but were careful not to use gang-related signs. To do so would be considered "false flagging," and would be met with considerable reprobation by gang members. Those familiar with gang-related hand signs could readily discern the difference. Nongang members, including backpackers, however, frequently deployed similar symbolic practices outside of gang-related settings. One of the most common communicative practices I witnessed at Chicago concerts occurred when rappers—gang members or otherwise—would implore concertgoers to "throw your C's up." Amenable spectators would respond by configuring their hands into a C shape and hoisting them toward the ceiling. The "C" hand sign was not gang-related; it indexed Chicago. This was a danger-free variation of the gang ritual, rooted in the symbolic communicative practices of street gangs. Repeating this custom safely aligned performers with Chicago gang culture, a desirable status, and attempted to build consensus among the crowd, rather than division.

The performance of gang identity at live concerts was also achieved through sartorial practices. For example, gang members who rapped sometimes wore clothing that featured gang-related colors or symbols. This included color-coded shirts, jackets, shoes, hats, bandanas, wristbands, headbands, sunglasses, watches, jewelry, and other accessories. For example, at one Bully Boyz's show at the Capitol Club, the band members were heavily draped in brown and gold, the colors of the IOAs. Phantastic sported a brown leather bomber jacket with an elaborate gold pattern embroidered on the back and chest. During the show, he removed the jacket to reveal a yellow shirt with a brown and gold eagle on the front.[8] Brown Timberland boots, a gold watch, and a gold chain accentuated the outfit. To outside observers, Phantastic would not have looked like a gang member. To those familiar with the coded meaning of these colors, he might as well have had a bullhorn announcing his IOA affiliation.

Clothing was also used to index a rapper's People/Folks affiliation or his gang's association with one of Chicago's multigang alliances. This included the wearing of clothing on the left or right side of the body, signifying either People or Folks. A hat tilted to the left denoted affiliation with the People Nation; a bandana wrapped around the right wrist or an earring in the right lobe indicated association with the Folk Nation.

At times the use of clothing as gang signifier was overt, such as a T-shirt in bold gang-related colors. At other times, the symbolic uses of clothing were subtler. For example, at one concert, a member of the Gangster Disciples wore a black hoodie, accentuated by a thin blue cord through the hood. Blue and black are the Gangsta Disciple colors, but this understated display of color was less likely to attract attention from authorities and rival gang members. Sportswear was also popular. Gang members would wear the official jerseys, hoodies, and hats of professional sports teams whose colors matched those of the gang. For example, the Four Corner Hustlers' colors were black and gold; members wore sports garb from the New Orleans Saints, which featured the same color scheme. This symbolic practice represented the gang but also was functional because it was less conspicuous and gave a gang member plausible deniability that he was wearing gang colors.

Gang members who had been to prison touted this prized status during live performances as well. For example, while on stage, members of Xcons sometimes wore T-shirts with their prison mug shots printed on the chest. Their firsthand experience with the criminal justice system also made its way into their stage banter at live performances. For example, upon taking the stage one night at a Calumet City nightclub, Bleek greeted the audience by saying, "I feel good today 'cause I just got off parole. I been on that shit for about three years." Bleek's status as a parolee was a form of subcultural capital, so it came as no surprise that he mentioned it before rapping a single word. Doing so informed the audience that his lyrics were autobiographical, rather than the fictional accounts of a studio gangsta. Furthermore, being on parole for three years implied that whatever crimes Bleek committed must have been fairly serious.

Violence and Gangs in Chicago Nightclubs

In Chicago's gangsta-rap microscene, gang membership was a valuable resource, a culturally rewarded status that was used to accrue subcultural capital and derive tangible benefits. Deliberately signaling one's gang affiliation, however, could also be a magnet for trouble. Even mentioning the name of one's gang on stage could be viewed as provocation by members of a rival set. Boss Bee described the negative reactions he sometimes received from rival gang members upon stating his affiliation with the Four Corner Hustlers during concerts: "When I rap and say Four Corner Hustler, I'm not dissing a GD or a Stone or a Vice Lord, I'm reppin' my mob. I'm just rapping what I am," he said. "But motherfuckers be like, 'That Four Corner Hustler is disrespecting us.' I'm not disrespecting you, cousin. But motherfuckers don't know how to differentiate." These varied interpretations resulted in problems for everyone involved in the gangsta-rap microscene, particularly those who were members of gangs.

One ramification of the overlap between street gangs and the gangsta-rap microscene was an ever-present threat of violence. Concerts featuring gangsta rap attracted scores of gang members, often from rival sets. Typically, this was not problematic; most gangsta-rap shows took place without incident. But the threat of violence was ever present. "I don't like inviting people to shows anymore," Joka said. "I don't want you to die on my time. 'Cause I know that this is a powder keg. I've seen it many times. That shit is out of control, man. If gangs were a brick of fuckin' firecrackers that went off one at a time, that whole brick is on fire right now."

Rap concerts that prominently featured members of a certain gang or People/Folk Nation alliance sometimes attracted rivals looking to cause trouble. Gang-related acts that promoted their live shows simultaneously announced the time and date when they could be found at a certain location. Gangsta-rap concerts held at venues located in a particular gang's territory were almost certain to be patronized by members of that gang. "They see a flyer online, 'Oh this is where the Ds live; we're gonna go fuck 'em up,'" 40 Thief explained. "They go to the club knowing that other motherfuckers gonna be there and they gonna do some shit. Shit's gonna pop off. They gonna have a couple of drinks and then somebody's gonna throw a punch."

Some Chicago venues enacted policies specifically designed to forbid gang members from entering or flaunting their gang affiliation. This included the prohibition of hats, bandanas, hoodies, baggy pants, sportswear, and other garb that might be associated with gangs. Those wearing such items when trying to enter the venue were told to leave them in their cars or be denied entry.[9] Promotional flyers for concerts would sometimes include these regulations: "No headgear, no jerseys," read one. Such prohibitions, however, were easy to circumvent through subtle uses of garb, such as the side of the body upon which an item of clothing was worn or the color of one's T-shirt. Small items such as jewelry or bandanas could be stuffed into a pocket and then donned inside the club. Moreover, venues dedicated primarily to gangsta-rap concerts seldom featured such policies, or did not enforce them strictly. Some venues required that all patrons be patted down or frisked for weapons before entering; others had no such regulations.

At concerts that were heavily attended by gang members, the combustible mixture of hard-hitting gangsta rap, drugs and alcohol, women, and rival gangs sometimes proved inflammatory. "That's what happens with the territory," said CapPeela when asked about the number of fights at gangsta-rap concerts. "Niggas get the iron [i.e., gun], niggas get hot, niggas get drunk or high, whatever the fuck they do. It could be anything. Gangs, colors, whatever." It wasn't just gang members who were affected by these dynamics, it was anyone in the club. According to Shoota,

> There's a lot of people that rap in general that are gangbangers. That might not be the best situation for a concert; people get up there onstage and start throwing their [hand signs] up and all that. You gotta expect people beefing and fights. You got a hat on, you look the part, let me check you. You could be chilling in the back, and shit'll pop off. You gotta be careful.

Additionally, at venues dedicated to gangsta rap, the weaker performance frames, the more evenly distributed balance of power, and the lack of structural barriers between audience and artist increased the likelihood of interactions between these groups. Concertgoers at an arena show would have a difficult time picking a fight with a performer. Backpacker venues were more likely to have raised stages and backstage areas that separated musicians and fans. At the semitraditional and non-traditional venues that tended to host gangsta-rap concerts, starting a fight with the performer was often as simple as walking across the room.

Fights at these events ranged from standoffs and verbal altercations to full-blown brawls involving dozens of patrons. The venues and their clients sometimes sustained serious damage. Sissero described it this way:

> You go to a show and you're afraid for your life; we have fights all the time. You definitely become very afraid, especially when things escalate. When we have shows and you're a rapper and you're in a certain gang, another gang is gonna come and they're gonna wanna show they're better than you, they're more macho than you, so they're gonna start a fight. You look at them crazy and you're in another gang, they're gonna come at you, they're gonna fight you. You have to be really careful who you hang out with, who you're standing with. I've seen guns being pulled out, people being shot at.

Sissero's comment about guns was no exaggeration. Fights at gangsta-rap concerts sometimes escalated to more serious violence, including shootings. For example, just after midnight on December 5, 2012, four men were shot during a gangsta-rap concert held at the Ultra Lounge, a Logan Square nightclub. According to reports, the incident took place after two men began fighting and one pulled a gun. Eight to ten shots were reportedly fired inside the club. A firearm was later recovered, but no arrests were made and the crime went unsolved (Nickeas 2012). "When you bring out talent from all over the city, you bring out crowds from all over the city and you bring out enemies from all over the city," said Jay Thompson, who was spinning records at the event under his stage moniker DJ JT Da Don. It was the third shooting at a rap-related event Thompson had witnessed that week. "It's so common in certain neighborhoods," he told a reporter. "Certain crowds, certain communities, nobody's blinking an eye" (Ziezulewicz and Morris 2012). Bo Deal, a gangsta rapper who was performing onstage at the Ultra Lounge when the shooting occurred, later posted on his Facebook account, "It's crazy that niggas can't go out and have a good time without gun violence in my city!!" The rapper told a reporter, "You get used to it, which is not a good thing" (ibid.).

During the research for this book, authorities shut down some of the host nightclubs due to gang-related violence; other venues stopped booking gangsta-rap acts because they attracted too many gang members. According to Doctor Who, the relative scarcity of rap concerts in some parts of Chicago was due to the prevalence of gangs in those neighborhoods. "They don't have a lot of shows out South because there's a lot of gangbangers," he said. Whytenoiz, a South Side rapper, agreed. "A lot of clubs won't do hip-hop shows out this way. They're concerned about having a problem. They see hip-hop as bringing gangbangers in the place." Phillip Morris, the backpacker who sometimes performed at gangsta-rap shows, described the impact of violence and gang-related activity at concerts, and how it hindered progress for everyone.

> There's a lot of knuckleheads that don't know how to act when they're out at a spot, don't know how to respect a venue, and end up getting events shut down because of ignorance. I wish people were a little more conscious about how they act, and realize that an event might be small in their mind, but it could be helping to perpetuate hip-hop in the city. And it gets shut down because they're throwing gang signs or hit somebody in the head with a bottle. There was a freaking gunfight outside of [the nightclub] Exedus last year. There was mad paddywagons everywhere, and that brings a lot of unnecessary heat and negative attention, not only to the spot, but to hip-hop as well. I think that's one of the main problems that's plaguing Chicago hip-hop.

Violence at concerts was a nuisance for rap-music fans and artists who had no affiliation with gangs. "I've done a show and a fight kicked off and it had to do with the whole rap and gangbanging bullshit," Six Gun recalled. "I wasn't in the fight, but my fans were there; it scares away my people." Likewise, backpackers generally kept their distance from gangsta concerts, which further cemented divisions between the two microscenes. According to ReeVerse, the violence that occurred at gangsta concerts was the primary reason that backpackers stayed away.

At gangsta shows you gonna have gangstas, and gangstas are gonna start fights. Backpack rappers don't like that. We went to this club the other night, and we thought it was [rap music], but they changed it to rock because there were so many fights in there. They were telling people who were coming in, "It's rock [music] all night," and they were like, "Thank God!" 'Cause they didn't want all these gangsta rappers coming in there and starting a fight and acting a fool. A lot of backpack rappers in Chicago don't want to intermix because they're going out to have a good time, do their raps, spread their message and whatnot. So that's why it doesn't get intermixed so much. The backpackers don't want us there because they know that we roll with these kinds of people and some shit might happen.

The lack of interaction between the backpacker and gangsta-rap micro-scenes made it more difficult to create and maintain a thriving underground rap scene in Chicago. According to Lynx, "It's hard to build a big scene without both of those groups of people." The divide between backpackers and gangstas placed limitations on everyone trying to launch a career in Chicago's rap underground. For gang members who rapped, however, career opportunities were far more restricted. In the following chapter, I examine the career limitations for rapping gang members and the strategies they enacted to mitigate the risk of gang-related violence.

5

Capital Punishment

Crime and Risk Management in the Rap Game

The waiting room at Cook County Jail isn't a fun place to kill time. You can't bring anything with you, and the only entertainment is a rack of tattered romance novels and worn-out children's books slumped in the corner. We're sitting in Division Ten, the jail's maximum-security wing. One of the floors of the division is on lockdown today, and the prisoners housed there will not be allowed to receive visitors. Unfortunately, there's no way to know this in advance, so a steady stream of wives, girlfriends, parents, friends, and children are turned away and told to come back next week. There are few events in life more wrenching than watching a wide-eyed child being told that he will not be visiting his father in jail today. Tears and protests fly to no avail.

I'm sitting on a hard stone bench next to Bleek and Boss Bee, waiting. We've been here for nearly an hour before a staff member finally summons us. We walk through a metal detector and are patted down and frisked for the third time since our arrival. We walk down a narrow hallway and take an elevator to the third floor. We follow another hallway, which leads to a locked door with a small window. An electronic latch makes a loud click and the door opens. We go inside and wait. After about five minutes, Habit walks in, looking surprised and happy to see us.

He's dressed in a standard issue, beige jail uniform. His hair is cropped short, and he looks thinner and more muscular than I've seen him in a while. I can tell he's been working out. Visitation at Cook County isn't like you see in the movies, with both parties whispering intimately into phone receivers as they stare through a glass partition. The partition is there, but no phones, only a small speaker located at the bottom of the window. You have to lean down and shout through the speaker, while the person on the other side of the glass cups their ear to listen. There are five or six people on either side of you, also leaning and shouting, making it nearly impossible to hear.

Habit is in high spirits today, almost giddy. We take turns trying to talk to him. With all the noise, we can't discuss anything in depth, so we mostly yell short sentences back and forth. Habit asks how school is going; I ask how he's being treated in jail. After about twenty minutes, our time is up and Habit is escorted from the room. As he turns to leave, he throws a quick hand signal to a fellow inmate, a code of some sort. "See that, he's always on the hustle," Bleek says with a laugh.

We make our way back down the stairs and outside, passing another guard at the gate. We pile into Boss Bee's car and hit the road. "Habit needed that," Bleek tells me. "He needed to go back in to get that hunger back. We're prison artists, that's where we got our inspiration, that's where we got our drive."

I note that Habit seemed to be upbeat, all things considered.

"That's 'cause he knows what he's facing, and he knows what he's already been through," Boss Bee says.

I didn't hear about Habit's arrest until it was posted online. Someone wrote, "Free Habit" as part of a longer bulletin post. I sent the poster a private message and he responded with the news that Habit had been locked up. I immediately called Bleek to get the scoop.

Habit was arrested in the spring of 2008. He was pulled over by the police, who found two ounces of marijuana in the car, a felony. Habit, whom I'd never seen smoke pot, had been dealing it on the side to make a few bucks. With his previous convictions taken into account, Habit was facing four years in state prison. He was housed in Cook County Jail's maximum-security wing, awaiting trial. Bomb First, the group Habit formed after leaving Xcons, folded in the wake of his arrest. Habit was the main thrust of the group, and without him running the show, the entire endeavor instantly collapsed.

I located Habit's prisoner information online and sent him $150 through Western Union. I debated whether or not to bail him out of jail while he awaited trial, but couldn't afford it. Instead, I e-mailed his mother and offered to write to the judge on Habit's behalf. She responded with the necessary information, and I penned a letter and mailed it to the judge handling Habit's case. Apparently, it helped. Habit's sentence was reduced from four years to two. With the two-year sentence automatically cut in half, and given a day's credit for every day he stayed out of trouble, Habit would serve just six months. With time credited, he would be free in six weeks. It was a cause for celebration and probably helped explain his upbeat mood the day we visited.

That Habit, his friends, and family were thrilled that he would serve "only" six months in jail illustrates the different worlds inhabited by the backpackers and gangsta rappers in Chicago's rap underground. Most backpackers would be horrified at the thought of spending one minute in jail or prison, but for Habit this status served as subcultural capital, a certification of authenticity in a culture where claims to street "realness" were valued commodities. It also gave him a renewed sense of purpose and direction. Bleek and Boss Bee insisted that serving half a year in jail was the best thing that could have happened to Habit. "When you get down to jail, when you get in that cell, you have enough time to get inside yourself and really get a peace of mind," Boss Bee said. Jail would give Habit the opportunity to work on his music, virtually uninterrupted. In jail, Habit could dream.

Career Limitations

The fierce competition in Chicago's rap underground—the "crabs in a bucket" milieu described by so many MCs—created a winner-take-all environment that was fraught with competition and rivalry. Adding gangs to this already combustible atmosphere merely exacerbated tension between various groups. The number of gang members involved in Chicago's gangsta-rap microscene, the inflammatory "dis" tracks and music videos posted online, and the heavy presence of rival gangs at concerts created a volatile microscene fraught with enmity. "There's too much drama," a rapper named Conyazo said. "People focus on trying to be king of this, king of that, they trying to be better than everybody else. That's one problem with Chicago. You got underground rappers battling with underground rappers, killing each other off. We ain't never get anywhere. We killing each other out here."

Gang membership is problematic for any number of reasons, including exposure to arrest, delinquency, and violence. Criminologist Mike Tapia (2011) found that delinquency rates are significantly higher for gang members, and that merely being in a gang heightens the chances of arrest. Moreover, joining a gang increases the odds that one will become the victim of violence, including serious crimes such as aggravated assault and robbery, often by members of the same gang or rival organizations (Taylor 2008).

Most Chicago gangs operate in small slices of territory, often just a block or two, sometimes within a single building or residence (Venkatesh 2008). Large Chicago gangs, such as the Gangster Disciples and the Latin Kings, partition into smaller, hyperlocal branches, known as chapters or sections, which are easier to mobilize. "The primary unit in Chicago's gang organization is the turf-based branch, named after the street corner where the local homeboys hang out. As soon as a branch grows too large to accommodate the face-to-face intimacies that are the highly prized and defining quality of gang life, it subdivides into more manageable units, typically no more than 50 'heads'" (Conquergood 1994, 32). This resulted in a sprawling metropolitan area with a patchwork distribution of rival gangs and Nations that sometimes changed on a block-by-block basis.

Gang members who rapped and who traveled throughout the city to perform, record, promote, or network had to continuously assess prospective threats from other gang members. This was achieved through a dialectic of coded exchanges: symbolic gestures such as the flash of a hand sign, the slight tilt of one's hat, knowing a gang's "secret" handshake, wearing certain colors, or linguistic cues such as a particular gang's greeting. Gang researcher Robert Garot (2010) referred to this communicative ritual as "hitting up," and asserted, "On inner-city streets in the contemporary United States, demanding of another, 'Where you from' is the clearest, firmest way to distinguish oneself as a gang member, as one who is willing to stand up for one's gang and take whatever risks might arise from such an affiliation" (69–70). Failure to comprehend the symbolic cues of hitting up could result in misunderstandings, physical harm, and possibly even death. According to Sissero,

> You can't wear your hat to the right, and then somebody else is wearing their shit to the left. They're gonna fuckin' knock your ass out, just for the way you're wearing your hat, just for the way you got one pant leg up and not the other one. 'Are you Folks? Are you People? What gang are you?' The gangs here are serious. They'll kill you over colors; they'll kill you over looking at them the wrong way; they'll kill you for driving in a big car and just looking suspicious.

Ikon, a member of the Gangster Disciples who rapped, concurred, warning, "We still bang on colors. You better not wear that shit over here with your hat rolled the wrong way. We'll smack you. We'll twist your fuckin' head off, nigga. It's real."

Nene, a rapper who lived in Humboldt Park, was especially careful walking through his neighborhood, which was located on a border controlled by two rival gangs, the Black Disciples and the Latin Kings. "You step on Sacramento [Boulevard], that's the line. BDs on one side, Kings on another. You gotta watch your back all the time. Click clack pow! Motherfucker, you dead. That's how it is. Motherfuckers get shot for a penny on the street."

Hippo, a member of the Spanish Cobras who lived in a gang-occupied area, restricted his movements to early morning, when he felt secure enough to travel through his neighborhood unarmed. On most days he walked to a bandmate's house, where their group recorded in a basement studio. Returning home at night, he said, always seemed treacherous:

> Every day I go to the studio early in the morning, because I don't even feel safe where I live. That's how dangerous it is. I come out here and sit in this man's house all day, just to feel safe. Like man, Joe, we just going to the studio! And in the daytime I feel safe when I ain't got a gun. But right now when I leave out of here, I ain't strapped, so I don't know what's going to happen. It's a chance just walking in the dark in Chicago. That's how dangerous it is. People are dying everywhere, especially when you got do-rags and you wear braids and you look Latino. 'Cause some other Latinos or some black dudes come along and just air your ass out, leave you flat on the floor.

Walking was dangerous, but traveling by car did not guarantee safety. Joka cautioned members of his gang to maintain a distrustful viewpoint whenever leaving the house, and to be prudent when hit up by gang members in cars. "I train my crew to be defensive in this city, have their eyes open and be aware of anything. Because the creep is everywhere. Watch out for the war wagons. You'll see dudes roll up, look in your car just to see what's what."

Furthermore, violence was not restricted to turmoil between rival gangs; altercations sometimes occurred within gangs as well. "The game's changed so much," Black Soldier lamented:

Now there's no leadership, no respect for each other, everybody's vying for position. They beef with each other, everybody ratting on each other. Everybody thinks they're John Gotti. They're taking all this shit literal. So now you got thirty different 'hoods with thirty different motherfuckers thinking they're John Gotti. And it's nothing. It's a bunch of dummies killing each other in a circle. And that's falling into the rap world. That's part of our shit now.

In addition to exposure to violence, gang membership limited the interactions participants had with musicians and fans from rival gangs. This reduced opportunities for networking, collaboration, and building an audience, all vital to career advancement in Chicago's rap underground. "On the North Side we have the Kings, we have the Cobras, the Maniacs, the OAs. All on this one side," Flamethrowa said. "There's so many different gangs, and gang members don't get along. They don't chill, they don't hang out, that doesn't happen. So if you're in one gang and you're rapping, and I'm in another, we're not gonna interact with each other."

Gang-related rivalries restricted the regions of the city in which a rapper from a particular gang could carry out rap-related activities. Those who could travel securely in their own neighborhoods sometimes had problems as soon as they ventured outside these safety zones. "You have a lot of artists who are stuck to their area because of the music and their affiliation that they campaign with their music," Chopper explained. "If you have a record label that's pretty much put together by one organization, they tend to maybe not socialize or network with other organizations on the other side."

PLA added that rival gangs refused to perform at the same concerts due to the potential for violence. "As far as gangs in the music scene, people have their cliques," he said. "There's groups that can only do shows here or there, 'cause people from different sides can't really do shows with each other. There's fights and stuff. So that kind of slows people down; you can't do it to the fullest." These de facto regulations placed severe limitations on the career potential of the participants. According to Racket,

Let's say you're in this certain gang and you're a hot-ass rapper. People want you in their clubs, but you rep your [gang] so much that you can't go into a certain 'hood and perform. So you lose that whole crowd right there. The gangs are so real here that they want you to perform at club X. You walk in, pop, you get shot. Or you like, 'No I can't go into that 'hood.' What the fuck? You're a artist. How the fuck are you gonna tell somebody that's paying you that you can't go into that 'hood? You think people wanna market you? You think people wanna put millions of dollars behind you? How you gonna make your money selling CDs when you can't cross that border right there?

Many club owners didn't want to deal with the headaches related to a venue full of gang members. They either booked backpacker acts or refused to hire rappers altogether. Artists or groups that were known to be affiliated with gangs, or that attracted large numbers of gang members to their concerts had a harder time securing gigs. "You put a bad rep out there and that's gonna stick with you forever," Stackhouse said.

The atmosphere of arbitrary violence that pervaded Chicago's gangsta-rap microscene resulted in a sense of despair for some rappers who were members of gangs. There was an aura of hopelessness and unpredictability; many participants told me that they felt powerless to stop whatever hand fate might deal them. They seemed almost resigned to the consequences of their chosen lifestyles. "Niggas losing their families, whether it's being in prison or getting popped," Grafta said. "But war is war. Soldiers get killed in war. When it's your day, it's your day. But I don't even think about that, really. I try not to, at least. Could it happen? Yeah, of course. It could happen to me. My day could come tomorrow." Shank added, "You could be here today, and you could be gone tomorrow. You don't know how you gonna go out, you don't know what's gonna happen."

Sociologist Alexander Riley (2005) suggested that these "tragic narratives" are standard motifs in corporate gangsta rap. He examined themes of suffering and fate in the lyrics of Jay-Z, Tupac, and 50 Cent and linked them to a literary history of dramatic tragedies:

We can see similarities between the way in which these [rappers] position themselves and the position of tragic dramatic characters like Hamlet. Such characters are in possession of dreadful knowledge that others lack, and they recognize that this knowledge will ultimately prove fatal. Yet they accept that fact and proceed in action with that knowledge, essentially recognizing that there is no solution that can avoid the terms of the field of play and choosing affirmation rather than rejection of the hand they have been dealt. (305)

From this perspective, the sense of fait accompli described by Chicago's gangsta rappers exemplified their appropriation of mediated gangsta-rap culture. Tupac prophesied "death around the corner" in his lyrics and interviews, and the Chicago gangstas assumed this philosophy in the same manner that they emulated Tupac's baggy jeans and tattoos. The degree to which the Chicago gangstas (or Tupac, for that matter) were imitating the tropes of commercial gangsta rap is debatable, but the consequences of adopting a tragic outlook were unaltered. This aura of unpredictability and impending doom, the belief that they could become the victims of violence or that their lives could end at any moment, led some gang members to pursue their musical ambitions by any means necessary.

Criminal Activity

The overlap between street gangs and Chicago's gangsta-rap microscene led to difficulties related to crime and its intrinsic risks. Following Eazy-E's rap-hustler blueprint, many rapping gang members resorted to criminal activity to support their rap ambitions. In previous eras young rebels might have committed low-level offenses like shoplifting or vandalism; today, they sold drugs (Venkatesh 2008). Selling drugs was illegal, but it was also profitable and readily available to those willing to assume the risks. The unyielding demand for illegal narcotics has rendered drug dealing the cornerstone of underground economies in large inner-city neighborhoods throughout the country (Anderson 1999). Adding to the appeal was the drug dealer's outlaw status, glamorized in the media, including the corporate tier of the rap music industry. Riley (2005) noted that the lyrics of celebrity gangstas such as Jay-Z and 50 Cent equated authenticity with criminal behavior, including "such morally complex actions as the selling of drugs as a way out of poverty with the full knowledge that this necessarily involves the ruining of the lives of those addicted to those drugs and with full acceptance of the great personal risk (possible prison or death) involved in such activity" (309). Furthermore, Elijah Anderson asserted that gangsta rap promoted an "oppositional culture" that encouraged young black males from poor inner-city communities to enter the narcotics trade: "Nowhere is this situation better highlighted than in the connection between drugs and violence, as young men involved in the drug trade often apply the ideology glorified in rap music to the problem of making a living and survival in what has become an oppositional if not an outlaw culture" (1999, 107).

Most of those at the intersection of street gangs and Chicago's gangsta-rap microscene believed that illicit activities were the quickest and easiest means by which to support their rap careers. With low levels of education, lack of work experience, and in many cases criminal records, they had few legitimate employment opportunities, even in the low-wage service sector. According to Habit:

> There's a thousand ways to make money, we just tapping into 'em right now. We *have* to do some dirt; there's no other option for us. If rap don't happen, we can't have a decent life for us and our family. If rap don't happen, then it's penitentiary chances that we takin'. That's all that's left for us. 'Cause ain't no McDonald's and Burger Kings and White Castles and Kentucky Fried Chicken, there's none of them jobs for us. We can't get a job because everybody scared that we gonna rob them or shoot them. So if this shit don't happen right now, then it's gonna be a big ass problem.

I asked one rapping gang member, who dealt narcotics to fund his music aspirations, if he thought his lifestyle was risky. "Yeah, of course it is," he nodded. "Very much risky. Hell yeah. But it is what it is. It doesn't stop me, bro. I'm on a mission." Limited employment opportunities and an atmosphere of violence, combined with their risky lifestyles and sense of despair, resulted in enormous pressure to succeed at music as quickly as possible. "You can get popped, you can get locked up," insisted Hippo, a Spanish Cobra. "Time is running out. Time is precious. You gotta do something *now!*" Boss Bee, who dealt drugs to fund his rap ambitions, explained:

> I haven't found a investor; I haven't found nobody to support what I'm doing [musically]. So whatever I gotta do to get that support is justified. If I gotta get in the streets to try to back me, I'm gonna do that. If somebody right now was like, 'We got the money to

back you, we gonna put you in the studio,' fuck selling drugs in the streets and shit. But I haven't run across anyone that was willing to do that. This is my only shot.

By committing crimes to fund their music careers, gang members who rapped played a high-risk game that could—and sometimes did—lead to arrest and incarceration. Habit spent six months in jail after being caught with drugs; Rayzor dealt crack to support his rap career and landed in prison. Others were on probation or parole, which limited their ability to build careers in music. At the time of our interview, Zone Two was on house arrest that resulted from an altercation with police during a traffic stop. He sported an electronic ankle monitor that allowed the Cook County sheriff's office to track and restrict his movements. This eliminated his ability to perform in concert, network, or partake in anything related to music other than recording tracks in his home studio.

Shank claimed that he had been picked up by the police dozens of times for petty crimes. "I got locked up for weed or for just being on the block," he said. "Misdemeanors. Standing in front of somewhere you're not supposed to, chilling, gangbanging. One time I got stopped, I had twenty [one-gram] bags of weed on me." Shank alleviated the risks of drug dealing by carrying only small quantities of marijuana. At the time, Illinois law stated that possession of less than thirty grams of marijuana was a misdemeanor, rather than a felony. To avoid felony charges, Shank never carried more than thirty grams at one time. "I won't even carry twenty-five [grams]," he said. "Just because [the police] would be like, 'Oh, that's thirty.'"

There were a number of backpackers in Chicago who also dealt narcotics to fund their rap aspirations. To my knowledge, none were ever arrested for these crimes, and I did not meet a single backpacker who told me that he or she had ever served time. Thus, the risks associated with criminal activities were far greater for the gangsta rappers in this study, lower in social class than the backpackers and mostly black or Latino males. The criminal justice system's blatant targeting of this very demographic meant that gangsta rappers who committed crimes to fund their music aspirations were more likely to be stopped by police, arrested, charged with crimes, tried, and convicted (Alexander 2010). Those convicted by the courts faced stiffer penalties, including long stints of incarceration that put their music careers on hold. Indeed, the immense rise of the U.S. prison population since the 1970s is largely "attributed to sentencing disparities that put African Americans and Latinos in prison for drug crimes at higher rates than whites" (Wakefield and Uggen 2010, 392). The risks of drug dealing and other crimes also included being injured or even killed. Rayzor, who lived in the Cabrini Green housing project, was shot three times after his crack-dealing gang attempted to take over the selling rights to a neighboring building:

> I was big time drug dealing at Cabrini. Our clique was gonna take over another building; a lotta guys don't like that. This is how they eat and put food on the table for they shorties. But I mean it's like at the same time, you have to do the same thing. So as we moved into another building, we had static. People are not willing to give up they building like that. So of course there's gonna be gunplay. Shit is like that. That's how the streets are.

Even small-time narcotics dealers sometimes encountered high levels of violence. "You can get murdered quick, dog," said Hymnal, the Bully Boyz rapper who was shot twice. "Open your door, try to sell somebody some weed, get shot in the head. I done seen that happen. I done seen boys get lit up on avenues. Choppers. Hittin' 'em. Foul. Dirt."

Some believed that outcomes such as these were inevitable for gangsta rappers who were also members of street gangs. Their risky lifestyles and violent reputations made getting shot or locked up unavoidable. According to Gumbo,

> It's only so long you can do illegal shit before you get caught up. I don't care how good you think you are. It's a numbers game. The more time that go by, the more dudes know about you, the more haters there are, somebody gonna say something, some shit gonna happen, you gonna get locked up. So real hustlers, real Gs, go legal at some point and get a legal hustle.

Most of the gang members who rapped believed that they would get a legal hustle and make it in the music industry before becoming ensnared in the criminal justice system. But the clock was ticking, according to Bleek. "It's easier to go back in prison than it is to stay out. Every day that goes on, my chances of going back is getting greater and greater." Boss

Bee, who served five years in prison before taking a shot at the music industry, tried not to ponder a return to the penitentiary. "I know I'm taking these chances, but I don't think about going to jail," he said. "Could I see myself back in jail? Of course I could, me doing the things I do. 'Cause I know me, and I know my temper. If that day came around, I'm conditioned already. It's nothing. If it was to come to ten, twenty, thirty, forty, fifty years, I'm conditioned to do that. But I can't see myself in jail before I see myself at the top of the rap game."

The overlap between street gangs and Chicago's gangsta-rap microscene created serious risks for those at the intersection of these two worlds. Gang-related violence, rivalries between artists, fights and shootings at shows, clubs being shut down due to gang-related activity, restricted movements due to gang-marked territories, and the ongoing threat of arrest and imprisonment restricted career opportunities for gang members who participated in the gangsta-rap microscene. Moreover, as the murder of Lil JoJo demonstrated, the consequences of this relationship were not confined to quaint notions of career "limitations." Commingling within these two worlds was a fate-tempting strategy that sometimes resulted in death.

Risk-Management Strategies

Those who reside in neighborhoods with high rates of crime and violence often develop risk-management strategies to avoid victimization. A study of at-risk or delinquent black youths living in high-crime areas of Saint Louis found that risk-management strategies included "staying within the boundaries of their own neighborhoods [and] avoiding activities that might lead to retaliatory violence" (Cobbina, Miller, and Brunson 2008, 692). When these young people traveled to other neighborhoods, they employed tactics such as compliant body language, not speaking to others, traveling collectively, or carrying weapons.

One of the more interesting trends to emerge in recent research on gangs is Robert Garot's (2010) work on the selective, performative use of gang identity. While gang identity is sometimes viewed as fixed, Garot discovered that gang members invoked and concealed gang identity in differing situations. Similar practices were reported by Cobbina, Miller, and Brunson (2008): When the young men in their study adopted subservient body language, they downplayed gang identity; when they flashed weapons or traveled with fellow gang members, they displayed it. Both sets of behaviors served as risk-avoidance tactics. Garot also detailed strategies employed by gang members to evade physical fights when directly confronted by adversaries, including backing down, complimenting the would-be attackers, or asking authority figures to intervene. Garot concluded that

these tactics are much more common than many depictions of inner-city life might lead us to believe, and many young people take pride in their ability to draw on them as a resource in their everyday lives. Hence, despite claims that the facework of inner-city young men is routinely and manifestly violent, this analysis shows that the efforts of such young people to avoid violence are often quite subtle, creative, and mature. (2010, 142)

The hazards associated with gang membership resulted in the creation of risk-management strategies by the Chicago rappers who were gang members, designed to curtail the potential for violence and other dangers. As found in previous studies of street gangs, gang members who rapped stuck to their own neighborhoods when possible and avoided situations that might lead to retaliatory violence. Participating in Chicago's gangsta-rap microscene, however, often meant traveling to various parts of the city and engaging with members of rival gangs. When doing so, rappers who were gang members sometimes also adopted subservient, docile body language, avoided speaking to others, traveled collectively, and carried weapons. I detail below a range of additional risk-management strategies that were used by the participants in this study. These tactics—as clever and mature as those described by Garot—did not eliminate risk, but were designed to reduce or minimize it. Not every rapper used all strategies. Some used only one or two; others used more. No rapper employed every strategy simultaneously, which would be impossible because some tactics conflicted with others. Furthermore, the strategies were used in different contexts by different rappers, and successful tactics were employed more often than those deemed less meritorious. These techniques illustrated how gang-member status was used strategically and selectively in the participants' efforts to further their music-industry aspirations.

1. One risk-management strategy was achieved through the calculated use of gang-related clothing, especially during live performances. Concerts

held at nightclubs were fraught with the potential for gang-related violence because the acts appearing onstage could not directly control who attended the events. Gang members who rapped and wanted to advance their careers by networking and collaborating with microscene peers could do so with relative safety in recording studios and similarly "closed" locations. Traveling to and from these locations entailed some risk, but the spaces themselves were largely secure. By contrast, rival gang members frequently attended concerts, sometimes specifically looking for trouble. Managing the risk inherent in public performance settings was imperative.

Rappers who were members of gangs were selective in how they displayed gang membership while performing. This was contextually dependent; the rappers adjusted their clothing to fit the neighborhood in which the venue was located, which often drew patrons from the area who were affiliated with gangs in those locales. For example, when performing at the Capitol Club, Bully Boyz and their crew members, who were located both onstage and in the audience, sported mostly brown and gold. This display of IOA membership served as a show of force that declared the performance to be an IOA event. This reduced the potential for violence because members of rival gangs at a club filled with IOAs were going to have their work cut out for them if they wanted to start trouble.

By contrast, when Bully Boyz performed at the VIP Room, they downplayed their membership in the IOAs; the band members and their entourage wore almost no brown and gold that night. The group anticipated the heavy presence of other gangs in the audience that night, and prepared for this by adjusting their clothing to suit the setting. Phantastic's between-song banter that night—"No disrespect to nobody, but we sure the hell gonna rep the fuck out the A"—signified deference to members of other gangs.

2. The presence of an entourage consisting of gang members on stage or in the performing area served as another risk-management strategy. Having a posse on hand ensured greater safety for the performer at concerts, where there were often rival gangs present. The visual effect of the gang gathered together and performing was itself a disincentive for adversaries to start trouble. Furthermore, even in venues with weak performance frames there was some power differential between performer and audience. Having gang members present in the performance area tilted the power, however slightly, in favor of the rapper and his crew. This reduced

the possibility that rival gangs would start trouble, and also made interaction between these groups at least modestly more difficult. Were the entourage members amassed in the audience, rather than the performing area, the potential for gang-related interaction would be increased.

3. Another risk-management strategy, deployed in recording studios and during concerts, was achieved through discursive practices that emphasized the collective qualities of gang members. While some members of the gangsta-rap microscene invoked or stated the name of their gang on recorded songs, at concerts many of these same rappers referred to gangs collectively. Rather than shouting out their gang's name, rappers would employ terminology that emphasized the collective. For example, Phantastic's on-stage dedication of a song to "all my gangbanging-ass niggas" signified the mutual identity and collective characteristics of gang members. Smokestack, a member of the Gangster Disciples, told me that the group didn't claim GD in its music because "Everyone knows at this point that we GDs. That's why we really don't have to put as much emphasis on it. People know where we from. We just making it more broader. We're trying to make everyone a part of it, every set." This emphasis on the collective had the potential to reduce violence through consensus building.

4. Another risk-management strategy was to separate gang membership and rapping to the greatest possible extent. This tactic was employed physically, musically, and rhetorically.[1] Physically, this meant that when a rapper engaged in music-related practices, he subsumed his identity as a gang member and foregrounded his identity as an MC. This technique involved, for example, keeping the members of his gang physically separated from the spaces related to rap music, such as recording studios and nightclubs. For some, this strategy involved participating in rap music in locations that were removed from their neighborhood of residence, where most of their gang-related activities took place. This limited the potential for violence in the rap-music settings via sheer lack of proximity, and enabled the rapper to work with others without the burdens related to gang membership. According to Platinum,

> I was a straight banger, Chicago, South Side representative. I went to over fifty funerals. I was used to hearing gun shots. I was accustomed to that lifestyle and I didn't see no way out of it. I thought I was gonna be dead or locked up. And I accepted it. Now, I live outside the city, but I do my [music] business inside the

city. I do as much as I can to stay focused and be out here as much as I can.

This tactic was also employed musically; some gang members declined to rap about gang life or demonstrate affiliation to their gang in any meaningful way on stage. In doing so, they downplayed their gang affiliation and emphasized their identities as rap musicians. This did not necessarily mean distancing themselves entirely from the gang, but downplaying gang membership or making gang references less overt. "You can't stop your lifestyle and the people who are in your lifestyle. All you can do is control it a little more and make it look different," CapPeela said. "So basically what you're doing is you're holding up one of those signs and it's blurry as fuck, but if you shake your head you can see it. People know what we are, they know who are we, they can hear it through the music, but it's more of a clean feel. So it's basically like camouflage."

Some of those who employed this strategy linked it to authenticity. Real gangstas, they asserted, would never dare to rap openly about their criminal exploits, lest they draw the attention of the authorities.[2] Rapping about one's gang-related exploits was framed as a form of "dry snitching"—indirectly revealing the gang's secrets to authority figures and other gangs. Joka rapped about Chicago gangs in general terms, but offered no lyrical specifics about his gang, its criminal pursuits, or cultural practices. He had been arrested a few times, but refused to detail his own criminal history on wax. Instead, his songs warned of the dangers of gangs and attempted to steer young people away from gangs and gang-related activity. According to Joka,

> It's about playing the game; it's about having game. It's about understanding, seeing, being observant, being smart about it—not just being reckless. Reckless is not gangsta to me. To me, dry snitching on yourself is not cool. That's just buffoonery. People are telling on themselves on the records, talking about their hustle and really breaking it down. You're ratting yourself out, you're screaming these gang names. These cops will use this against you in a court of law.

This distancing technique was also employed rhetorically. By stating outright that rap and gangs were separate, the rappers created psychosocial

distance between these two identities. Dustup proclaimed that, "We trying to get away from gangbanging and get more into our music. I take
this more serious than gangbanging. Gangbanging don't got anything to
do with the music. There's music, there's gangbanging. Gangbanging's
not gonna be out of our lives, but we ain't gonna be into it like we were
into it when we were young."

5. Another risk-management strategy was to make the gangsta-rap microscene a sort of no-fly zone, where violence and gang-related rivalries
were off limits. When MCs participated in rap music and its related practices, gang affiliation was set aside and a temporary truce was called. This
tactic curtailed the potential for violence by allowing rappers from adversarial gangs to work together without hostility. Chopper insisted, "We'll
collaborate with whoever. If you rap raw and you ain't gangbanging at me
in the studio, let's do this. I don't care if you a King or opposition, I don't
care what colors you wear in your 'hood. The money's green."

6. While some rap groups featured only members of a specific gang,
another risk-management strategy was to recruit members from other
gangs from different neighborhoods and form a single rap group. For example, Bully Boyz, which was based in Logan Square and populated primarily by members of the Insane Orchestra Albany, also featured members of the Gangster Disciples from the South Side of Chicago. This
strategy reduced potential violence between IOAs and GDs, and also allowed Bully Boyz to travel to the South Side more safely.

Others actively recruited members of rival gangs. This tactic alleviated risk by decreasing the odds that adversarial gang members who did
not participate in the gangsta-rap microscene would act violently towards members of the rap group. The technique also improved the odds
for networking. Xcons, which was composed of members from seven different street gangs, utilized this strategy both in and out of prison. According to sometime Xcons member Trilogy:

> We have members of damn near every organization. When we
> come together, or when we wanna network, it's nothing. We can
> send [a member of the same gang] to go holla at them. I can talk
> to them, he can go talk to them. They lookin' at him like, "Well
> he gonna help him make it." They lookin' at me like I'm gonna
> help him make it. If somebody in my organization say "Man,
> that's all you do is hang out with them," okay, that's what we

doing. If I make it, you know you straight. So they respect what we're doing.

7. Some gang members who rapped were careful not to insult other gangs in their songs, another risk-management strategy. This tactic decreased the potential for violence because rival gangs would not get offended and feel the need to retaliate. "I write raps for all type of mobs," Shoota explained. "That's why I would never get on a track [and dis other gangs] or disrespect a mob." This policy extended to music videos as well. For example, one night, shortly after videotaping a concert and posting the footage online, I received an e-mail from Deckstarr, a rapper who had performed that night. He explained that in the video footage, a gang member—who was not a rapper, but part of the group's entourage—could be seen throwing down the pitchfork hand sign as an insult to members of a rival gang. Deckstarr asked me to edit the clip and repost it with the offending footage removed. He explained:

> That guy was throwing down the pitchfork 'cause they hate Maniac Latin Disciples, but more than just the Maniacs run under the pitchfork and I'd hate to be associated with that on YouTube. The last thing I need is to be performing somewhere and someone says 'I saw you in a video with a nigga dropping forks.' It's a question of safety, sorry.

Some rappers took this strategy one step further and offered verbal praise to rival gangs in their songs and music videos. "I keep it respectful," Trilogy told me. "I'm not trying to dis no other organization. You may hear me say one line where I'm reppin' my organization and then the next bar I'm reppin' my nigga's organization."

8. Those who did insult rival gangs in their songs would sometimes get a member of that same gang to do the insulting, another strategy designed to minimize risk. This tactic reduced the potential for between-gang violence and supposedly decreased the threat of retaliation.

9. Another risk-management strategy was to maintain a sense of perspective when being disrespected by a rival gang. Using this technique, retaliation for a verbal slight might result in an oral retort, but not a physical one. When he and Xcons were embroiled in the online feud with Bully Boyz, Habit told me that "we can only take it to a certain level." The

tactic worked—the two groups waged a musical and symbolically violent battle that did not result in physical aggression. Garot (2010) noted that "Skills for avoiding fighting in such circumstances involve substantial personal discipline in managing one's emotions and redefining the situation so that it is possible to live with one's face/identity, even as the moment may have transformed it" (119).

10. Another risk-management strategy was to change musical styles to something other than hard-core gangsta rap. This alleviated risk by distancing the artist from the music and audiences associated with the subgenre. A group called Urban Wasteland began as a gangsta-rap act, but found that the number of gang members attending their concerts and the related violence and other problems made it increasingly difficult to book live shows. After some consideration, the group decided to change its musical style in hopes of attracting a different audience and securing more concert bookings. "This year we switching it up, cutting all that gangbanging stuff," group member Stackhouse told me. "You ain't got to gangbang to be 'hood. So we do hip-hop, R&B, we do lovey dovey. We're not trying to provoke anybody to be violent."

11. Changes in musical style were sometimes accompanied by other alterations. Groups whose reputations became damaged due to their association with gangs sometimes changed their band names. In doing so they hoped to attract fewer gang members to their concerts, reduce violence, and improve their chances of success.

12. A final risk-management strategy was to extract oneself from the gang lifestyle and use rap as a justification for doing so.[3] This technique enabled rappers to remove themselves from gang-related violence and criminal activity without losing face. Quitting a gang outright is a taboo that, in some instances, can be met with violence or death (Pih et al. 2008), but most street gangs have "easily transcended codes of loyalty and informal rather than formal roles for members" (Klein 2004, 59). Pursuing a career in rap music gave participants a legitimate reason to serve at the periphery of the gang and be less involved in its day-to-day activities. "Now that I've been away from gangbanging for a while, I can really focus and get right on the music scene by going legit and still hustling," Zone Two told me. "It's still the same game; now instead of flipping dope, I'm flipping music." By framing his rap pursuits in the same language used to describe gang-related criminal activity, Zone Two legitimized his distancing behavior. He was still a hustler, he was still in the game, he was

still flipping product, but now his hustle was legal. The gang, he said, respected and supported the decision. Others told me that their gangs had policies that allowed for such behaviors; members who were trying to do something positive with their lives were not required to be involved in the gang's day-to-day activities.

The media-fueled image of gangs is that youth who join them are committed to lifelong membership. Numerous studies, however, refute this myth.[4] Gang membership is typically transient and short lived, generally lasting between one and four years; as gang members get older, they tend to age out of gangs. For Chicago's gang members who rapped, this was no different. As they matured, got older, and began to take on adult responsibilities, they generally reduced their commitment to the gang or quit altogether. This process typically did not occur overnight, but was gradual. As gang scholar James Howell (2007) noted, "youths can dissolve their gang membership by reversing the process by which they joined, by gradually disassociating with other members" (44). Fathering children, in particular, seemed to serve as a turning point that spurred a transition out of the gang.

Economic studies of drug-dealing street gangs report that members of these organizations who traffic at the street level earn approximately minimum wage (Levitt and Venkatesh 2000). A recent study of youth gang membership suggested that these low earnings provided little economic incentive to remain in a gang. "This might explain why youth in our sample who reported joining a gang to make money were more apt to leave the gang after one wave, as these youth likely turned from their gang when they learned that it could not fulfill their monetary needs and/or desires" (Melde, Diem, and Drake 2012, 494). This finding, combined with a celebrity culture that makes it look easy to become famous, may have made rap music appear to be a more lucrative career move.

Crucially, however, even if they had distanced themselves from gangs, the claim to gang member status remained a resource for those aspiring to build careers in the music industry. Even those members who had distanced themselves from gangs were quick to remind me—and others—of their affiliation. "I'm always gonna be a Four," said Boss Bee, referring to the Four Corner Hustlers. "No matter if I drop my flags or not." This aligned with the findings of scholars who report that gang involvement assumes myriad forms, including peripheral members who still claim the gang's name but have reduced involvement in gang-related criminal exploits. "A number of young men claimed to be involved in a gang but said they did not need to 'prove themselves' by becoming involved in dangerous activities" (Garot 2010, 106).

This transitional process was already under way for most of the rapping gang members I met in Chicago. Although many were involved with street gangs when I first encountered them, their participation in the day-to-day activities of gangs diminished during the course of my fieldwork. All of them viewed rap as a way out of gangs and poverty. A better life, they insisted, was on the horizon.

A Day in the Park

It's a perfect afternoon in Humboldt Park, one of those summer days that make you temporarily forget Chicago's long, cruel winters. The scent of roast lechón and arroz con gandules mixes with freshly cut grass, and a steadily growing crowd amasses in front of a sprawling outdoor stage, pitching umbrellas and lounging on blankets. The people always come out en masse for the Puerto Rican Festival, an annual weeklong celebration of Boricua pride.

The first familiar face I see is Bleek's. With Habit still locked up in Cook County Jail and everyone else busy with other pursuits, Xcons is down to two members, Bleek and Boss Bee. As we survey the audience, which looks to be at least a couple thousand strong, I ask Bleek if he gets nervous playing to a crowd this size. He shakes his head. "Naw. In prison we did shows every day. We went through artist development in there. So I never get stage fright. The more people that are there in the crowd, the better I am. I feed off the energy."

Today's show marks the first time Xcons and Bully Boyz will share a bill since before the clash broke out between the two groups more than a year ago. The animosity between them seems to have dissipated, as evidenced by Bleek's recent mixtape, which includes a guest appearance from none other than Shank. More than a mere song, the track symbolizes a truce between two once-warring camps. I tell Bleek that I was shocked upon hearing the sonic cease-fire. He laughs. "That song shocked a *lot* of people. But they don't understand. They been online hearing things. We could walk inside of a club and Bully Boyz'll be in there, and people will think there's about to be a fight or we gonna start shooting or something."

True to form, Bleek's mixtape is packed wall-to-wall with hard-hitting gangsta rap and violent street themes, but Bleek's life has taken a turn with the recent birth of Bleek Jr., who's also on hand today. Bleek is every inch the proud father, showing off his son, who looks a lot like his old man, right down to the diamond earring sparkling from his right lobe. "Are you happy?" Bleek asks, tickling the boy, who squeals with delight. Bleek Jr. is a charmer, just like his dad.

Shank is next to arrive, greeting Bleek with a one-armed hug. There are dozens of acts slated to appear today, each only getting to play two songs before turning the mic over to the next in line. Bleek has asked Shank to join Xcons onstage to debut their new song. This I have to see.

A nondescript rapper wraps up his set to mild applause, but the crowd perks up as the emcee announces Xcons: "Let's keep it going; let's get everybody involved. Give it up for Xcons y'all." Bleek and Boss Bee take the stage, with Bleek greeting the masses: "Yeah, what up? How y'all doin'? Humboldt Park, let me hear y'all make some noise! Xcons is in the building." The crowd cheers. "We gonna get right into this," Boss Bee tells the audience. "They got us on a time schedule."

Bleek and Boss Bee hammer out a track from Bleek's new mixtape. Underground gangsta-rap music is a lot less effective in a park on a summer day. The subgenre all but demands the milieu of a sweaty, packed nightclub to be truly effective. The atmosphere in the park this afternoon is more like a company picnic.

In part this is due to the festival's family-friendly vibe, which includes a strict no-swearing policy for all performers. That's a bit tough for Xcons, whose outlaw anthems feature wall-to-wall cursing. Boss Bee lets a couple of "motherfuckers" slip, and the emcee shoots the musicians a look of warning. Shank watches from the side of the stage, ready to join the pair for song number two. A couple of "motherfuckers" later and the emcee pulls the plug on Xcons, the music coming to a quick demise. Looks like the Shank-Xcons summit won't be taking place today.

A chorus of booing emanates from the audience.

"Hey, it's not me," the emcee retorts defensively. "Can't have the swearing up here, I just can't do it. That's my man right there. [He points to Bleek.] That's my dude for real. I'm not even trying to hate on him; I just can't have it. Trust me, y'all, it ain't me."

Hymnal, Chilly, and Grafta arrive about an hour later. We stand backstage and wait for Bully Boyz to go on. They look a little anxious, an emotional state I don't generally associate with these guys. The nerves are not without good reason. Today marks the group's first major appearance on stage since Phantastic's passing. They're still working on the second album, honing and perfecting tracks in the studio with Grafta at the helm. The new album, they assure me, is going to cement their legacy once and for all.

After a few more acts, the emcee announces the group's arrival: "All right cha'll. This next group, you already know about them. They been rockin' it a long time. They need no introduction, so let me bring 'em to the stage. Put your hands together for Bully Boyz."

Bully Boyz saunter to the stage, and the audience springs to life. This is home turf for the Boyz and their supporters are out in full effect. For once, it's not gang members or clubgoers on hand, but wives, girlfriends, grandparents, and children. The group is all smiles, and no one is sporting brown, gold, or orange today. Hymnal's wearing jeans shorts, for heaven's sake!

"What's good baby, who know about Bully Boyz in this motherfucker?" Hymnal asks the crowd with a cocky grin. The emcee immediately dashes onstage and warns, "No cursing, no cursing!"

"They don't want us to curse, and that's makin' me feel like cursing," Chilly retorts with a cackle.

"We bringing Logan Square to Humboldt Park!" Shank announces to applause from the crowd. "This is for Phantastic. R.I.P. Phantastic."

True to form, Bully Boyz has somehow finagled twice as much stage time as the other acts, four songs instead of two. They start with "Clock Dollers," a Phantastic-era number that the group had performed several times in concert just before he passed. Chilly raps new lyrics over Phantastic's verses, flouting the no-cursing policy with glee. Beside him, Hymnal sports a backwards White Sox baseball cap, its bill cocked jauntily to the right. He throws the IOA gang sign a couple of times. Even in jeans shorts, Hymnal's a gangsta.

Bully Boyz try out some new material from the forthcoming album, performing it live for the first time. I haven't heard these songs before, and notice a decided change in direction. The music is as hard hitting as ever, but the lyrics no longer detail the minutiae of gritty gang life, dodging bullets and serving drug fiends. The new songs are all about money.

Obsessed with it, in fact. Making money, getting money, spending money. The lyrics are rife with terms like swag, balling, Hugh Hefner, pesos, dough, green, and cheddar. But it's good to see the band onstage again, and the crowd eats it up. As their set closes, everyone in the audience is on their feet, and the group departs the stage to a thunderous ovation. Phantastic would have loved a moment like this.

"That was one of the hardest shows emotionally, like physically, everything," Shank tells me later. "We wanted to do it just to let people know, but we didn't want to do it 'cause it hurt us so much. We did it, though, and it was a success. Everybody was going crazy. It felt like the revival of Bully Boyz. 'Cause we go through so much shit. We keep going down, but we keep coming back up."

Rap Hustlers or Sucker MCs?

On January 17, 2013, Keith Cozart, better known by his stage moniker Chief Keef, stood before a Cook County judge, tears streaming down his cheeks. "I am a very good-hearted person," said the seventeen-year-old rapper, who added that he had two young daughters to support. "I am sorry for anything that I have done wrong. . . . Give me a chance" (Main 2013).

It was a bad time for the Chicago gangsta-rap sensation to wind up in court. His career had exploded in the months that passed since the gang-related slaying of his adversary, Lil JoJo. Cozart's major-label debut, *Finally Rich,* had been released a month earlier to acclaim. He had collaborated with some of the biggest names in the industry: 50 Cent, Rick Ross, Kanye West, and others. Tour dates were booked in the United States and abroad.

The court hearing stemmed from a video interview Cozart had given to the webzine *Pitchfork.tv* (Pitchfork Media 2012), which took place at a New York shooting range. Prosecutors contended that Cozart's firing a rifle in the *Pitchfork* video was a violation of his probation terms. Keef— who had two drug arrests on his record, including one for dealing heroin— was on probation for pointing a gun at a police officer in 2011. Cozart's lawyer argued that holding a rifle while conducting an interview was not criminal behavior, but a gangsta-rap marketing ploy. "It was a promotion, just like a movie," he told the judge.

Cozart was also reprimanded by the court for moving from Chicago's South Side to Northbrook, a wealthy suburban enclave located north of the city. Doing so without notifying the state was another infringement of his probation.

Prosecutors contended that Cozart's gangsta-rap song lyrics—in which the rapper boasted about the gun conviction, his taste for drugs, and his loyalty to the Black Disciples street gang—indicated a demonstrable lack of remorse. "People say whatever they want in a song," Cozart's attorney countered. "I'm sure that the Beatles said really goofy things in songs. It doesn't mean they were out there to commit a crime." Cozart's mother told a reporter from the *Chicago Tribune* that her son was "just rapping about what he lived next to" (Gorner 2013).

Cozart was sentenced to two months in a Cook County youth detention center. At the time of his conviction, he had the eighth-best-selling rap album in the country. Lil JoJo's unsolved murder remained under investigation.

Reward and Risk

Studies of culture often take place in a vacuum. Yet, as described in this book, people are members of overlapping entities, and identities and cultural practices are shaped and negotiated within a complex array of social forces. The microscenes perspective offers a more complete understanding of Chicago's underground rap music scene, whose gangsta-rap component contains a social reality divergent from its backpacker counterpart.

Considering the social and economic consequences of class-based division is critical to understanding the differences between these microscenes. Class-based divisions are found in many facets of social life, and they were replicated here, at the micro level. The class differences between backpackers and gangstas are significant but not sweeping. Yet even when the strata are relatively narrow, opportunities and outcomes diverge for different social classes.

At the corporate tier of the rap music industry, backpacker rap is less commercially viable than gangsta rap, which outsells its conscious counterpart by a wide margin. While those who opt for the less commercial backpacker music earn respect from their microscene peers for having artistic purity, the corporate music industry tends to focus its efforts on some derivative of gangsta rap. The chances of a backpacker act being signed to a major label are small, relative to commercial gangsta-rap artists. That said, the backpackers I met in Chicago had a wider array of career options. Some opted to become hobbyists or realists, who enjoyed making music but did not perceive rap to be their only means of obtaining upward mobility. If things didn't pan out with music, they could always fall back on day jobs, college, or even support from their parents. Those backpackers who doggedly pursued musical careers did not have to interact with members of the gangsta-rap microscene—and most did not. This reduced the backpackers' exposure to the types of risks regularly encountered by the gangstas. Even those backpackers who committed crimes to fund their musical ambitions encountered fewer career limitations than the gangsta rappers. While members of the gangsta-rap microscene were arrested, jailed, exposed to violence, and even killed, the backpackers encountered none of these hardships.

Backpackers also benefited from a system of local venues that favored the backpack subgenre, both structurally and technologically. Prestigious venues dedicated to live music were more likely to book backpacker rap. Venues principally devoted to backpacker rap tended to be centrally located in safer neighborhoods that were close to public transportation; this accessibility brought in larger crowds. Backpacker concerts were more likely to take place in traditional venues that were dedicated to live music. Raised stages, lighting and sound systems, seating directed toward the performance space, and other conventions created a stronger performance frame that increased the physical and symbolic distance between spectators and performers. As a result, audiences were more likely to acknowledge the performance, and less likely to perceive performers as approachable. Thus, relative to gangsta shows, backpacker-audience interactions were more likely to align with conventional performer-audience behaviors.

Commercial gangsta rap outsells backpacker music, and those who pursued this subgenre had a sound and image that was more appealing to the corporate tier of the rap industry. Gangsta rappers who were also members of gangs accrued some benefits from this dual status. Gang membership supplied social and economic capital, and gave gang members who rapped prestige and credibility in an industry where authenticity is paramount.

Overall, however, gangsta rappers had fewer career options than backpackers. Outside the microscene, the stigma attached to the gangsta persona, as well as its behavioral and performative requirements, made it difficult for gangstas to attend school or obtain traditional employment. With low levels of education and few prospects, the gang members viewed rap as their only legitimate ticket to achieving upward mobility. Some may argue that this denoted a refusal to explore other potential options or simply regurgitated "all or nothing" tropes from pop culture, but the consequences were unaltered—if things did not pan out with music, few had backup plans. This by itself made gangsta rap a riskier proposition.

Furthermore, gangsta rap was hindered by a system of local venues that favored the backpack subgenre, both structurally and technologically. Prestigious venues dedicated to live music were less likely to book gangsta rap. Venues principally devoted to gangsta rap were peripherally located in neighborhoods with higher crime rates that were further from public transportation. This reduced the number of attendees. Gangsta concerts were more likely to take place in semitraditional and nontraditional venues that were dedicated to activities other than live music. Audiences were freer to tune out or ignore performers, particularly attendees who were at the venue for other purposes. The lack of structural conventions such as raised stages resulted in weaker performance frames that reduced the physical and symbolic distance between spectators and performers. As a result, relative to backpack shows, audiences were more likely to perceive performers as approachable and to interact with them, including violent exchanges.

The atmosphere of the gangsta-rap microscene was charged with violence and other hazards. Gangsta concerts were the sites of fights and shootings, and served as a breeding ground for tensions between local gangs. The majority of gangsta rappers were not gang members, but their proximity to gang members exposed them to many of the related hazards. For gang members who rapped, prospects were reduced and risks were greater. Their inability to travel freely throughout the city limited opportunities to collaborate, network, and promote, all crucial to career building. Gang members who followed the rap-hustler blueprint and committed crimes to fuel their rap ambitions encountered the highest level of risk, including the potential for violence, arrest, incarceration, and even death. Gang membership complicated an already difficult struggle: trying to succeed in the music industry, despite the odds.

"Jus Lyke Compton"

Social reproduction theory posits that environment plays a key role in the generational propagation of social classes. The social environment of the backpackers and gangstas helped shape their identities and cultural practices, and influenced the opportunities available to the rappers and the choices made by them. Social class and environment, however, were not deterministic.

Not all backpackers were members of the middle or upper classes. A number of backpackers came from circumstances similar to those of the rapping gang members. Some even grew up and resided in the same neighborhoods. Many of these backpackers had high hopes for their prospects in the music industry, but did not follow the rap-hustler blue-print in trying to achieve their goals. Disciples of the American dream, they also believed in hard work, motivation, and personal effort but saw little value in becoming criminals. For example, Blaze grew up in the slums of Puerto Rico and saw plenty of trouble during his formative years. He now resided in a poor Chicago neighborhood, worked a low-wage day job, and pursued a rap career at night:

I grew up in the 'hoods in Puerto Rico. When you're six, seven, seeing your friends get shot, seeing your friends get stabbed, get beat up, it shocks you. Young bucks grow up today and they're like, "I wanna be a gangster when I grow up." There's no point in being a gangster. You turn a gangster, there's only two ways you're gonna end up. You're gonna end up being dead or locked up. You know what? None of 'em's good.

A backpacker named Reg had a similar story. He grew up in a gang-occupied community but saw no value in mixing gangs and rap music. Reg believed that his surroundings could be useful only in that they motivated him to get out:

These little knuckleheads over here, they wanna take it to another level. Why not just keep it into the music? Take all that frustration and that shit out in the music. Put that shit to use. Don't try to go out here and get on some bullshit and hurt a motherfucker. You can hurt a motherfucker with your words, believe that. A lot of artists don't make it under the gangbanging thing. A motherfuck-er will get slapped with one [prison] sentence that will fuck they whole life up. And a motherfucker probably would have made something of hisself.

Backpackers from the bottom rungs of the socioeconomic ladder insist-ed that rapping kept them away from the crime and gang-related activity in their environs. "Without hip-hop, I'd probably be in a really bad world right now," a backpacker named Jam One told me. "I grew up in a bad neighborhood—a lot of gangbangers, a lot of drug dealers, stuff like that. Hip hop kept me away from all of that." Others insisted that rap's great gift was that it provided such alternatives. "If you really wanna get into the old school of hip-hop and the history and all that, it wasn't brought for fighting, it was brought so cats wouldn't be killing, shooting, and fighting in the street, they could do it with words," a backpacker named Wondur said. Conversely, there were middle-class rappers in Chicago who became enamored with the rap-hustler blueprint and joined gangs. Phantastic hailed from a middle-class family and was raised in a strict, religious household. He started out as a backpack rapper. "He was never a hustler, he was never on the streets," an associate recalled. Enlisting in the gang-affiliated Bully Boyz and following the rap-hustler blueprint proved fatal for Phantastic. The young man thrilled with the gangsta lifestyle was ultimately consumed by it. As Mary Pattillo-McCoy (1999) wrote, "sometimes, when you dress like a gangsta, talk like a gangsta, and rap like a gangsta, soon enough you *are* a gangsta" (123).

The rap-hustler blueprint popularized by Eazy-E more than twenty-five years ago continues to resonate with today's rap musicians, aspiring or otherwise. The heavily publicized criminal exploits of celebrity gangstas such as Chief Keef, Rick Ross, and T.I. often overshadow whatever musical contributions they have to offer. If anything, the violent songs and music videos produced by these artists are vehicles for the reinforcement of their outlaw images. The music industry and media are complicit in this process, emphasizing the criminal backgrounds of gangsta rappers to boost sales. Gangsta rap's outlaw culture glorifies street crime and promotes risky behavior.

Identification and distinctiveness theories help explain how audiences can absorb these gangsta-rap fantasies and reproduce them in local settings. South Central gangsta rapper DJ Quik rapped about this phenomenon in his 1991 song "Jus Lyke Compton," where he described touring the United States only to discover that the gang-related attitudes and behaviors embedded in LA gangsta rap were being reenacted in cities such as Denver and Saint Louis. "Citing the gang signs and ubiquitous red and blue colors associated with Blood and Crip gang members seen at his various concerts, Quik reveals mixed emotions of pride and horror in his description of the multiple ways in which the California gang culture has been adapted and integrated in to the daily practices or locally meaningful experiences of audiences residing throughout the American heartland" (Forman 2002, 201). In the song, Quik decried these "wannabe" gangstas and chided them for watching too many Hollywood films, but the damage was already done.

Aspiring rappers no longer needed to visit Compton to experience gang culture; it was available right outside their front doors.

Notably, even the pioneering gangsta-rap artists of Los Angeles experienced this life-imitating-art phenomenon personally. Dan Charnas (2010) described an incident in which an associate of Dr. Dre and Eazy-E was shocked to find them preparing for an early tour by purchasing shotguns and pistols. Dre and Eazy "were solidly middle-class people. They had all grown up around gangs and guns—in South Central, that was the reality. But Dre, Eazy, and [Ice] Cube were turning that reality into theater, and now that theater was becoming real, too. *Of course* they were buying guns. Everywhere they went now, *real* gangsters were trying to test them" (222, emphasis in original).

Rap's obsession with authenticity is another culprit. While the early gangsta rappers in Los Angeles could get away with narrativizing their surroundings, the requirement that gangsta rappers be stamped-and-certified criminals seems to have increased. Tupac Shakur and The Notorious B.I.G. went to deadly extremes to prove that their criminal yarns were the real thing. Chief Keef may be on a similar path, nudged along by the various branches of the culture industry. Criminal records sell rap records, but nothing moves product quite like a dead legend.

Habit's entry into the world of hustling helps illustrate the process of assuming the gangsta persona. He started out as a backpacker, or hip-hopper as he called it. In time, however, Habit was drawn to gangsta rap because he believed it better reflected his surroundings.

> As a gangsta rapper or as a hardcore rapper, it always starts hip-hop for everybody. I started hip-hopper. And every rapper get to that point in they life where they gotta make a decision which way they gonna go. I was straddling the fence on that back in the day. One way was more dominant in my area than the other way. The gangsta shit was more relevant to people like me. It's based on real life in the worst possible circumstances. We are the underachievers. If you been through some shit, you'll *know* this is real rap, this is real-life shit.

Habit's description includes a sense of agency; Chicago's aspiring rappers did not perceive themselves to be pawns of larger societal structures, but as empowered actors making rational calculations. One such calculation was to assume the risks that went along with becoming a rap hustler. According to Habit, gangsta rap had greater commercial viability; he believed there was more money in becoming a gangsta. His working-class background and firsthand experience with gangs and prisons gave him the pedigree to follow the rap-hustler blueprint with credibility.

Forever Money

The rap-hustler blueprint held forth the promise that street smarts derived from criminal behavior, combined with the American-dream ideology of hard work and motivation, were a path to upward mobility. Were they successful at following this blueprint, gangstas could appropriate the dominant markers of elite status, upend existing hierarchies of social class, and give the finger to white America. Because the rap-hustler blueprint involved the symbolic representation of the so-called street, it demanded experience with economic struggle, gangs, crime, and the criminal justice system. Following the rap-hustler blueprint was a high-stakes gamble that offered great reward but required great risk.

The belief that they would be selling music instead of narcotics and filling concert halls rather than prison cells was ubiquitous for those at the intersection of Chicago's street gangs and its gangsta-rap microscene. Every rapping gang member I interviewed was convinced that music was his ticket to upward mobility. "Yeah, that's my ticket out the 'hood," Hymnal affirmed. "But I'm still gonna be in the 'hood. I'm fittin' to buy blocks in my 'hood. Buy a crib and shit like that."

Unlike the backpackers—who wanted to earn a living from music, but whose goals and aspirations were often relatively modest—the gang members who rapped dared to dream big. It was a dream that few, if any, of them were likely to achieve. This had nothing to do with their talent, motivation, ambition, or work ethic; it is that the odds were stacked against them. They dreamed big anyway.

In his study of social-class reproduction, Jay MacLeod ([1995] 2009) reported that members of the lower classes often have reduced career ambitions. For those at the bottom rungs of the socioeconomic ladder, MacLeod wrote, ambitions were tempered by realistic assessments of the chances of achieving upward mobility within a societal structure that limits opportunities for the poor at every turn. "A lower-class child growing up in an environment where success is rare is much less likely to develop strong ambitions than is a middle-class boy or girl growing up in a social world peopled by those who have 'made it' and where the connection between effort and reward is taken for granted" (15). In Chicago, however, the opposite phenomenon occurred; those with the objectively least chances of achieving success were those with the highest ambitions.

A question I asked everyone I interviewed was where they envisioned themselves in five years. The members of Xcons uniformly described a bright future, one that included wealth, status, and personal fulfillment. They would achieve this, they insisted, by following the rap-hustler blueprint. Through grinding, the world would be theirs:

HABIT: We see ourselves rich in the game, succeeding, being ambitious, taking bold business moves, and being artists. I see myself five years from now in the game making business power moves. That's where I see myself in five years—financially comfortable, in a beach chair. And that's guaranteed. You can mark my fuckin' words. There's no way we can't make it.

BLEEK: Five years? I see myself as a well-established artist and CEO in the music business, with a few businesses throughout the city—automotive, auto body, sounds, and a couple more business ventures that I'm looking into. I see myself in five years as a very well-established, successful, up-and-coming artist and businessman.

BOSS BEE: Filthy dirty by thirty. Rich. Rich. Just Xcons doing our thing at the top of the rap game. That's where I see myself, at the top.

The members of Bully Boyz predicted similar futures in five years' time:

GRAFTA: I see myself in a motherfuckin' office, signing these motherfuckin' checks. Really doing this shit for real, on a corporate level. Maybe six, seven years it might take me, but I don't see it like that. It could happen two months from now. But either way, if I don't make it in this business, I'm gonna make it doing something. Motherfuckers don't think I got a plan B, C, or D.

live years from now I see myself making a lot of money. That's all I see is money. I'm not gonna even lie to you. years from now all I see is happiness. No problems. Everybody eating right. Five years from now, I want to be eating, feeding, making sure that my kids got that money.

HYMNAL: In five years? Shit. Gone. I'll be gone from here. I'm gonna be in Disneyland. I'm gonna get money, live life, dog. But I'm gonna work hard as hell to live that lifestyle, I'm gonna have the bad car, bitches, jewelry. I'm gonna be a multimillion-aire. Money to burn. We call that forever dough, forever money. That's what we reaching for. You got forever money, my nigga, you living good. You living right, your kids are gonna live right, their kids are gonna live right. So when I'm gone, they got money to spend, college, anything they need. If they need to buy a house or they need to buy a car, they got that money. All because you did what you had to do for that. You went through them struggles so they don't have to do that. So in five years we gonna be livin' good. No more hustlin', you dig?

It is striking how the ambitions of the Xcons and Bully Boyz were framed using mainstream, middle-class measures of achievement. They did not envision themselves hustling in the streets, selling drugs, and committing crimes. Their desire was not to be Tony Montana, the cocaine kingpin from the movie *Scarface*. Quite the opposite. In their estimation, happiness and "living right" were indexed by markers that aligned with traditional capitalism and the American dream. They envisioned them-selves as CEOs, businessmen making power moves, owning side compa-nies, and holding investments. They saw themselves working in corpo-rate offices, signing checks. They wanted to send their children to college and purchase homes and cars. And yes, they wanted to be rich, wealthy beyond imagination. Forever money.

It is tempting to assert that, for all of the criticisms aimed at gangsta rap, its primary contribution to young, disenfranchised ethnic minority males may be its ability to provide hope to the hopeless. For the young men in Chicago who were gang members, dreams and optimism were central to their identities. "You know the crazy part? The audacity we have to still have the dream," Habit told me. "Guys I been knowing all my life are like, 'You're still rapping? What the fuck is that? Why aren't y'all gangbanging like you used to?' We dreaming right now. What the fuck is wrong with that?"

To paraphrase George Carlin, the problem with the American dream is that you have to be asleep to believe it. The unyielding faith that hard work leads to success and that failure is the result of laziness is problematic because it obscures the hegemonic structures that maintain existing socioeconomic inequalities. Positive symbols of nonwhite success, be they Barack Obama or Chief Keef, instill ethnic minorities with hope, but also sustain the falsehood that the playing ground is level. Buying into the myth that anyone can make it if they work hard turns a blind eye to the hegemonic structures that limit opportunities for the poor and maintain existing systems of power. In other words, buying into the American dream may make it more difficult to achieve.

False consciousness was the term Karl Marx used to describe how working-class people failed to see how the game was rigged in favor of powerful elites. Though they did not lack motivation, effort, or talent, Chicago's aspiring rap hustlers did not see how the game was rigged so that they would lose. The game was rigged by the music and media corporations, which cynically shilled racism and criminality in the sheep's clothing of empowerment. The game was rigged by the technology corporations, which promoted the myth that anyone who purchased expensive equipment could turn their home studio into a dream factory. The game was rigged by shoe and clothing manufacturers, who insisted that by sporting overpriced, brand-name products, poor rappers could—literally—walk in the rich man's shoes. The game was rigged by the branded rap moguls, who hawked so many products that they added up to a total lifestyle. And worst of all, the game was rigged by a criminal justice system that targeted young men who dressed, talked, and rapped like gangstas, filling court dockets and prisons with those who adhered most convincingly to the rap-hustler blueprint. What Chicago's rap hustlers did not see was the degree to which they were being hustled.

Epilogue

Six Years Later

I'm standing at the address Shank gave me on the phone earlier, in front of a nondescript brick warehouse in the southern end of Chicago's downtown Loop. It's early November 2012, and the icy winter air has arrived. I haven't seen or heard from anyone in Chicago's rap underground for a couple of years. This is largely because I finished gradaute school in 2010 and took a teaching job in the Middle East.

When I returned to Chicago a few days ago, I assumed that tracking down my former contacts would be easy, but none of the information I had amassed during my fieldwork was of any use. Phone calls went unanswered or were picked up by strangers; e-mails were unreturned or bounced back. MySpace and Facebook were ghost towns—no one used them anymore, nor had anyone seemingly logged in to their accounts for months. Twitter was the new virtual home for the rappers in Chicago, and after numerous attempts, I was able to get a hold of Shank through Twitter.

I found Xcons on Twitter, too. To my surprise, Habit had given up on music entirely. He spent about a year working on a new dream, to become a mixed martial arts fighter. He trained for months and even had a few fights. But he lost more bouts than he won, and gave up that dream, too. No one had heard from him in a while.

Bleek was still in the rap game, grinding hard as ever. He'd released a couple of new mixtapes and continued to perform live on a regular basis. He'd also moved into video directing, and seemed to have a good side business making music videos for local gangsta-rap artists. He assured me via Twitter that we would catch up soon.

Boss Bee's story was a heartbreaker. In early 2012, he was caught in possession of a quantity of narcotics sufficient to justify felony charges, and was currently serving a six-year sentence in the Illinois prison system. Now in his early thirties, Boss Bee's chances of succeeding in the youth-centric rap-music industry were forever diminished. I found his prison mug shot online, and the pain and ferocity in his stare were devastating. I hoped to pay him a visit the next time I was in town.

As I stand, shivering in the cold and waiting for Shank to arrive, I think about all that had changed in a few short years. I feel utterly removed from Chicago's gangsta-rap underground, back to square one. Things are certainly different in my life. I now have a PhD from a prestigious university, and have spent the last two years teaching and conducting research in the Middle East. I've traveled extensively, journeying to Lebanon, Iraq, India, and China. Just before leaving Chicago in 2010, I got married and now have a son due in a few months. I feel older and significantly more mature, transformed by my experiences abroad. My once-brown hair is now a shock of salt and pepper, and there are a few more lines on my face. I wonder what it will be like to reconnect with Bully Boyz, Xcons, and everyone else I met during the years when I was a plucky graduate student, hitting the rap-music clubs night after night. Gaining access to this group wasn't easy in the first place, and now we couldn't be more different. But I still have incredible fondness for these guys. I think about them often, listen to their music regularly, and although none have achieved fame or recognition, I still want good things for them.

It is fascinating and frustrating to me that Chicago's hard-core gangsta-rap music has exploded, with artists like Chief Keef, Lil Reese, and Lil Durk inking major-label record deals, touring the world, and garnering international press and acclaim. Those young upstarts are finishing what "my" guys started, which strikes me as both cruel and unfair, a bad joke played by a music industry with no sense of humor.

After about forty-five minutes, Shank finally rolls by in a black SUV, honking and waving with a huge, familiar smile. I can't wait to see him.

Shank parks around back, and ushers me inside a few minutes later with a warm hug. He's the first to arrive, and we go upstairs and sit down in Bully Boyz's recording studio. Shank hasn't changed much. He's the same guy I remember from six years ago, and he remains youthful and boisterous. The main difference seems to be that his once-elaborate braids are now shorn into a military buzz. After a few minutes of small talk, Shank plays me a bunch of newly recorded tracks and updates me on the continuing saga of Bully Boyz.

To my surprise, the group has changed its name to The Almighty Dollar. Shank tells me that the Bully Boyz moniker gained a bad reputation in the gangsta-rap microscene, permanently associated with gangs, crime, and violence. "The Bully Boyz name started getting tarnished," he explains. "People wouldn't book shows because they would say the crowd we would bring was too rowdy and crazy. And people just keep thinking about gangbanging. The Almighty Dollar was a clean name, a clean slate, a fresh start."

I understand, but I'm still astonished that Bully Boyz would change its name under any circumstances. It's a moniker I so completely associate with everyone in the group, a name tattooed on Shank's forearm in huge black script. But he has a new tattoo now, a huge Almighty Dollar logo in equally bold lettering. "It's always gonna be Bully Boyz, 'cause it's Bully Boyz 'til we die," Shank proclaims. "Bully Boyz is a way of life, and that's what we created. That life is never gonna die."

Why the name change then? "'Cause we was banging, and now we getting money."

I'm skeptical that the group is earning much from music, but I get the point. Shank is one of the lucky ones. "I should be a felon," he says. "I should be locked up. Doing all the stuff, the people I was with, the things that I've done, the things that I've seen. But I dodged all that. I made the right choices every time that I did. And I'm the one here still." Others have not fared so well. Several of the original Bully Boyz members have gone astray. CapPeela and Ikon have vanished. "They just got lost in life," Shank says. "I don't know what happened. They just disappeared, bro. I guess that West Side life just got to them or something." Nfamous is facing hard time in prison. "He kind of drifted off on his own," Shank explains. "He got mixed with the wrong crowd."

The most surprising change in membership, however, is the departure of Grafta, the band's longtime producer and leader, who founded the group with Shank when they were high-school students with million-dollar dreams. Grafta has gone straight, and no longer makes music on a regular basis. Married with two young children, he works a nine-to-five job at a suburban real-estate corporation. "I push keys," Grafta once crowed, referring to his recording studio. Today, he spends his weekends coaching his daughters' little-league team. His departure was not acrimonious, according to Shank:

> He's more of a businessman now. And I say that respectfully. He's got a family, he owns buildings, he works, he's a real-estate agent. He does everything. The man is a man of a lot of crafts. But he's

not into the music like before, where he was more forced being into the music because he was the boss—he had to run shit. But right now he's just chilling, doing his thing. He's living life, he's a grown-up. He's got responsibilities now. Us, we're still hungry so we're here.

I ask Shank how he thinks things might be different today had Phantastic not died just as Bully Boyz's career was ascending. "Man, I think we would have been rich already," Shank says with a heavy sigh. "Honestly, I'm not gonna even lie to you. I don't think we'd still be sitting right here talking about this. We'd be somewhere in LA. But he passed, and it was a big piece taken away from the puzzle. You were there for that era of me and Phantastic and Hymnal. What we made together is crazy. I felt like we gave the city something so great that they didn't even acknowledge to how it should have been."

Like me, Shank is surprised that Chicago-style gangsta rap is suddenly all the rage in the corporate music industry. He shares some of my frustration over this turn of events, too: "You know, Geoff, that kind of tweaks me out a little bit. If you think about it, all of that shit that they was so rowdy about is the music that's selling now. And we were doing that but people didn't understand. They just didn't give it a chance. I don't understand how I'm not a signed artist. I don't understand how I'm not touring the world right now."

There don't appear to be any world tours on the horizon for The Almighty Dollar. Once a stalwart on the gangsta-rap microscene, the group is now ensconced in the studio, honing tracks for various future releases and filming music videos that they upload to YouTube. The much-anticipated follow-up to their 2006 debut remains unreleased, and they haven't performed live in Chicago for months. "It's not like before," Shank admits. "We making a lot of music and trying to build a super catalog, so when we do do what we do, it'll be a lot easier. So we haven't done shows as much or stuff like that. We've just been filming videos and making music and building relationships."

Hymnal strolls into the studio about an hour into my conversation with Shank. Nineteen years old when I met him, Hymnal is now twenty-five. He's filled out a bit and looks like a grown man instead of the acne-scarred teenager of yesteryear. Back then Hymnal was brash and cocky to a fault, impulsive and quick to anger. I ask Hymnal how he's changed since 2006. "I've just matured more," he says. "I understand the streets better. I understand life a little better than I did when I was eighteen, nineteen. I still got a temper, but I'm more calmed down than what I used to be. I *think* now. Before, I just react. And I seen how reacting without thinking, people ended up in fucked-up situations. So I learned from other people's mistakes. When you get to that point, you don't do the same shit."

I ask Hymnal if he still hangs out with members of the IOAs. "I still see some of the guys, but I'm older," he says. "When I was younger, I used to be like, 'I'll sacrifice myself for this neighborhood.' 'Cause you're young. But now, there's a generation that's newer. I see them and they do the same thing that we were doing."

I point out that Chief Keef seems to garner as much attention for his affiliation with the Black Disciples as he does his music. If anything, the Chicago rap sensation plays up his gang association in his songs and music videos. "Those dudes are seventeen, not twenty-nine," Shank responds. "I'm not seventeen no more. They're young, they're obnoxious. They're doing what we did. So his life and what he's seen, he's representing that. And he's not gangbanging, obviously, he's making music. You can see him traveling, making money. So that part is dead; he's just talking about it."

Shank and Hymnal insist that the gang life is dead to them, too, that they've made the transition from gangbangers to artists. According to Shank, this is all part of getting older. "When I was seventeen or eighteen or nineteen, I was gangbanging—on the songs, everything. I'm not doing that no more. I'm not in the streets like before. I'm in the studio trying to make something of this. Everybody understands what I'm doing now is positive, so I don't have to do the same shit I used to do or be around the same people I used to be around. I'm not saying that I'm retired because I'm not, but I left gangbanging alone by making music."

Shank also attributes this change to his musical ambitions and the birth of his three children.

I have goals. See, when you're young, your mentality isn't the same as when you have something that you wanna do. When you're young, you're just thinking everybody's doing it, I'm doing it too. Fuck it. I'm living for right now. When you get older, you can't live that life no more. I have to be a role model, I can't just be

gangbanging. I have three kids, and I'm thinking of them. Once
I had a responsibility and I had to show a character to another
person who's gonna want to be just like me, there's no way that I
can be out there gangbanging and throwing up gang signs. 'Cause
if they see that then they're gonna be that theirselves. And I'm just
recreating the same circle over and over. So basically fuck that life.
That part of me is dead.

Hymnal nods in agreement. As with Shank, the birth of his son three
years ago changed everything. The only thing that mattered now was
music. Hymnal wasn't the multimillionaire that he predicted he'd be at
this point, but his faith in the American-dream ideology had not wavered
in the slightest. "We just got, not to say tired, but we just older now. We're
grown," he says. "If you want to do something, you gotta do it. And we
doing it. The work ethic is getting harder and harder—we're working
harder than ever. That's good. Hard work pays off."
I wonder if this causes any problems with the IOAs who are still active, if they have a problem with Shank and Hymnal's distancing themselves from the gang. Shank shakes his head:

This is how I look at it. If guys say like, "Hey, why aren't you
gangbanging?" this is what I say: When I was gangbanging,
I didn't complain about who wasn't gangbanging. When I was
sleeping in the streets, in them vans, and doing whatever I was
doing, I didn't complain about the next person who wasn't there.
For the simple fact that I didn't care about that. I was doing what
I had to do, whenever I had to do it. So for you to sit there and
look at me and say why isn't he gangbanging, then you're not
doing what you should be doing. Because now you're watching
me. But what I love about my brothers is they don't knock me for
doing positive. People are allowed to retire. Don't get me wrong. I
love the streets. I ain't never gonna not love the streets. But there
comes a time in life when you got to change shit and do it the
right way.

For Shank and Hymnal, doing it the right way means grinding, putting their energy into music instead of gangbanging. The most effective
risk-management strategy for gang members who rap is to use rap music

as a justification to exit the gang and leave the life of crime. For all the criticisms of gangsta rap, it was valuable for these two young men. It may very well have saved their lives. It got them out of the gang without losing face, and it continues to give them a sense of hope that they may not have had otherwise. Obtaining freedom from gangs is easier than achieving upward mobility, of course, but it's a step in the right direction. Long may they grind.

Notes

Introduction

1. The term "hip-hop" is generally defined as a culture encompassing rap music (whose lyrics are performed by rappers or MCs), breakdancing, DJ-ing, and graffiti art. The term is contested and used differently by scholars, journalists, musicians, and fans. To avoid confusion and because this book examines rap music, I avoid use of the term "hip-hop," unless quoting an author or research participant or specifically indexing hip-hop culture, rather than rap music.

2. The gangs referred to throughout this book are institutionalized street gangs, which differ from, for example, loosely affiliated rebellious adolescent groups or highly structured organized crime outfits. An institutionalized street gang is an established street gang that "persists despite changes in leadership, has an organization complex enough to sustain multiple roles of its members, can adapt to changing environments without dissolving, fulfills some needs of its community, and organizes a distinct outlook of its members" (Hagedorn and Rauch 2007, 452).

3. The reason for the disparity in these figures is that gang membership is fluid and often short-lived.

4. Harrison (2009) uses the term "underground hip hop" to denote "literate, middle-class, bohemian" rap music (the focus of his study). He distinguishes this from "thug rap," which I term "gangsta rap," denoting rap music whose themes include violence, misogyny, drug and alcohol use, and anti-social behavior. The term "underground," when used in the context of rap music, typically refers to rap music or rap-music scenes that are not connected to the major music corporations. (Harrison uses the term "independent" as a proxy for this concept.) Because there are three tiers to Chicago's rap music scene, only two of which exist independently from the major music corporations, I use the term "underground" to denote the bottom of these three tiers, which consists of aspiring musicians who do not earn a living wage from music.

5. These depictions are not unique to Chicago, though they were perceived to be. I would venture that most musicians describe their local music scenes using similar terms. When I was working as a music journalist in the Kansas

City area, local musicians portrayed their music scenes as crabs-in-a-bucket Hatervilles, too.

6. A comprehensive review of the scenes literature is provided by Bennett (2004). *Music Scenes: Local, Translocal, and Virtual* (Bennett and Peterson 2004) is an edited volume that contains thirteen case studies of music scenes.

7. Harrison used the word "unprecedented" to describe underground rap music's "capacity to blur distinctions between musicians and fans" (2009, 39). Morgan noted that the call-and-response of rappers and audience members at Project Blowed "became an echo chamber that reverberated back on itself until the artist became the audience and vice versa. This was especially true for whoever was on the mic. People were not there just to enjoy and to listen; they also came to evaluate and to play a part in building their culture" (2009, 10–11).

8. Sociologist Wendy Griswold (2012) defined a cultural object as "a socially meaningful expression that is audible, visible, or tangible or that can be articulated. A cultural object, moreover, tells a story, and that story may be sung, told, set in stone, enacted, or painted on the body" (12). In this book, references to cultural objects primarily index cultural forms or practices related to the musical output of the Chicago rappers: songs, song titles, lyrics, albums, album titles, CD artwork, merchandise, promotional items, music videos, and live performances.

9. Throughout this book, I use the contested term "backpack" to index the myriad derivations of socially conscious, progressive, and political rap that have coexisted alongside—and in opposition to—the gangsta subgenre. My use of the term is an aesthetic choice. Socially conscious rap predates the term backpack. Likewise, there has always been some form of so-called street rap, although "gangsta rap" did not become part of the hip-hop lexicon until the late 1980s. The term "backpacker" derives from "graffiti writers who kept all their cans and nozzles in backpacks" (Morgan 2009, 207), although the term is used by Chicago rappers (and in this book) to denote any member of the backpack microscene.

10. A symbolic boundary is a socially constructed barrier that differentiates various groups of people. Cerulo (1997) notes that boundaries "create distinctions, establish hierarchies, and renegotiate rules of inclusion" (394–95). Boundaries "generate feelings of similarity and group membership. They are an essential medium through which people acquire status and monopolize resources" (Lamont and Molnar 2002, 168).

11. Scholars of rap music have spent a good deal of energy parsing out the various subsets of the genre. For example, ethnomusicologist William E. Smith (2005) situated his ethnographic case study of a Washington, D.C., rapper with a brief discussion of genre that illustrates the differences between backpackers and gangstas. Early "old school" rap music, Smith wrote, was divided into three categories: party rap, conscious rap, and gangsta rap. Current rap music consists of

two categories: "pop hip hop" (including gangsta rap) and underground/conscious rap. Smith defined pop hip-hop music as being primarily concerned with "cars, clothes, sex, and violence, whereas the underground styles of conscious rap . . . deal with more substantive issues such as black history, community and personal development, literature, and current events" (2–3). Sociologist Jennifer Lena (2004) unearthed no less than thirteen subgenres of rap music in her content analysis of rap songs that charted in *Billboard Magazine* from 1979 to 1995: crossover, parody, rock, booty, pimp, don, jazz, new jack swing, race, G funk, dirty South, gangsta rap from the east and west coasts. Viewed on a continuum, with backpack rap at one end and gangsta at the other, all varieties of rap music fall somewhere between these polarized extremes.

This dichotomous view of rap music was shared by many of the musicians I interviewed in Chicago. "I just really break it down into two categories," a rapper named Jae Lee said when I asked him to describe how he categorized the various subgenres of rap music. "There's rap, there's hip-hop. Hip hop is like real, from the heart that everybody in the world can relate to. And then there's rap, which is like money, cars, clothes, females, jewels and gangsta things."

Like many others I interviewed, Jae Lee used the terms "hip-hop" and "rap" to distinguish backpacker and gangsta rap. Gangsta rap was also described using terms such as "hardcore," "street," "gritty," "trap music," and "commercial," while backpacker rap was described as "underground," "conscious," "abstract," "lyrical," and "progressive." Some backpackers believed that only a backpacker could be considered an "MC," while they described gangstas using what they considered to be the more negative term, "rappers." (I use the terms interchangeably throughout the book and do not make this distinction.) In addition to making personal judgments as to which rapper in this book belonged to what category (based on the eight characteristics described in this chapter), I also listened to the opinions of others and asked rappers to which of these two broad categories they would assign themselves. Some rappers were quick to align themselves with either backpackers or gangstas; others were reluctant to categorize themselves at all. The latter response generally came from rappers who believed that they had been miscategorized as a backpacker or gangsta by others, and/or did not appreciate the inherently restrictive nature of the label. I also asked about this indirectly in interviews. For example, I asked subjects to describe how they categorize the various subgenres of rap music, which ones they liked and disliked, and why.

12. A content analysis of songs from rap albums that sold at least one million copies from 1992 to 2000 found violent themes in 65 percent of them (Kubrin 2005; see also Adams and Fuller 2006; Armstrong 2001). A handful of scholars (Cross 2003; Perry 2008; Quinn 2005) have defended—sometimes grudgingly—gangsta rap's ability to shed light on the social problems encountered by inner-city youth, including poverty, crumbling infrastructures, gang-related violence,

disenfranchisement, and police harassment. "Gangsta rap, amid its numerous negative overtones, has many positive attributes, including the fact that it presents the real crisis of inner-city living from the inside out, offering an intimate portrayal of the failure of many social service and governmental aid programs and bringing to the forefront the persistent problems of police brutality, racial profiling, and a broken legal system" (Price 2006, 61). Others (Alim 2006; Neff 2009; Smitherman 1997) have positioned gangsta rap as part of a historical legacy of African-diasporic linguistic, performative, and communicative practices. Still others (Hagedorn 2008, 107) have placed gangsta rap within a history of ethnic music that includes the Mexican *corrido* folk songs of the 1800s, which celebrated rebellious *banditos* (see Morales 2003), and the indigenous *milo* music created in Sierra Leone circa the late 1940s by *rarray boys*, who were described as "pimps, pickpockets and petty criminals" (Abdullah 2002, 23).

13. In a 2003 interview, Rock stated that the idea for the routine came from the Ice Cube song "Us," which critiqued the black community for apathy, jealousy, materialism, and antisocial behavior. "I stole more from Ice Cube than from any artist," Rock said (Edwards 2003, 96).

14. This point bears emphasis, because I have been asked repeatedly, "What about rapper X?" who does not fit neatly into either category. No rapper does. The backpacker and gangsta categories are polarized ideal types that serve as analytical tools.

15. There were also divisions—and thus symbolic boundaries drawn—within these groups. Many gangstas estimated that only a small percentage of gangsta rappers were telling true stories in their rhymes. The majority, they claimed, were studio gangstas, phonies with no lived experience with the streets they rapped about. Socially conscious rappers also debated what constituted a "real" backpacker. For example, some decried peers who toted expensive, name-brand backpacks. Such critiques illustrated how notions of authenticity, even within these groups, were rooted in social class.

16. Social class was determined via responses to demographic questions asked during interviews or in a brief written survey.

17. Education was measured on a five-point Likert Scale as follows: (0) no high school, (1) some high school, (2) high school graduate, (3) some college, (4) college graduate.

18. According to the 2011 census, the three largest ethnoracial groups in the United States are white (63.4 percent), Hispanic or Latino (16.7 percent), and black or African American (13.1 percent). Asians are 5 percent of the country's total population and 2.3 percent of people identify as being of two or more races.

19. I asked participants to self-identify race or ethnicity. The category "some other race" was not used by anyone, which likely explained the disparity between this category and the "two or more races" category.

20. Asians and Arabs are underrepresented. In six years of fieldwork, I observed very few Asian or Arab rappers in Chicago. Besides one participant who identified as half Korean, half white, no participants claimed Asian ancestry. In part, this reflected Chicago's ethnoracial demographics, where the total population of all Asian ethnic groups is 5.5 percent. By contrast, Harrison's (2009) study of the San Francisco rap-music scene, which included analysis of Filipino-American rappers, was set in a city where Asians constituted nearly a third of the population. While Asians and Arabs remain largely absent from scholarly studies of rap music, the works of Condry (2006), Kahf (2007), Sharma (2010), and Wang (2007) provide welcome change.

21. Shoes are an important yet understudied aspect of hip-hop culture. Nearly all of the rappers in this study paid careful attention to footwear, and most of them—even the poorest—had any number of expensive shoes. When a particularly "cool" pair of shoes was released by one of the major footwear corporations, the local rap-related message boards would light up with reviews, opinions, and photos. The emphasis on shoes in hip-hop style may also be rooted in its masculinized culture. It might not be considered "manly" to talk about sweaters or color combinations, but shoes are acceptable because they imply function rather than fashion. Those interested in this topic should read the work of Mary Pattillo-McCoy (1999), who devoted a chapter of her book *Black Picket Fences* to the prevalence of Nike footwear in the black community. Pattillo-McCoy linked the popularity of Nike shoes among blacks to a confluence of rising mass marketing and brand-conscious consumption.

22. Pattillo-McCoy (1999) noted that poor blacks employ conspicuous consumption to upend hegemonic hierarchies of wealth, status, and power, "buying things they often cannot afford in order to give others the impression that they can. . . . The real gap in economic status can be minimized at least symbolically by just looking good . . . African Americans use material goods as symbolic affronts to the power of whites" (147). Pattillo-McCoy concluded that this symbolic consumption and display of high-status material goods, however, had essentially no impact on the structural inequalities they were designed to address.

23. The word "urban" is sometimes used by scholars and writers as a proxy for blackness. I intentionally distinguish "urban" from "race" here and elsewhere in recognizing rap music as primarily reflective of life in cities, rather than rural areas. Though a few popular rap acts have depicted the rural experience, and rap music is popular in rural areas, the vast majority of rap music, particularly the gangsta subgenre, contains descriptions and aural recreations of city life. The greatest challenge to urban primacy in rap music has come from Southern rap artists. While the bulk of popular Southern rap has stemmed from large cities such as Miami, Houston, New Orleans, and Atlanta, some rural Southern artists have achieved success and Southern rap in particular signifies the rural. A more

complete discussion of these topics is provided by Miller (2004) and Sarig (2007; see especially chapter 8).

24. Jennifer Hochschild (1995) notes that "people most often define success as attainment of a high income, a prestigious job, and economic security," but points out that definitions vary (15). According to Hochschild, success can be measured along three scales: absolute, relative, and competitive (see 16–18). The Chicago rappers in this study operationalized success as the attainment of some degree of financial security and status (i.e., fame) via rap music. This includes hobbyists, who had few expectations of earning money from their efforts, but who sought recognition as musicians. One criterion for participating in this study was that subjects had to be active members of the underground rap music scene, meaning that they recorded and distributed their music and/or performed live on a regular basis. "Amateurs," who made music strictly for their own pleasure and who had no interest in money or recognition, are not included in this study.

25. Of the 135 participants, 78 were classified as gangsta rappers, 55 of whom did not claim to be active gang members. Gangsta rappers who were not gang members aligned themselves with "storytellers" such as Ice Cube who grew up in proximity to gangs but were not members. As one such MC stated, "If I rap about a certain subject, it doesn't mean that I personally did it. It's storytelling. I don't never claim that I'm a gangbanger, but I know the streets."

1. Who Shot Ya?

1. Habit is referencing the first track ("Intro/Bomb First (My Second Reply)") on Tupac's 1996 posthumous release, *The Don Killuminati: The 7 Day Theory*, which was issued under the pseudonym Makaveli.

2. The Blueprint

1. See Armstrong 2004; Calhoun 2005; Hess 2005; Rodman 2006; Watts 2005; White 2006.

2. See Harrison 2009; Rodriquez 2006; Sharma 2010.

3. Harrison provides a comprehensive review of this literature in a 2008 article, "Racial Authenticity in Rap Music and Hip Hop."

4. Legatum Institute (2013).

5. See also Carter 2003; Clay 2003.

6. See Lyons and Pettit 2008; Western and Pettit 2005.

7. Massoglia 2008; Schnittker and John 2007; Western and Wildeman 2009.

8. Sociologist Karyn Lacy makes a convincing argument that the black middle class is now large enough to justify a more nuanced analysis. In her 2007 book *Blue-Chip Black,* Lacy provides a class differential model that partitions

the black middle class into three socioeconomic subcategories: lower-middle, core, and elite. Analysis of phenomena such as discriminatory housing practices, rates of home ownership, and the recent foreclosure crisis typically conceptualizes the black middle class as a singular entity, but as Lacy asserts in a 2012 article, "intraclass distinctions, and their consequences for achieving the good things in life, must be factored into the calculus too" (1568).

9. Kelley (1996) provides a thorough sociocultural analysis of LA gangsta-rap lyrics from this era.

10. Bronx outfit Boogie Down Productions' 1987 *Criminal Minded* LP is also considered to be a key contribution to early gangsta rap.

11. Quinn (2005) asserted that labeling these cultural responses mechanistic, knee-jerk reactions to structural inequalities was an oversimplification. For example, young people join street gangs for any number of reasons, including the desire for belonging to a community-based group, the search for identity, lack of familial ties, a means of gaining a street education, and the desire for wealth and status. Gangs also reduce fears related to violence, and provide income for those with little training or education, and thus few job opportunities (Keiser 2006; Melde, Taylor, and Esbensen 2009). Finally, gang membership can be exiting and fun (Katz 1988).

12. While only tangentially related to gangs, there are numerous historical links between gangsta rap and underground economies, the bread and butter of most street gangs. Houston's Rap-a-Lot Records, home to the Geto Boys, was purportedly started with $200,000 in funds from drug kingpin Michael Harris (Quinn 2005). Similarly, it has been widely rumored that Death Row Records was funded through $1.5 million in seed money from Harris to founder Suge Knight (ibid.). A detailed journalistic account of the links between New York rappers and drug-selling syndicates can be found in Ethan Brown's 2005 book *Queens Reigns Supreme*.

13. Eazy-E's legend as a drug kingpin may have been exaggerated for the sake of publicity. According to childhood friend and N.W.A band mate MC Ren, Eazy still lived at home and was on the verge of becoming a postman at the time that N.W.A's career took off (Ogg and Upshal 2001).

14. The hustler archetype, which draws upon the broad range and history of African American "street" types, was not invented from scratch. Judy (1994) explores the connection between gangsta rappers and the "badman" figure from African American folklore. Some scholars view the hustler archetype as being at least partially beneficial. For example, Dyson (2007) asserted that Jay-Z offers a "political aesthetic of entrepreneurship. . . . He's taken hustling savvy and corporate smarts . . . to the next level. . . . You can spit venom at white supremacy, social injustice, the personal limitations imposed by a dominant culture, and still use . . . the master's tools to dismantle the master's house" (53, 56).

15. Sociologist Jennifer Lena described how the shift in rap music from content distributed by independent record companies to major labels impacted the genre's lyrical content. "Rappers developed particular tropes of artistic legitimacy to cope with the threat of corporate incursion into the market reflected by the 'hustler' character. . . . They felt pressure to craft an identity suitable (and saleable) in the mainstream recording industry while 'keepin' it real,' remaining congruent with an older value system. The hustler is still an outsider, but one with a comfortable relationship to commercial culture and material success" (2006, 489).

3. Bangin' on Wax

1. Leyshon (2009) provides an extensive overview of the impact of these technologies on recording studios in the United Kingdom.

2. The word "hook" had a different meaning in Chicago's rap underground than the definition typically found in genres such as rock. A hook is popularly understood to be a musical or vocal device used in a song to "hook" the listener into paying attention (see Burns 1987). According to this definition a hook is any device that achieves this goal, be it an instrumental or verbal flourish, infectious vocal tics or phrases, or a particularly thrilling musical break. In Chicago's rap underground, this concept existed but there was no fixed term for it. Instead, the word "hook" was synonymous with what musicians usually refer to as a song's "chorus."

3. Drug use, mostly marijuana, was not limited to the gangsta-rap micro-scene, and there were several gangsta rappers who eschewed all drugs. Moreover, there were a number of backpack rappers who, like Hymnal, supported themselves and funded their music careers through small-scale drug dealing.

4. The benefits described here are related specifically to music careers. The rappers in this study also derived benefits from the gang (income, transportation, protection, solidarity) that had nothing to do with music.

4. In Da Club

1. Nielson (2010) and Shipley (2009) describe how recording technology can serve purposes that are similar to live rap performances.

2. Lee (2009b) provides an in-depth exploration of street-corner ciphers in Los Angeles, describing how the seemingly improvised rhymes combine previously written material with "spontaneous and unpredictable events from the immediate situation" (313).

3. Harrison (2009) described his experience as an aspiring MC at a weekly open-mic night as key to his research. The coffee shop that hosted the event enabled rappers to "gain confidence and make a name for his or herself. Perform-

ing in public is crucial to having a social identity as an emcee. At Rockin' Java, an aspiring emcee could be assured the opportunity to perform in front of several dozen people each week. In this way it was a port of entry for many" (75–76).

4. Battles carry symbolic significance that goes beyond competition or wordplay. Alim, Lee, and Carris (2011) studied battles between black and Latino MCs in Los Angeles and wrote that these exchanges "coproduce and contest hip hop as a black space, one that foregrounds working-class street-affiliation and supports masculinist, heteronormative ideologies of gender and sexuality" (423).

5. Goffman (1974) defined frames as "definitions of situations [that] are built up in accordance with principles of organization which govern events—at least social ones—and our subjective involvement in them" (10–11). In other words, the conventions and obligations that comprise the performance frame exist external to one's subjective experience of it. For example, the performance frame includes the behavioral obligation that audience members will demonstrate appreciation through applause, but this convention is not always followed in practice. We know when a comedian "bombs" because we understand the performance frame and recognize when it has been compromised. Goffman wrote that almost any public performance in front of an audience was "pure," including "dramatic scriptings, nightclub acts, personal appearances of various sorts, the ballet, and much of orchestral music" (125). Less pure were performances such as weddings, funerals, and lectures, where spectators were invited or where the performance was not intended to entertain. Building on Goffman's theory, Mullen (1985) asserted that the purity of a performance was contextually dependent on the degree to which the conventions of traditional performance were followed: A play held in an ornate theater was purer than a bluegrass musician strumming an acoustic guitar in a coffee shop.

6. There were myriad complications that could affect a performance. Among the most discussed was stage fright, the anxiety that arose before, during, and sometimes after performances. Stage fright was part of a larger set of psychological or emotional challenges, internal issues that were largely imperceptible to audiences (and researchers), but that sometimes impacted performance (see also Sanders 1974). I do not include them here because: (1) some rappers said that stage fright was helpful and productive, (2) stage fright was part of rap's live-performance script; when discussing stage fright, several rappers indexed the opening scene from 8 *Mile*, where Eminem's character vomits before going onstage, (3) I never saw stage fright disrupt a show; those who suffered from it still performed.

7. Émile Durkheim ([1912] 1995) pioneered the sociological study of these types of symbolic exchanges. Such symbols, which Durkheim called totems, were crests or signs that symbolized a clan, usually in the form of a plant or an animal. Clans would draw them on objects such as weapons or the walls of houses

and engrave them on their bodies. During religious ceremonies, totems were heavily featured as a means of creating group cohesion and unity. Such rituals were a means by which to achieve collective effervescence, the intense feelings of unity that took place during large tribal gatherings. "The very act of congregating is an exceptionally powerful stimulant," Durkheim wrote. "Once the individuals are gathered together, a sort of electricity is generated from their closeness and quickly launches them to an extraordinary height of exaltation. . . . [F]rom every side there are nothing but wild movements, shouts, downright howls, and deafening noises of all kinds that further intensify the state they are expressing. . . . [T]hese gestures and cries tend to fall into rhythm and regularity, and from there into songs and dances" (217–218). Although Durkheim was interested in religion, his ideas have been applied to sporting events, elections, and television viewing (see Grazian 2010, chapter 2).

8. The eagle signified Logan Square, home to most of the IOA members. The Logan Square eagle, which was invoked by rappers in both stagewear and lyrics, referred to the Illinois Centennial Monument, erected in 1918 to celebrate the 100th anniversary of Illinois' entry into the union. The marble monument consists of a 68-foot-tall Greek column with an eagle perched on a dais at the top. Its location in Logan Square—at the intersection of Logan Boulevard, Kedzie Boulevard, and Milwaukee Avenue—is considered the heart of the larger Logan Square neighborhood. Representing Logan Square was not unique to gang members, though most gang members regularly invoked symbols of their neighborhoods via performative practices.

9. Such policies were not without controversy. In October 2009, six black college students were denied entry to a Chicago bar called the Original Mother's for being in violation of the club's "no baggy pants" policy. The students complained of racism and claimed that white patrons in similar garb were allowed to enter. An employee from Mother's countered that the policy was in place to curb gang members from entering the club. "Holding a sheaf of Chicago police gang intelligence reports and pointing to security video of two black members of the group with backward ball caps, Mother's human resource manager Dan Benson said gang violence was common nearby" (Janega 2009).

5. Capital Punishment

1. Pop-rapper Tone Lōc employed a similar strategy, "playing down his former membership in the Westside Tribe Crips to make his smash party raps on Delicious Vinyl Records" (Quinn 2005, 56).

2. Lyrics to gangsta-rap songs are increasingly being used as evidence in court cases. For example, in 2013 Antwain Steward, a Virginia-based rapper who goes by the stage name Twain Gotti, was indicted for the 2007 murder of two men.

Steward, a purported gang member, boasted of a murder in a song entitled "Ride Out," which caught the attention of local detectives. Lyrics from "Ride Out" were included in an affidavit for a search warrant related to the case, and a witness testified in court about the recording of the song, which took place a few days after the murders (Speed 2013).

3. According to Quinn (2005), Snoop Dogg and MC Eiht, two famed MCs with gang ties, employed a similar strategy. Watkins (2005) noted that Afrika Bambaataa was "an active member of the Black Spades. But like a number of his peers he was drawn to the magnetic powers of hip hop. At some point he started to believe that the energy, loyalty, and passion that defined gang life could be guided toward more socially productive activities" (22–23).

4. Gatti, Tremblay, Vitaro, and McDuff 2005; Hill, Lui, and Hawkins 2001; Melde, Diem, and Drake 2012; Melde and Esbensen 2011; Peterson, Taylor, and Esbensen 2004; Thornberry et al. 2003.

Bibliography

Abdullah, Ibrahim. 2002. "Youth Culture and Rebellion: Understanding Sierra Leone's Wasted Decade." *Critical Arts* 16:19–37.

Adams, Terri M., and Douglas B. Fuller. 2006. "The Words Have Changed but the Ideology Remains the Same: Misogynistic Lyrics in Rap Music." *Journal of Black Studies* 36:938–57.

Alba, Richard, and Victor Nee. 2003. *Remaking the American Mainstream.* Cambridge, Mass.: Harvard University Press.

Alexander, Michelle. 2010. *The New Jim Crow: Mass Incarceration in the Age of Colorblindness.* New York: The New Press.

Alim, H. Samy. 2006. *Roc the Mic Right: The Language of Hip Hop Culture.* New York: Routledge.

———, Jooyoung Lee, and Lauren Mason Carris. 2011. "Moving the Crowd, 'Crowding' the Emcee: The Coproduction and Contestation of Black Normativity in Freestyle Rap Battles." *Discourse and Society* 22:422–39.

Anderson, Elijah. 1999. *Code of the Street: Decency, Violence, and the Moral Life of the Inner City.* New York: W. W. Norton and Company.

———. 2008. "Against the Wall: Poor, Young, Black, and Male." In *Against the Wall: Poor, Young, Black, and Male,* edited by Elijah Anderson, 3–27. Philadelphia: University of Pennsylvania Press.

Appiah, Osei. 2002. "Black and White Viewers' Perception and Recall of Occupational Characters on Television." *Journal of Communication* 52:776–93.

Armstrong, Edward G. 2001. "Gangsta Misogyny: A Content Analysis of the Portrayals of Violence against Women in Rap Music, 1987–1993." *Journal of Criminal Justice and Popular Culture* 8:96–126.

———. 2004. "Eminem's Construction of Authenticity." *Popular Music and Society* 27:335–55.

Bauman, Zygmunt. 2000. *Liquid Modernity.* Cambridge: Polity Press.

Bayton, Mavis. 1990. "How Women Become Musicians." In *On Record: Rock, Pop, and the Written Word,* edited by Simon Frith and Andrew Goodwin, 238–57. New York: Pantheon.

Becker, Howard. 1974. "Art as Collective Action." *American Sociological Review* 39:767–76.

———. 1982. *Art Worlds*. Berkeley: University of California Press.

Bennett, Andy. 2004. "Consolidating the Music Scenes Perspective." *Poetics* 32:223–34.

———, and Richard A. Peterson, eds. 2004. *Music Scenes: Local, Translocal, and Virtual*. Nashville, Tenn: Vanderbilt University Press.

Bourdieu, Pierre. 1984. *Distinction: A Social Critique of the Judgment of Taste*. Cambridge, Mass.: Harvard University Press.

Bowen, Lawrence, and Jill Schmid. 1997. "Minority Presence and Portrayal in Mainstream Magazine Advertising: An Update." *Journalism and Mass Communication Quarterly* 74:134–46.

Boyd, Todd. 2003. *Young, Black, Rich & Famous: The Rise of the NBA, the Hip Hop Invasion, and the Transformation of American Culture*. Lincoln: University of Nebraska Press.

Britz, Marjie. 2008. "A New Paradigm of Organized Crime in the United States: Criminal Syndicates, Cyber-gangs, and the Worldwide Web." *Sociology Compass* 2:1750–65.

Brown, Ethan. 2005. *Queens Reigns Supreme: Fat Cat, 50 Cent, and the Rise of the Hip-Hop Hustler*. New York: Anchor Books.

Burns, Gary. 1987. "A Typology of 'Hooks' in Popular Records." *Popular Music* 6:1–20.

Calhoun, Lindsay. 2005. "Will the Real Slim Shady Please Stand Up? Masking Whiteness, Encoding Hegemonic Masculinity in Eminem's *Marshall Mathers LP*." *Howard Journal of Communications* 16:267–94.

Caramanica, Jon. 2012. "Chicago Hip-Hop's Raw Burst of Change." *New York Times*, October 4.

Carter, Prudence L. 2003. "'Black' Cultural Capital, Status Positioning, and Schooling Conflicts for Low-Income African American Youth." *Social Problems* 50:136–55.

Cerulo, Karen A. 1997. "Identity Construction: New Issues, New Directions." *Annual Review of Sociology* 23:385–409.

Chang, Jeff. 2005. *Can't Stop Won't Stop: A History of the Hip-Hop Generation*. New York: St. Martin's Press.

Charnas, Dan. 2010. *The Big Payback: The History of the Business of Hip-Hop*. New York: New American Library.

Chen, Meng-Jinn, Brenda A. Miller, Joel W. Grube, and Elizabeth D. Waiters. 2006. "Music, Substance Use, and Aggression." *Journal of Studies on Alcohol* 67:373–81.

Chicago Crime Commission. 2012. *The Chicago Crime Commission Gang Book: A Detailed Overview of Street Gangs in the Chicago Metropolitan Area*. Chicago: Chicago Crime Commission.

Chicago Police Department. 2010. *2010 Annual Report.* Chicago: Chicago Police Department, Bureau of Administrative Services, Research and Development Division.

"Chief Keef and Lil JoJo: A Rap Feud Straight outta Englewood." 2012. *Chicago Sun-Times,* September 9.

Cho, Sumi K. 1995. "Korean Americans vs. African Americans: Conflict and Construction." In *Race, Class, and Gender: An Anthology* (2nd ed.), edited by Margaret L. Anderson and Patricia Hill Collins, 461–70. Belmont, Calif.: Wadsworth Publishing Company.

Císař, Ondrej, and Martin Koubek. 2012. "Include 'Em All? Culture, Politics, and a Local Hardcore/Punk Scene in the Czech Republic." *Poetics* 40:1–21.

Clay, Andreana. 2003. "Keepin' It Real: Black Youth, Hip-Hop Culture, and Black Identity." *American Behavioral Scientist* 46:1346–58.

Cobbina, Jennifer E., Jody Miller, and Rod K. Brunson. 2008. "Gender, Neighborhood Danger, and Risk-Avoidance Strategies among Urban African-American Youths." *Criminology* 46:673–709.

Cohen-Marks, Mara A., and Christopher Stout. 2011. "Can the American Dream Survive the New Multiethnic America? Evidence from Los Angeles." *Sociological Forum* 26:824–45.

Collins, Patricia Hill. 2006. *From Black Power to Hip Hop: Racism, Nationalism, and Feminism.* Philadelphia: Temple University Press.

Condry, Ian. 2004. "Cultures of Music Piracy: An Ethnographic Comparison of the US and Japan." *International Journal of Cultural Studies* 7:343–63.

———. 2006. *Hip-Hop Japan: Rap and the Paths of Cultural Globalization.* Durham, N.C.: Duke University Press.

Conley, Dalton. 2009. *Elsewhere U.S.A.: How We Got from the Company Man, Family Dinners, and the Affluent Society to the Home Office, BlackBerry Moms, and Economic Anxiety.* New York: Pantheon Books.

Conquergood, Dwight. 1994. "Homeboys and Hoods: Gang Communication and Cultural Space." In *Group Communication in Context: Studies of Natural Groups,* edited by Lawrence R. Frey, 23–55. Hillsdale, N.J.: Lawrence Erlbaum Associates.

Cross, Brian. 1993. *It's Not about a Salary: Rap, Race, and Resistance in Los Angeles.* London: Verso.

Cutler, Cecelia. 2007. "The Co-Construction of Whiteness in an MC Battle." *Pragmatics* 17:9–22.

Daloz, Jean-Pascal. 2010. *The Sociology of Elite Distinction: From Theoretical to Comparative Perspectives.* Houndmills, United Kingdom: Palgrave Macmillan.

Décary-Hétu, David, and Carlo Morselli. 2011. "Gang Presence in Social Network Sites." *International Journal of Cyber Criminology* 5:876–90.

Decker, Scott H., and David Pyrooz. 2012. "Gang Offending and Online Behavior." *JRSA Forum* 30:1–4.

Dennis, Christopher. 2012. *Afro-Colombian Hip-Hop: Globalization, Transcultural Music, and Ethnic Identities.* Lanham, Md.: Lexington Books.

Dimitriadis, Greg. 1996. "Hip Hop: From Live Performance to Mediated Narrative." *Popular Music* 15:179–94.

———. 1999. "Hip Hop to Rap: Some Implications of an Historically Situated Approach to Performance." *Text and Performance Quarterly* 19:355–69.

———. 2009. *Performing Identity/Performing Culture: Hip Hop as Text, Pedagogy, and Lived Practice* (rev. ed.). New York: Peter Lang Publishing.

Dowd, Timothy J., Kathleen Liddle, and Jenna Nelson. 2004. "Music Festivals as Scenes: Examples from Serious Music, Womyn's Music, and Skatepunk." In *Music Scenes: Local, Translocal, and Virtual,* edited by Andy Bennett and Richard A. Peterson, 149–67. Nashville, Tenn.: Vanderbilt University Press.

Dowdy, Michael. 2007. "Live Hip Hop, Collective Agency, and 'Acting in Concert.'" *Popular Music and Society* 30:75–91.

Du Bois, W. E. B. (1903) 1994. *The Souls of Black Folk.* Toronto: Dover Publications.

———. 1935. *Black Reconstruction in America 1860–1880.* New York: Atheneum.

Duffett, Mark. 2009. "'We Are Interrupted by Your Noise': Heckling and the Symbolic Economy of Popular Music Stardom." *Popular Music and Society* 32:37–57.

Durkheim, Émile. (1912) 1995. *The Elementary Forms of Religious Life.* New York: The Free Press.

Dyson, Michael Eric. 2005. *Is Bill Cosby Right? Or Has the Black Middle Class Lost Its Mind?* New York: Basic Civitas Books.

———. 2007. *Know What I Mean? Reflections on Hip Hop.* New York: Basic Books.

Edwards, Gavin. 2003. "Smart Mouth." *Rolling Stone,* September 4.

Fine, Gary A. 1979. "Small Groups and Culture Creation: The Idioculture of Little League Baseball Teams." *American Sociological Review* 44:733–45.

Flores, Juan. 2000. *From Bomba to Hip-Hop: Puerto Rican Culture and Latino Identity.* New York: Columbia University Press.

Forman, Murray. 2002. *The 'Hood Comes First: Race, Space, and Place in Rap and Hip-Hop.* Middletown, Conn.: Wesleyan University Press.

Frank, Richard, Connie Cheng, and Vito Pun. 2011. "Social Media Sites: New Fora for Criminal, Communication, and Investigation Opportunities." Paper prepared for Research and National Coordination Organized Crime Division, Law Enforcement and Policy Branch: Public Safety Canada.

Fujioka, Yuki. 2005. "Emotional TV Viewing and Minority Audience: How Mexican Americans Process and Evaluate TV News about In-Group Members." *Communication Research* 32:566–93.

Garot, Robert. 2010. *Who You Claim: Performing Gang Identity in School and on the Streets.* New York: New York University Press.

Gatti, Uberto, Richard E. Tremblay, Frank Vitaro, and Pierre McDuff. 2005. "Youth Gangs, Delinquency and Drug Use: A Test of the Selection, Facilitation, and Enhancement Hypotheses." *Journal of Child Psychology and Psychiatry* 46:1178–90.

George, Nelson. 1998. *Hip Hop America.* New York: Penguin.

Glaeser, Edward, and Jacob Vigdor. 2012. *The End of the Segregated Century: Racial Separation in America's Neighborhoods, 1890–2010.* Manhattan Institute Civic Report No. 66, January.

Glasgow, Douglas G. 1980. *The Black Underclass: Poverty, Unemployment and Entrapment of Ghetto Youth.* San Francisco: Jossey-Bass.

Goffman, Erving. 1974. *Frame Analysis: An Essay on the Organization of Experience.* Cambridge, Mass.: Harvard University Press.

Gorner, Jeremy. 2013. "Chief Keef Jailed After Judge Finds Probation Violation." *Chicago Tribune,* January 15.

Grazian, David. 2003. *Blue Chicago: The Search for Authenticity in Urban Blues Clubs.* Chicago: University of Chicago Press.

———. 2010. *Mix It Up: Popular Culture, Mass Media, and Society.* New York: W. W. Norton.

Greenburg, Zack O'Malley, ed. 2012. "Cash Kings 2012: Hip-Hop's Top Earners." *Forbes,* September 5. http://www.forbes.com/special-report/2012/0905_hip-hop-cash-kings.html.

Griswold, Wendy. 2012. *Cultures and Societies in a Changing World.* 4th ed. New York: Sage Publications.

Grogger, Jeffrey. 2011. "Speech Patterns and Racial Wage Inequality." *Journal of Human Resources* 46:1–25.

Haenfler, Ross. 2012. *Goths, Gamers, and Grrrls: Deviance and Youth Subcultures.* 2nd ed. London: Oxford University Press.

Hagedorn, John. M. 1988. *People and Folks: Gangs, Crime, and the Underclass in a Rustbelt City.* Chicago: Lake View Press.

———, and Brigid Rauch. 2007. "Housing, Gangs, and Homicide: What We Can Learn from Chicago." *Urban Affairs Review* 42:435–56.

———. 2008. *A World of Gangs: Armed Young Men and Gangsta Culture.* Minneapolis: University of Minnesota Press.

Hammett, Daniel. 2012. "Reworking and Resisting Globalising Influences: Cape Town Hip-Hop." *GeoJournal* 77:417–28.

Hanson, Sandra L., and John Zogby. "The Polls—Trends: Attitudes about the American Dream." *Public Opinion Quarterly* 74:570–84.

Harkness, Geoff. 2011. "Backpackers and Gangstas: Chicago's White Rappers Strive For Authenticity." *American Behavioral Scientist* 55:57–85.

———2012a. "True School: Situational Authenticity in Chicago's Hip-Hop Underground." *Cultural Sociology* 6:283–98.

———. 2012b. "The Spirit of Rapitalism: Artistic Labor Practices in Chicago's Hip-Hop Underground." *Journal of Workplace Rights* 16:251–70.

Harris, Cherise A., and Nikki Khanna. 2010. "Black Is, Black Ain't: Biracials, Middle-Class, and the Social Construction of Blackness." *Sociological Spectrum* 30:639–70.

Harrison, Anthony Kwame. 2006. "'Cheaper than a CD, Plus We Really Mean It': Bay Area Underground Hip Hop Tapes as Subcultural Artefacts." *Popular Music* 25:283–301.

———. 2008. "Racial Authenticity in Rap Music and Hip Hop." *Sociology Compass* 2:1783–1800.

———. 2009. *Hip Hop Underground: The Integrity and Ethics of Racial Identification.* Philadelphia: Temple University Press.

Hebdige, Dick. 1979. *Subculture: The Meaning of Style.* London and New York: Routledge.

Hess, Mickey. 2005. "Hip-Hop Realness and the White Performer." *Critical Studies in Media Communication* 22:372–89.

Hill, Karl G., Christina Lui, and J. David Hawkins. 2001. "Early Precursors of Gang Membership: A Study of Seattle Youth." *Juvenile Justice Bulletin.* December.

Hochschild, Arlie Russell. 1983. *The Managed Heart: Commercialization of Human Feeling.* Berkeley: University of California Press.

Hochschild, Jennifer L. 1995. *Facing up to the American Dream: Race, Class, and the Soul of the Nation.* Princeton, N.J.: Princeton University Press.

Hoplamazian, Gregory J., and Osei Appiah. 2013. "Viewer Responses to Character Race and Social Status in Advertising: Blacks See Color, Whites See Class." *Journal of Current Issues & Research in Advertising* 34:57–76.

Howell, James C. 2007. "Menacing or Mimicking? Realities of Youth Gangs." *Juvenile and Family Court Journal* 58:39–50.

Hunnicutt, Gwen, and Kristy Andrews. 2009. "Tragic Narratives in Popular Culture: Depictions of Homicide in Rap Music." *Sociological Forum* 24:611–30.

Hunt, Matthew O. 2007. "African American, Hispanic, and White Beliefs about Black/White Inequality, 1977–2004." *American Sociological Review* 72:390–415.

———, and Rashawn Ray. 2012. "Social Class Identification among Black Americans: Trends and Determinants, 1974–2010." *American Behavioral Scientist* 11:1462–80.

Hunter, Margaret. 2011. "Shake It, Baby, Shake It: Consumption and the New Gender Relation in Hip-Hop." *Sociological Perspectives* 54:15–36.

Janega, James. 2009. "Students from Washington University in St. Louis Raise Civil Rights Complaints about Original Mother's Club in Chicago." *Chicago Tribune*, October 23.

Jankowski, Martin S. 1991. *Islands in the Street: Gangs and the American Urban Society*. Berkeley: University of California Press.

Jeffries, Michael. 2011. *Thug Life: Race, Gender, and the Meaning of Hip-Hop*. Chicago: University of Chicago Press.

Jhally, Sut, and Justin Lewis. 1992. *Enlightened Racism: The Cosby Show, Audiences, and the Myth of the American Dream*. Boulder, Colo.: Westview Press.

Jiménez, Tomás R. 2010. "Affiliative Ethnic Identity: A More Elastic Link between Ethnic Ancestry and Culture." *Ethnic and Racial Studies* 33:1756–75.

Johnson, E. Patrick. 2003. *Appropriating Blackness: Performance and the Politics of Authenticity*. Durham, N.C.: Duke University Press.

Johnson, James H., Walter C. Farrell, and Melvin L. Oliver. 1993. "Seeds of the Los Angeles Rebellion of 1992." *International Journal of Urban and Regional Research* 17:115–19.

Judy, Ronald A. T. 1994. "On the Question of Nigga Authenticity." *boundary 2* 21:211–30.

Jurgenson, Nathan. 2010. "The De-McDonaldization of the Internet." In *McDonaldization: The Reader* (3rd ed.), edited by George Ritzer, 159–70. Thousand Oaks, Calif.: Pine Forge Press.

Kahf, Usama. 2007. "Arabic Hip Hop: Claims of Authenticity and Identity of a New Genre." *Journal of Popular Music Studies* 19:359–85.

Katz, Jack. 1988. *Seductions of Crime: Moral and Sensual Attractions in Doing Evil*. New York: Basic Books.

Kealy, Edward. 1982. "Conventions and the Production of the Popular Music Aesthetic." *Popular Culture* 16:100–15.

Keiser, Lincoln. 2006. "The Vice Lords Today: Sociocultural Change in an African American Street Gang." In *Globalization and Change in Fifteen Countries: Born in One World, Living in Another*, edited by George Spindler and Janice E. Stockard, 73–96. Belmont, Calif.: Thompson Wadsworth.

Kelley, Robin D. G. 1994. *Race Rebels: Culture, Politics and the Black Working Class*. New York: The Free Press.

———. 1996. "Kickin' Reality, Kickin' Ballistics: Gangsta Rap and Postindustrial Los Angeles." In *Droppin' Science: Critical Essays on Rap Music and Hip Hop Culture*, edited by William Eric Perkins, 117–58. Philadelphia: Temple University Press.

Kelman, Herbert C. 1961. "Processes of Opinion Change." *Public Opinion Quarterly* 25:57–78.

Kenna, Laura Cook. 2008. *Dangerous Men, Dangerous Media: Constructing Ethnicity, Race, and Media's Impact through the Gangster Image, 1959–2007.* Washington D.C.: The George Washington University.

Keyes, Cheryl L. 2000. "Empowering Self, Making Choices, Creating Spaces: Black Female Identity via Rap Music Performance." *The Journal of American Folklore* 113:255–69.

———. 2002. *Rap Music and Street Consciousness.* Urbana and Chicago: University of Illinois Press.

Kibby, Marjorie D. 2000. "Home on the Page: A Virtual Place of Music Community." *Popular Music* 191:91–100.

Klein, Malcolm W. 2004. *Gang Cop: The Words and Ways of Officer Paco Domingo.* Walnut Creek, Calif.: AltaMira Press.

Knox, George W. 2005. "The Problem of Gangs and Security Threat Groups (STG's) in American Prisons Today: Recent Research Findings from the 2004 Prison Gang Survey." Peotone, Ill.: National Gang Crime Research Center.

Konkol, Mark, Kim Janssen, and Allison Horton. 2012. "Lil JoJo Slain in Chicago; Cops Look at Chief Keef's Tweets." *Chicago Sun-Times,* September 6.

Kot, Greg. 2012. "Chicago Hip-Hop War of Words Turns Violent." *Chicago Tribune,* September 6.

———, and Jeremy Gorner. 2012. "Cops Investigating Whether Hip-Hop Feud Linked to Slaying." *Chicago Tribune,* September 6.

Kubrin, Charis E. 2005. "Gangstas, Thugs, and Hustlas: Identity and the Code of the Street in Rap Music." *Social Problems* 52:360–78.

Lachmann, Richard. 1988. "Graffiti as Career and Ideology." *American Journal of Sociology* 94:229–50.

Lacy, Karyn R. 2004. "Black Spaces, Black Places: Strategic Assimilation and Identity Construction in Middle-Class Suburbia." *Ethnic and Racial Studies* 27:908–30.

———. 2007. *Blue-Chip Black: Race, Class, and Status in the New Black Middle Class.* Berkeley: University of California Press.

———. 2012. "All's Fair? The Foreclosure Crisis and Middle-Class Black (In)Stability. *American Behavioral Scientist* 56:1565–80.

Lamont, Michèle. 2000. *The Dignity of Working Men: Morality and the Boundaries of Race, Class, and Immigration.* Cambridge, Mass.: Harvard University Press.

———. 2002. "Symbolic Boundaries and Status." In *Cultural Sociology,* edited by Lynn Spillman, 98–107. Oxford and Malden, Mass.: Blackwell Publishers.

———, and Virag Molnar. 2002. "The Study of Boundaries in the Social Sciences." *Annual Review of Sociology* 28:167–95.

Lareau, Annette. 2011. *Unequal Childhoods: Class, Race, and Family Life.* Berkeley: University of California Press.

Lee, Jooyoung. 2009a. "Battlin' on the Corner: Techniques for Sustaining Play." *Social Problems* 56:578–98.

———. 2009b. "Escaping Embarrassment: Face-Work in the Rap Cipher." *Social Psychology Quarterly* 72:306–24.

———. 2009c. "Open Mic: Professionalizing the Rap Career." *Ethnography* 10: 475–95.

Lee, Steve A., and Richard A. Peterson. 2004. "Internet-Based Virtual Music Scenes: The Case of P2 in Alt.Country Music." In *Music Scenes: Local, Translocal, and Virtual,* edited by Andy Bennett and Richard A. Peterson, 187–204. Nashville, Tenn.: Vanderbilt University Press.

Legatum Institute. 2013. "Legatum Prosperity Index." http://www.prosperity.com.

Lena, Jennifer C. 2004. "Meaning and Membership: Samples in Rap Music, 1979 to 1995." *Poetics* 32:297–310.

———.2006. "Social Context and Musical Content of Rap Music, 1979–1995." *Social Forces* 85:479–95.

———. 2012. *Banding Together: How Communities Create Genres in Popular Music.* Princeton, N.J.: Princeton University Press.

Levitt, Steven D., and Sudhir A. Venkatesh. 2000. "An Economic Analysis of a Drug-Selling Gang's Finances." *Quarterly Journal of Economics* 115:755–89.

Lewis, Oscar. 1968. *A Study of Slum Culture: Backgrounds for "La Vida."* New York: Random House.

Leyshon, Andrew. 2009. "The Software Slump: Digital Music, the Democratisation of Technology, and the Decline of the Recording Studio Sector within the Musical Economy." *Environment and Planning A* 41:1309–31.

Lyons, Christopher, and Becky Pettit. 2008. "Compound Disadvantage: Race, Incarceration, and Wage Growth." National Poverty Center Working Paper Series 08–16. October. University of Michigan National Poverty Center, Ann Arbor. http://www.npc.umich.edu/publications/working_papers/?publication_id=166&.

MacLeod, Jay. (1995) 2009. *Ain't No Makin' It: Aspirations and Attainment in a Low-Income Neighborhood.* Boulder, Colo.: Westview Press.

Main, Frank. 2013. "'Tearful Chief Keef Gets 60 Days in Juvenile Jail for Violating Probation." *Chicago Sun-Times,* January 17.

Marsh, Kris, William Darity, Phillip Cohen, Lynne Casper, and Danielle Salters. 2007. "The Emerging Black Middle Class: Single and Living Alone." *Social Forces* 86:1–28.

Marshall, Wayne. 2006. "Giving Up Hip-Hop's Firstborn: A Quest for the Real after the Death of Sampling." *Callaloo* 29:868–92.

Massey, Howard. 2009. *Behind the Glass Volume II: Top Record Producers Tell How They Craft Their Hits.* Milwaukee: Backbeat Books.

Massoglia, Michael. 2008. "Incarceration, Health, and Racial Disparities in Heath." *Law & Society Review* 42:275–306.

Mastro, Dana E., and Susannah R. Stern. "Representations of Race in Television Commercials: A Content Analysis of Prime-Time Advertising." *Journal of Broadcasting & Electronic Media* 47:638–47.

Maxwell, Ian. 2003. *Phat Beats, Dope Rhymes: Hip Hop Down Under Comin' Upper.* Middletown, Conn.: Wesleyan University Press.

McGuire, William J. 1984. "Search for the Self: Going beyond Self-Esteem and the Reactive Self." In *Personality and the Prediction of Behavior,* edited by Robert A. Zucker, Joel Aronoff, and Albert I. Rabin, 73–120. New York: Academic Press.

McLeod, Kembrew. 1999. "Authenticity within Hip-Hop and Other Cultures Threatened with Assimilation." *Journal of Communication* 49:134–50.

Melde, Chris, Chelsea Diem, and Gregory Drake. 2012. "Identifying Correlates of Stable Gang Membership." *Journal of Contemporary Criminal Justice* 28:482–98.

———, and Finn-Aage Esbensen. 2011. "Gang Membership as a Turning Point in the Life Course." *Criminology* 49:513–52.

———, Terrance Taylor, and Finn-Aage Esbensen. 2009. "'I Got Your Back': An Examination of the Protective Function of Gang Membership in Adolescence." *Criminology* 47:565–94.

Miller, Matt. 2004. "Rap's Dirty South: From Subculture to Pop Culture." *Journal of Popular Music Studies* 16:175–212.

Mitchell, Tony. 1996. *Popular Music and Local Identity: Rock, Pop, and Rap in Europe and Oceania.* London: Leicester University Press.

Moore, Joan. 1990. "Gangs, Drugs, and Violence." In *Drugs and Violence: Causes, Correlates, and Consequences,* edited by Mario De La Rosa, Elizabeth Y. Lambert, and Bernard Gropper, 160–76. Rockville, Md.: National Institute on Drug Abuse.

Morales, Gabe. 2003. "Chicano Music and Latino Rap and Its Influence on Gang Violence and Culture." *Journal of Gang Research* 10:55–63.

Morgan, Marcyliena. 2009. *The Real Hiphop: Battling for Knowledge, Power, and Respect in the LA Underground.* Durham, N.C.: Duke University Press.

Motley, Carol M., and Geraldine Rosa Henderson. 2007. "The Global Hip-Hop Diaspora: Understanding the Culture." *Journal of Business Research* 61:243–53.

Mukherjee, Roopali. 2006. "The Ghetto Fabulous Aesthetic in Contemporary Black Culture: Class and Consumption in the *Barbershop* Films." *Cultural Studies* 20:599–629.

Mullen, Ken. 1985. "The Impure Performance Frame of the Public House Entertainer." *Journal of Contemporary Ethnography* 14:181–203.

Nagel, Joan. 1994. "Constructing Ethnicity: Creating and Recreating Ethnic Identity and Culture. *Social Problems* 41:152–76.

National Collegiate Athletic Association. 2012. "Probability of Competing in Athletics Beyond High School." National Collegiate Athletic Association.

http://ncaa.org/about/resources/research/probability-competing-beyond -high-school.

National Drug Intelligence Center. 2008. *Attorney General's Report to Congress on the Growth of Violent Street Gangs in Suburban Areas.* Washington, D.C.

National Gang Center. http://www.nationalgangcenter.gov/Survey-Analysis/ Measuring-the-Extent-of-Gang-Problems#estimatednumbergangs, http:// www.nationalgangcenter.gov/Survey-Analysis/Prevalence-of-Gang-Problems, http://www.nationalgangcenter.gov/Survey-Analysis/Demographics.

Nayak, Anoop. 2003. *Race, Place and Globalization: Youth Cultures in a Changing World.* Oxford: Berg.

Neff, Ali Colleen. 2009. *Let the World Listen Right: The Mississippi Delta Hip-Hop Story.* Jackson, Miss.: University Press of Mississippi.

Neff, Gina, Elizabeth Wissinger, and Sharon Zukin. 2005. "Entrepreneurial Labor Among Cultural Producers: 'Cool' Jobs in 'Hot' Industries." *Social Semiotics* 15:307–34.

Negus, Keith, and Patria Roman Velazquez. 2002. "Belonging and Detachment: Musical Experience and the Limits of Identity." *Poetics* 30:133–45.

Nickeas, Peter. 2012. "4 Shot during Private Party at Logan Square Club" *Chicago Tribune,* December 5.

Nielson, Erik. 2010. "'We Are Gone': 'Black Steel' and the Technologies of Presence and Absence." *Popular Communication* 8:120–31.

———. 2012. "'Here Come the Cops': Policing the Resistance in Rap Music." *International Journal of Cultural Studies* 15:349–63.

Ogg, Alex, and David Upshal. 2001. *The Hip Hop Years: A History of Rap.* New York: Fromm International.

Packman, Jeff. 2009. "Signifyin(g) Salvador: Professional Musicians and the Sound of Flexibility in Bahia, Brazil's Popular Music Scenes." *Black Music Research Journal* 29:83–126.

Padilla, Felix M. 1992. *The Gang as an American Enterprise.* New Brunswick, N.J.: Rutgers University Press.

Pager, Devah. 2003. "The Mark of a Criminal Record." *American Journal of Sociology* 108(5):937–75.

Pattillo-McCoy, Mary. 1999. *Black Picket Fences: Privilege and Peril Among the Black Middle Class.* Chicago: University of Chicago Press.

Perry, Imani. 2004. *Prophets of the Hood: Politics and Poetics in Hip Hop.* Durham, N.C.: Duke University Press.

———. 2008. "'Tell Us How It Feels to Be a Problem': Hip Hop Longings and Poor Young Black Men." In *Against the Wall: Poor, Young, Black, and Male,* edited by Elijah Anderson, 165–77. Philadelphia: University of Pennsylvania Press.

Peterson, Dana, Terrance J. Taylor, and Finn-Aage Esbensen. 2004. "Gang Membership and Violent Victimization." *Justice Quarterly* 21:793–815.

Peterson, Richard A. 1997. *Creating Country Music: Fabricating Authenticity.* Chicago: University of Chicago Press.

———, and Narasimhan Anand. 2004. "The Production of Culture Perspective." *Annual Review of Sociology* 30:311–34.

———, and Andy Bennett. 2004. "Introducing Music Scenes." In *Music Scenes: Local, Translocal, and Virtual,* edited by Andy Bennett and Richard A. Peterson, 1–15. Nashville, Tenn.: Vanderbilt University Press.

———, and Roger M. Kern. 1996. "Changing Highbrow Taste: From Snob to Omnivore." *American Sociological Review* 61:900–907.

Pew Charitable Trusts. 2012. "Pursuing the American Dream: Economic Mobility Across Generations." Report prepared by the Pew Charitable Trusts. Washington, D.C.

Pih, Kay Kei-ho, Mario De La Rosa, Douglas Rugh, and KuoRay Mao. 2008. "Different Strokes for Different Gangs? An Analysis of Capital among Latino and Asian Gang Members." *Sociological Perspectives* 51:473–94.

Pitchfork Media. 2012. "Watch Chief Keef Freestyle at a Gun Range." Pitchfork Media, July 2. http://pitchfork.com/news/47032-watch-chief-keef-freestyle -at-a-gun-range/ (removed September 6, 2012).

Price, Emmett G. III. 2006. *Hip Hop Culture.* Santa Barbara, Calif.: ABC-CLIO.

Quinn, Eithne. 2005. *Nuthin' but a "G" Thang: The Culture and Commerce of Gangsta Rap.* New York: Columbia University Press.

Reinikainen, Santtu. 2005. "Representations of Women and Wealth in Hip Hop Videos." Pro Gradu Thesis. University of Tampere.

Richardson, Jeanita, and Kim A. Scott. 2002. "Rap Music and Its Violent Progeny: America's Culture of Violence in Context." *The Journal of Negro Education* 71:175–92.

Riley, Alexander. 2005. "The Rebirth of Tragedy out of the Spirit of Hip Hop: Some Suggestions for a Cultural Sociology of Gangsta Rap Music." *Journal of Youth Studies* 8:297–311.

Rodman, Gilbert B. 2006. "Race . . . and Other Four Letter Words: Eminem and the Cultural Politics of Authenticity." *Popular Communication* 4:95–121.

Rodriguez, Gregory. 1996. "The Emerging Latino Middle Class." Pepperdine University Institute for Public Policy. Malibu, Calif. http://publicpolicy.pepperdine .edu/davenport-institute/content/reports/latino.pdf.

Rodriquez, Jason. 2006. "Color-Blind Ideology and the Cultural Appropriation of Hip-Hop." *Journal of Contemporary Ethnography* 35:645–68.

Rose, Tricia. 1994. *Black Noise: Rap Music and Black Culture in Contemporary America.* Hanover, N.H.: Wesleyan University Press.

———. 2008. *The Hip Hop Wars: What We Talk about When We Talk about Hip Hop—And Why It Matters*. New York: Basic Books.

Rothfield, Lawrence, Don Coursey, Sarah Lee, Daniel Silver, and Wendy Norris. 2007. *Chicago Music City: A Report on the Music Industry in Chicago*. Chicago: Cultural Policy Center.

Sampson, Robert J. 2012. *Great American City: Chicago and the Enduring Neighborhood Effect*. Chicago: University of Chicago Press.

Sanders, Clinton R. 1974. "Psyching Out the Crowd; Folk Performers and Their Audiences." *Journal of Contemporary Ethnography* 3:264–82.

Sarig, Roni. 2007. *Third Coast: OutKast, Timbaland, & How Hip-Hop Became a Southern Thing*. Cambridge, Mass.: Da Capo Press.

Scarborough, Roscoe C. 2012. "Managing Challenges on the Front Stage: The Face-Work Strategies of Musicians." *Poetics* 40:542–64.

Schilt, Kristin. 2004. "'Riot grrrl is . . .': Contestation over Meaning in a Music Scene." In *Music Scenes: Local, Translocal, and Virtual*, edited by Andy Bennett and Richard A. Peterson, 115–30. Nashville, Tenn.: Vanderbilt University Press.

Schloss, Joseph G. 2004. *Making Beats: The Art of Sample-Based Hip-Hop*. Middletown, Conn.: Wesleyan University Press.

Schnittker, Jason, and Andrea John. 2007. "Enduring Stigma: The Long-Term Effects of Incarceration on Health." *Journal of Health and Social Behavior* 48:115–30.

Security Threat Intelligence Unit, Florida Department of Corrections. "Gang and Security Threat Group Awareness." Florida Department of Corrections. http://www.dc.state.fl.us/pub/gangs/index.html.

Shank, Barry. 1994. *Dissonant Identities: The Rock'n'Roll Scene in Austin, Texas*. Hanover, N.H.: Wesleyan University Press.

Sharma, Nitasha. 2010. *Hip Hop Desis: South Asian Americans, Blackness, and a Global Race Consciousness*. Durham, N.C.: Duke University Press.

Shelton, Jason E., and Anthony D. Greene. 2012. "Get Up, Get Out, and Git Sumthin': How Race and Class Influence African Americans' Attitudes about Inequality." *American Behavioral Scientist* 56:1481–1508.

Shipley, Jesse Weaver. 2009. "Aesthetic of the Entrepreneur: Afro-Cosmopolitan Rap and Moral Circulation in Accra, Ghana." *Anthropological Quarterly* 82:631–68.

Shusterman, Richard. 1992. "Challenging Conventions in the Fine Art of Rap." In *Rules and Conventions: Literature, Philosophy, Social Theory*, edited by Mette Hjort, 186–214. Baltimore: Johns Hopkins University Press.

Skolnick, Jerome H., Theodore Correl, Elizabeth Navarro, and Roger Rabb. 1990. "The Social Structure of Street Drug Dealing." *American Journal of Police* 9:1–41.

Smith, Christopher Holmes. 2003. "'I Don't Like to Dream about Getting Paid': Representations of Social Mobility and the Emergence of the Hip-Hop Mogul." *Social Text* 21:69–97.

Smith, William E. 2005. *Hip Hop as Performance and Ritual: Biography and Ethnography in Underground Hip Hop*. Washington, D.C.: CLS Publications.

Smitherman, Geneva. 1997. "'The Chain Remain the Same': Communicative Practices in the Hip Hop Nation." *Journal of Black Studies* 28:3–25.

Speed, Ashley K. 2013. "Newport News Rapper Charged in Killings Was Targeted by Cops, Friends Say." *Daily Press,* October 10.

Stahl, Garth, and Pete Dale. 2012. "Creating Positive Spaces of Learning: DJers and MCers Identity Work with New Literacies." *The Educational Forum* 76:510–23.

Stout, Christopher Timothy, and Danvy Le. 2012. "Living the Dream: Barack Obama and Blacks' Changing Perceptions of the American Dream." *Social Science Quarterly* 93:1338–59.

Straw, Will. 1991. "Systems of Articulation, Logics of Change: Communities and Scenes in Popular Music." *Cultural Studies* 5:368–88.

Street, Paul. 2001. *The Color and Geography of Prison Growth in Illinois*. Chicago: Chicago Urban League.

———. 2002. *The Vicious Circle: Race, Prison, Jobs, and Community in Chicago, Illinois, and the Nation*. Chicago: Chicago Urban League.

Tapia, Mike. 2011. "U.S. Juvenile Arrests: Gang Membership, Social Class, and Labeling Effects." *Youth & Society* 43:1407–32.

Taylor, Terrance J. 2008. "The Boulevard Ain't Safe for Your Kids: Youth Gang Membership and Violent Victimization." *Journal of Contemporary Criminal Justice* 24:125–36.

Thornberry, Terence P., Marvin D. Krohn, Alan J. Lizotte, Carolyn A. Smith, and Kimberly Tobin. 2003. *Gangs and Delinquency in Developmental Perspective*. Cambridge: Cambridge University Press.

Thornton, Sarah. 1995. *Club Cultures: Music, Media, and Subcultural Capital*. Middletown, Conn.: Wesleyan University Press.

Venkatesh, Sudhir. 2006. *Off the Books: The Underground Economy of the Urban Poor*. Cambridge, Mass.: Harvard University Press.

———. 2008. *Gang Leader for a Day: A Rogue Sociologist Takes to the Streets*. New York: The Penguin Press.

Visher, Christy, Nancy La Vigne, and Jill Farrell. 2003. Illinois Prisoners' Reflections on Returning Home. Washington, D.C.: Urban Institute. http://www.urban.org/publications/310846.html and a pdf of the report is available here: http://www.urban.org/UploadedPDF/310846_illinois_prisoners.pdf.

Vroomen, Laura. 2004. "Kate Bush: Teen Pop and Older Female Fans." In *Music Scenes: Local, Translocal, and Virtual*, edited by Andy Bennett and Richard A. Peterson, 238–53. Nashville, Tenn.: Vanderbilt University Press.

Wakefield, Sara, and Christopher Uggen. 2010. "Incarceration and Stratification." *Annual Review of Sociology* 36:387–406.

Wang, Oliver. 2007. "Rapping and Repping Asian: Race, Authenticity, and the Asian American MC." In *Alien Encounters: Popular Culture and Asian America*, edited by Mimi Thi Nguyen and Thuy Linh Nguyen Tu, 35–68. Durham, N.C.: Duke University Press.

Watkins, S. Craig. 2005. *Hip Hop Matters: Politics, Pop Culture, and the Struggle for the Soul of a Movement*. Boston: Beacon Press.

———. 2012. "Black Youth and the Ironies of Capitalism." In *That's the Joint!: The Hip-Hop Studies Reader* (2nd ed.), edited by Murray Forman and Mark Anthony Neal, 690–713. New York: Routledge.

Watts, Eric King. 1997. "An Exploration of Spectacular Consumption: Gangsta Rap as Cultural Commodity." *Communication Studies* 48:42–58.

———. 2005. "Border Patrolling and 'Passing' in Eminem's *8 Mile*." *Critical Studies in Media Communication* 22:187–206.

Western, Bruce. 2002. "The Impact of Incarceration on Wage Mobility and Inequality." *American Sociological Review* 67:526–46.

———, and Becky Pettit. 2005. "Black-White Wage Inequality, Employment Rates, and Incarceration." *American Journal of Sociology* 111:553–78.

———, and Becky Pettit. 2010. "Incarceration and Social Inequality." *Dædalus* (Summer): 8–19.

———, and Christopher Wildeman. 2009. "The Black Family and Mass Incarceration." *Annals of the American Academy of Political and Social Science* 621:221–42.

White, Russell. 2006. "'Behind the Mask': Eminem and Post-Industrial Minstrelsy." *European Journal of American Culture* 25:65–79.

Wilson, William Julius. 1987. *The Truly Disadvantaged: The Inner City, the Underclass, and Public Policy*. Chicago: University of Chicago Press.

———. 2009. *More Than Just Race: Being Black and Poor in the Inner City*. New York: W. W. Norton.

Wimsatt, William U. 1994. *Bomb the Suburbs: Graffiti, Freight-hopping, Race, and the Search for Hip-Hop's Moral Center*. Chicago: Subway and Elevated Press.

Womer, Sarah, and Robert J. Bunker. 2010. "Surños Gangs and Mexican Cartel Use of Social Networking Sites." *Small Wars and Insurgencies* 21:81–94.

Ziezulewicz, Geoff, and Emily Morris. 2012. "Shooting at Logan Square Club Is the Third for Local DJ in a Week." DNAinfo.com. December 5.

Index

Aces. *See* Insane Orchestra Albany
Aesop Rock, 74
American dream, 91–93, 201;
  backpacker adherence to, 194–95;
  and criminal activity, 96, 100;
  gangsta adherence to, 27, 32,
  93–96, 102–3, 124, 133, 156, 198,
  208; resilience of, 92–93; and
  social class, 80, 84, 91, 120;
  symbols of, 101
Anderson, Elijah, 13, 24, 87–90,
  174–75
Appropriating Blackness (Johnson), 72
Armstrong, Edward G., 77
artistic purity, 9, 26, 192, 219n5
audiences, 25–26, 142, 154–58
authenticity, 9; and criminal activity,
  30, 35, 126–33, 169, 174, 182, 197;
  defined, 76; definitions of, 10; and
  gang membership, 29–30, 99–100,
  132, 193; of gangsta vs. backpacker
  rap, 17, 24, 27, 32; and identity, 77,
  79; Latino, 90; measurement of,
  77–78; and race, 73; situational,
  75–79, 131–33; and whiteness/
  blackness, 20

backpacker rap music: and American
  dream, 194–95; as anti-violence,
  165–66; audience characteristics,
  25–26; career options, 192–95;
  characteristics of, 14–27; criminal

activities, 176–77; ethnoracial
  groups in, 19–20; vs. gangsta, 11–13,
  15, 165–66, 192; lyrics, 24; musical
  aesthetics, 23; origins of, 12; social
  class background, 15–17, 22, 176;
  style, 20–22; use of term, 212n9;
  venues, 193–94
"Batterram" (Toddy Tee song), 97
Bauman, Zygmunt, 79
Bay Area rap, 6–7
Bayton, Mavis, 116
Becker, Howard, 5
Biggie Smalls. *See* Notorious B.I.G.,
  The
Black Disciples (gang), 2, 171, 191, 207
blackness. *See* race
Bone Thugs-N Harmony, 146–47
Boogie Down Productions, 217n10
Bourdieu, Pierre, 5, 14, 84–85, 127
Boyd, Todd, 96
"Boyz-N-The Hood" (N.W.A. song),
  99
Bridge Wars, 58

CDs. *See* mixtapes
Charnas, Dan, 197
Chess Records, 3
Chicago Crime Commission, 57
Chief Keef. *See* Cozart, Keith
code switching, 79
Coleman, Joseph, 1, 2, 191
Combs, Sean "Diddy," 21, 97

OAs. *See* Insane Orchestra Albany
Obama, Barack, 93, 95, 201
Occupy Wall Street movement, 80
Ocean, Frank, 79
Odd Future, 79
O'Reilly, Bill, 13, 24

Pager, Devah, 86
Pattillo-McCoy, Mary, 88–89, 95, 129,
  196, 215nn21–22
People Nation (alliance), 28–29, 53,
  159, 161, 170
performances and performance
  frame, 141–46; audience conflicts,
  154–56; battles, 144–45; ciphers,
  144; concerts, 145–46, 150–54;
  and gang identity, 157–63, 178–79;
  open-mic nights, 43–46, 144; and
  social class, 155–56; structural
  issues, 150–52; technical issues,
  153–54; violence in, 60–63, 162–66,
  183; as workspace, 149–50. *See also*
  nightclubs
Peterson, Richard, 76
prison-industrial complex, 39, 40–41,
  86
prison rappers, case studies, 33–50
Project Blowed, 7–8, 9, 10, 11,
  212n7
Pro Tools recording system, 106,
  112–13
"P.S.K." (Schoolly D song), 97
Public Enemy, 12
punk rock, 10

race: and authenticity, 73, 77–78; in
  rap music, 17–20, 30, 73–75, 79;
  and social class, 87–88, 89; speech
  patterns, 89
rags-to-riches narrative, 91–92, 96,
  101. *See also* American dream

rap music: ethnoracial groups in,
  18–20, 73–75; global, 8, 74; live
  performance, 141–46; microscenes,
  8–11, 19–20, 141–44, 192; mixtapes,
  51–53; rap hustler archetype,
  100–103, 196, 198, 217n14; scenes,
  5–8; and social class, 15–17, 22,
  71–72, 79, 143–44; subgenres,
  212–13n11. *See also specific genres*
recording studios, 105–7; emotional
  labor in, 121–22; entrepreneurial
  labor in, 122–23; home studios,
  111–13, 114; and identity, 116;
  isolation booths, 114–15; networking in, 122; role of, 108,
  110; stacking technique, 120; as
  symbolic space, 107–9, 110–11, 113,
  120; technological advances,
  111–13; as work space, 117–26
reggaeton, 148
Richardson, Jeanita, 124
Riley, Alexander, 173
Rock, Chris, 13
Rodriquez, Jason, 19–20
Rolling Stone magazine, 11
Rose, Tricia, 73
Ross, Rick, 12–13, 101, 191, 196
Run-D.M.C., 12
Ruthless Records, 100

Sanders, Clinton, 155
Scarface, 36
Schoolly D, 97
Scott, Kim, 124
segregation in Chicago, 5
Shakur, Tupac, 2, 6, 12, 14, 52, 58, 59,
  88, 100, 173–74, 197, 216n1
Shank, Barry, 113
"6 in the Mornin" (Ice-T song),
  97–99
slavery, legacy of, 87

GEOFF HARKNESS is assistant professor of sociology at Morningside College.